Phillips Brooks

The Mystery of Iniquity

And other Sermons

Phillips Brooks

The Mystery of Iniquity
And other Sermons

ISBN/EAN: 9783744742252

Printed in Europe, USA, Canada, Australia, Japan

Cover: Foto ©Lupo / pixelio.de

More available books at **www.hansebooks.com**

THE
MYSTERY OF INIQUITY

AND OTHER SERMONS

BY THE

RT. REV. PHILLIPS BROOKS, D.D.

LATE BISHOP OF THE DIOCESE OF MASSACHUSETTS

London

MACMILLAN AND CO.

1893

CONTENTS.

The dates given are those on which the Sermons were first preached.

SERMONS.

I.

THE MYSTERY OF INIQUITY.

"The mystery of iniquity." — 2 Thess. ii. 7.

In this season of Lent, the one thought which we want to bring and keep before ourselves is the thought of our own sinfulness. These weeks are set apart for the very purpose that we may make familiar to ourselves the idea of human sin, its sources, its nature, its effects, its remedy. We turn that idea over and over, look at it on this side and on that, try to know it by every point of access, try to let it completely get possession and control of us. And thus there are many subjects which are proper to be treated — the extent of human sin, its enormity, its variety, its tenacity, its sorrow, its penalty, the ingratitude of man in committing it, and the great love of God in pardoning it — all these are fit and familiar topics for Lenten consideration.

In our text Paul suggests another, — not less fit, though perhaps not so familiar, — "The Mystery of Iniquity," the mysterious character of human sin. Let us try to turn one or two of the many sides of this subject into view to-day and see if we cannot get some idea of it.

What does he mean, then, by the mystery of sin? Is not sin the one great present palpable thing which everybody understands by the clear witness of his own experience? But remember what a mystery is. A mystery I take to be the general name for any event whose reality or fact is evident, but whose method or way of accomplishment it is not in our power to understand. Thus, for instance, we call the force of gravitation a mysterious power. Every falling apple, every steady mountain, bears witness that such a force really exists; but what it is, how it works, where its causes and conditions lie, who can tell? So we talk about the mystery of life. Life is self-conscious. It testifies itself in every living action. The fact of life runs in the blood, beats in the pulse, speaks in the voice, thinks in the brain. But the mystery lies deeper, in the unfound methods, in that long-sought something which neither physician nor metaphysician has yet tracked to its hiding-place, that unnamed essence in which the true cause of life resides. And yet again of God — we speak of Him as the great all-embracing Mystery. You see again, it is not the fact but the method of His existence that is mysterious. We know that He is: Creation, Providence; the Human Consciousness, the Divine Revelation, — all tell us that. How He is; what is meant by eternal and uncaused existence; how the sacred union of the three persons is bound into the single life of Deity; what it is to be omnipotent, omniscient, omnipresent, — these are the things we do not know. It is our ignorance of these that makes God a mystery to us. Shall we take yet another? Look at death —that one great solemn fact, which nobody can hide, the gap in a household that stares itself into our remembrance day after day—or in a nobler way, the certainty of a won victory of a soul freed from its earthly suffering and entered on its endless joy. Either way the fact is past our doubting, but who knows how it comes or what it means? The silver cord is slowly loosed, or the golden bowl is suddenly broken, and we can only stand by and wonder into what new ways of life this death ushers the departing soul.

In all these cases, then, you see what we mean by a mystery. Some event whose fact is evident but whose methods and modes are dark. Now, if we apply this to the phrase of Paul, the " Mystery of Iniquity," it must mean the same. Iniquity or sin is one of the great evident patent facts of the world. No man with his eyes open doubts that it exists. But the more we have to do with it, the more we feel that the ways of its existence and operation are obscure. It is a subtle, elusive, inapprehensible thing, if we attempt to grasp all its movements. We understand why in the first sin it took as its first typical representation the figure of the serpent, which cheats the eye with sinuous changes of place continually, refuses to be located, and while it leaves no doubt of its existence is seen only in flashes and a wavering indistinctness.

My object to-day is to exhibit in some of its aspects this mysterious nature of human sin. Do not suppose that I wish to occupy your time with a merely curious or speculative study. I have no right to do that. I wish to speak earnestly and practically, and I think we shall find an abundance of practical lessons resulting on all sides of us as we go on.

1. First, then, iniquity or sin is mysterious in its origin. How did sin begin? It is the old question which has rung through all the philosophies as well as all the theologies and found no answer. And see how it fulfils our description of a mystery. The fact of a beginning of sin is one of those which very few men have had the hardihood to doubt. Not merely revelation to those who received it, but even human reason to those who made it their teacher, has always signified that the wrong was an importation, an intrusion, an invasion in the world. That there was a time when it was not, there was a moment when it began to be. This has been always one of the dearest and most precious thoughts of men, one that they laid hold of the most eagerly, one that they let go of last. And men have always seemed to carry a certain sort of proof of their idea about with them in the very pictures and ideals of perfect goodness, — which all ages have treasured and kept alive. I suppose there is no other way of explaining the strange fact that amid all the personal badness, and social corruption that is in the world, the human mind has been able to preserve the ideal of a pure society and a perfect life, to dream of it, sometimes to strive after it, except by acknowledging the reality of an entrance of iniquity into the world, and looking back to a time before that invasion when the world was sinless.

But readily and widely as men grant the fact, this does not touch in the least the method of the great intrusion of sinfulness. Still the " Mystery of Iniquity " remains as dark as ever. How the hard questions crowd up which any of us can ask and no wisdom yet is wise enough to answer! If sin came in, whence came it? Nay, what is it? Is it an active thing forcing itself violently upon unwilling humanity, or is it the new result of a fermentation of the ingredients, the passions, and powers of that humanity itself? If it came from without, how was it that a pure will with no evil habit or tendency could receive or adopt the evil of temptation? Where is the bridge by which a nature can pass over from innocence to guilt? All these are questions without answers, and in their doubt and darkness looms up the great " Mystery of Iniquity."

And this which is true in general history is repeated in the history of each single life. How does a new responsible immortal get the taint of sin? How is it that every being born into the world, without exception, born sinless, gets the evil habit into him and begins to sin? The fact is there — written clear as daylight whenever man has lived and sinned. But the explanation is not found yet. We talk to one another about "original sin," as if that explained it. Well, what do we mean by " original sin "? Not surely that each being comes into the world guilty, already bearing the burden of responsible sin. If that were so, every infant dying before the age of conscious action must go to everlasting punishment, which horrible theology, I think, nobody holds to-day. Original sin means some sort of tendency or possibility of sinfulness. I take it to express nothing more than something vague and indefinite — it does not say what — something in man which makes it certain that as he grows up into manhood he shall grow up into transgression; and that you see is only the statement of the same " Mystery of Iniquity " in other words.

There is something oppressive, something terrible, in this great mysterious presence of sin right in our midst, so that nothing goes on save in its shadow, — no state is formed, no family grows up, no social compact is organized, no character matures without its blighting mixture. Right in our midst, and yet no voice of man or God is opened to tell us how it came here. The Gospel does not tell us. The Gospel finds it here, deals with it, does not explain it. It stands here shading all life, tainting all action, the great unread, terrible " Mystery of Iniquity."

My brethren, with such a shadow on the world, how dare we live the lives we do? I do not say it ought to make us miserable, sad, or gloomy. I do not say it ought to crush us and dishearten us; but surely it ought to make us earnest, to put into our lives something of that quality, call it awe, or reverence, or solemnity, — the Bible groups it into its great word " Fear." That quality which should banish mere trifling and nonsense to the winds. It ought to make us sober — a happy soberness, but yet a sober happiness. It ought to make it dreadful for us to think of the lives that half of us are living, dancing and singing and idling in a world on which so vast a mystery abides. It ought to make us afraid of the miserable frivolity that trifles up to the very door of Lent,—and then wearies over its prayer-book and its church-going till the Easter door shall open to let it out into its butterfly life again.

2. From this mystery which belongs to the very presence of sin on earth, I pass on now to speak of some of the mysteries which belong to its special operations. Remember throughout our definition of a mystery.

Is there not something very mysterious in the pervasiveness and inveteracy of sin as compared with goodness? Look at it. We believe in goodness as the superior power. We hold that wherever they are brought to a fair struggle, goodness as the superior power must prevail. We look for the day whose signs we think we see already when "the might with the right and the truth shall be." This is our creed drawn from the nature of the things themselves. And all our observation of the larger experience of the world proves our creed true. The history of human life shows everywhere this gradual assertion of the victory of right over wrong. Civilization everywhere encroaches upon barbarism, order on disorder, religion upon heathenism, purity upon corruption. Slowly, surely, serenely, the banners of God everywhere, with His light upon them, press forward, and the dark masses of God's enemies fall back before them. We believe in this steady gain. Truth is stronger than error, mercy than cruelty, love than hate; and yet with this great creed I think few things are more bewildering than the way in which, in special cases, the evil is always seeming to be more pervasive and powerful than the good. We all feel as if as soon as there is one bad spot in a man's life there were more chance of the life becoming all bad, than with one good spot of the whole life being filled with goodness. It is almost an instinctive feeling. You take a poor miserable reprobate, one of those men who seem to have no goodness left in them, an outcast, an accepted bad man. Suppose some day some sign of a better spirit makes itself seen in him; his life is a long lie, but somewhere in it an impulse of truth surprises you; his life is black with impurity, but at some point a bright and better light breaks in. What do you say of him? Is not that glimmer of good swallowed up and lost in the great general mass of evil? You do not look on it as likely to come to anything. You expect it to go out. But now, suppose we have a good man's life, a long, bright stretch of goodness, clear, almost without stain; but somewhere in it you discern one taint, somewhere you find one falseness creeping in among the truth, one hate among the love,—at once you are distressed and frightened, at once you picture to yourself this bad spot spreading till the whole is bad. One bad spot seems so much more likely to taint, than one good spot does to purify the whole.

And so of the pervasive power of sin among masses of men. We send one good man into a crowd of villains and we vaguely and dimly hope that he may make them better. We send one villain into a company of saints and begin to look at once to see stains on their robes and tarnish on their crowns. You send your boy to college, and if he goes there pure you hardly expect him to purify the air about him. You only ask, with trembling lips, of God, that he himself be not defiled. But you hear of your neighbor's bad boy that has gone there, and in a moment you see the badness that there is in him spreading itself and taking root in others. I think we all can recognize this feeling. Vice is a hardy plant. Let it alone and it will grow on of itself. Virtue is a delicate and fragile thing, and needs all the care and petting it can get. Put this along with our firm belief in the essential superiority and final victory of goodness, and it certainly forces on us a conviction of the subtlety and energy of the power of evil, and is one of the most perplexing illustrations of the "Mystery of Iniquity."

3. I ask you again to notice the mysterious personalness with which sin presents itself as a tempter to the hearts of men. This is what we usually hear stated as the doctrine of "besetting sins." The idea is that every nature is by its constitution specially liable to certain forms of transgression, and that opportunities and inducements to transgress always multiply themselves on that side of the nature which is most inclined to yield. I know how easy it is for a man to imagine something of this kind, and to suppose, because the attacks which come to him on his weaker side give him the most trouble, therefore there are the most of them; but still, I think we have all felt the truth of the personal malignity of

sin too often not to recognize its truth. Why is it that he who is most liable to pride, has such continual incitements to an overweaning vanity? Why is it that the poor inebriate trying to give up his drink, finds the whole world full of beckoning fingers and tempting voices that keep calling back again his dying passions into life. To the light and over-frivolous character all nature shapes itself into a chorus and sings siren songs to scare incipient thoughtfulness away. To the morose and bitter nature all life gathers itself up gloriously to deepen and darken the wicked dreariness of his existence. We get the idea of a man's being personally persecuted by sin. A man is proud, and everything seems to minister to his pride. He is rich, prosperous; everything goes well with him. Some day he loses it all. He is cast down into humility and poverty. What then? Does his pride forsake him? In some form or other you see the man still proud of his very humility and poverty. His "besetting sin" has hunted him out and found him down in the depths. It is like nothing but the old Greek stories of the implacable furies that gave their victims no rest till they had chased them into their graves. What one of us sits here to-day and does not know his own besetting sin? Why is it that everywhere one of us goes, the lips shape themselves to lie; wherever another goes, the limbs sink down into sloth and self-indulgence; whatever turn another takes, the air burns hot with passion which he cannot escape? It is this personality of sin, this gradual conviction that certain sins are our sins, set apart, set down to us — it is this which gives the sense of helplessness to our condition. We get at last to settling down and shaping our lives to it, and making up our minds that there is no hope for us, but that this one bad thing we are delivered to do. Consciously or unconsciously we make for it a standard of responsibility different from that which we have for all other acts.

And not only on our weakest points, but at our weakest times does the special attack always seem to come. This is still more mysterious. We read of Christ, that He went up into the wilderness, and "when He was an hungered," the devil came to Him. So it is always. The offer of stones turned into bread comes "when we are an hungered." Why is it that just when we are most tried in good works, the road smooths itself and the banks grow green, and we are tempted to lie down in slothfulness? Why is it that just when we are poorest, and so find the readiest excuses for meanness, the sin of meanness comes; just when we are sore with some insult or blow, another always comes and makes us sin with angry words; just at the moment of all moments when some disappointment has shaken our faith in all truth and honor, comes a lie into our lips and insists on being told? It is very startling and bewildering sometimes to find the chance of sin occurring just when we are weakest to resist it. Surely in this personalness and timeliness of temptation is one of the most remarkable features of the "Mystery of Iniquity."

Now take yet another point in the mysteriousness of sin — its power of self-disguise. There is something encouraging and something disheartening in the way in which sin is constantly inducing us to commit it, by presenting itself to us as something different from what it really is. It is disheartening, because there is no sin which people, keeping the dread of it all the time before their own consciences, no sin so heinous that people may not be brought to commit it; and yet it is encouraging to see that people do need to have vice present itself to them under the cloak of virtue before they will heartily give up to it their allegiance. Is it not wonderful to see how few sins in this world are done flatly, fairly, blankly, as sins? We carry our consciences by side attacks, by elaborate strategies and artifices. We almost never charge up in the face of our sense of right and take it by assault. It is a very rare thing, I think, much rarer than we are often ready to suppose, for a man to say to himself, this thing is bad, bad and not good, certainly and necessarily and nothing but bad, and yet I will do it. Go and sit down by the murderer in his cell, by the traitor in his camp, stand with the persecutor before his burning victim, look into the hot heart of the adulterer or the blasphemer, tie the liar down to give an account of the disgraceful falsehood he has uttered, and every one of them has his fair mask to spread before the face of the iniquity to which he has yielded himself. Covetousness dresses itself in the decent robes of prudence, idleness calls itself innocence, prodigality goes garbed as generosity, they all masquerade through society and trap the souls of men. This is the meaning of the conviction of sin, this is what the Gospel does, — it strips the false shows off, and it is then, when men see their lives as what they are, when the inner nature of acts writes out their true titles on their foreheads; then that that terrible humiliation comes of which we hear the subjects of the Gospel speak; then that some strong men stand and tremble like children before the barrenness and wickedness of their whole lives, and others fall and press their faces in the dust to shut out the reproaching sight, and cry out before their convicted selves their wild "unclean! unclean!"

One cannot stand before a crowd of his fellow-men, and not think what would come to pass if the Gospel in one sudden moment did its work for all of them. O we are self-complacent as we sit and look into one another's faces here to-day! We have our sins here all decently labelled, all decently clad. What if He came, the Spirit of all truth, and wiped out every false name and wrote up every true one! We tremble to think of what these walls must see. We should not dare look up on one another's shame bowed down each with the supreme shamefulness of his own. We should leap at once into a self-abhorrence like to Job's. This would turn to a Lenten afternoon then indeed. "Out of the deep" we should cry unto God together. Out of the deep of our honest humiliation! Of all the mysteries of iniquity is there any stranger, more bewildering, than this — this power of self-disguise? There is no sin that may not be made to look like holiness, no holiness that may not be made the cloak of a sin. What does it mean? Is there a vice for every virtue, a shadow for every sunlight? Is there an iniquity cut into the shape and painted in the hue of every goodness; and is the power of substituting the evil for the good intrusted to the cunning and unscrupulous hands of some infernal malice? What a strange association and correspondence between the good and evil it suggests! Is it that the arch-fiend, the fallen angel, took with him when he fell out of the skies the patterns of the heavenly glory, and makes the curses that he sends upon the earth after their blessed shapes? However it may come, there is something fearful in having to live in the distrustfulness, and confusion, and perplexity that grows out of this strange Mystery of Iniquity.

These, then, I have specified as some of the mysteries in the character and operations of human sin; some of the phenomena whose reality we are compelled to recognize, but whose methods and means it is totally out of our power to understand. If we tried to generalize them, and find out thus something of the real nature of sinfulness, I do not think it would be hard to read one general character in all these various workings. They all show that wonderful activity, mobility, facility, malignity, which we always conceive of as belonging only to a personality. We have almost been driven to a personal phraseology in speaking of them. When we see some force working its way with restless energy against the sluggishness of higher forces, choosing its persons and points of attack, choosing its times of action with some marvellous discrimination, putting on, when need demands it, the cloak and mask of a diviner power, malignantly, dexterously, with such strange choice and ingenuity doing its work, what better conception can we form of it than that which the sublime language of the Scripture gives us of a personal evil, a Satan, a bad spirit set to the endless work of thwarting God and ruining the hope of man! Reason may find what difficulties she will in the doctrine of a personal Satan, but she has yet to harmonize and arrange, under any other idea, the phenomena of human sin. Till she does this, there stands forth this personal "Mystery of Iniquity," which Paul, with a sublime realism, sees working his devilish schemes in personal freedom and power among the sons of men.

We have spoken thus of the mysteriousness of sin in its origin and operations. It would be a cruel, a false, and an unchristian sermon if I closed without telling you of the diviner mystery in which human iniquity finds its cure. The first thought round which the grand wonder of the atonement grows into shape is this thought of sin as a real live thing standing forth to be fought with, to be conquered, to be killed. Not of a mere moral weakness to be strengthened, or an intellectual emptiness to be filled, but of an enmity to be slain, a giant to be subdued. To meet that enmity, to slay that giant, Christ comes forth with his wonderful nature. He undertakes a distinct and dreadful struggle. The sublime conflict goes on between Christ and Satan, in a region apart from, above, and separate from man. We see its outward manifestation in the agony of the cross. We see, but do not comprehend even that. All the deeper battle goes on out of our sight. We know not how it fares till the word of God comes to tell us that the victory is won by our Redeemer, and that Satan is trodden into death by the dying Christ. Of all the Mystery of Iniquity, where is the Mystery like this? You see how true a mystery it is. Nothing but the fact we know. That we know perfectly. That shining, splendid fact, that gracious, glorious fact — the fact of the Lord's victory and of Satan's fall — stands forth so clear that none can doubt it. It takes its place as the one certain, central fact of hope. By it the living live, by it the dying die; in it the glorified rejoice forever. But who shall go behind the fact, and tell its method? Who shall say how, why, where, that all-availing victory was won? Only the divine and human Christ met the power of sin and conquered it; and every human being in that triumph of the one great humanity stood possibly victor over his mighty and malicious foe.

O wondrous mystery! Who asks to know the way? Who does not take the glorious truth and fasten desperate hands upon it, and draw himself up by it into hope? Who will not stand content and let the clouds cover the awful mystery of his great Master's struggle, so long as out of the clouds he hears the assuring voice of God: " This is my beloved Son, in whom I am well pleased. Whosoever cometh unto me by him shall not perish, but shall have everlasting life " ?

The Mystery of Iniquity! This is the lesson of

all that we have said to-day, — that we are living in the midst of mysterious forces leagued against our souls, — that our enemy is mysterious, is superhuman. Mysterious and superhuman, then, must be our safety and defence. Our foe is a spirit. A higher spirit, then, even the Holy Spirit of God, must be our champion. "We wrestle not against flesh and blood, but against principalities, against powers, against the rulers of the darkness of this world, against spiritual wickedness in high places." Wherefore we must take unto ourselves the whole armor of God. Be strong in the Lord, and in the power of His might. Put on the whole armor of God, that we may be able to stand against the wiles of the devil, and having done all, to stand.

II.

THE VALLEY OF BACA.

"Who passing through the valley of Baca make it a well; the rain also filleth the pools."—PSALMS lxxxiv. 6.

THE prayer-book version of these words, you will remember, is a little different: "Who going through the vale of misery use it for a well; and the pools are filled with water." Let us try to keep both versions in mind while we are speaking of it.

The verse gathers its beauty from the circumstances of the Psalm. It is drawn out of the richness of that picture-land of Palestine. The more we read the Psalms, and indeed all the Bible, we are impressed with the remarkable value which belongs to the Holy Land as representing in a continual map or picture not merely the localities of certain historical events, but also by a higher association the geography of the spiritual life of man and the relations of spiritual truths to one another. The sacred names have passed from being merely the titles of hills and rivers and cities, and belong to principles and moral verities. In the world's great heart there will forever be a holy land besides that to which pilgrims travel halfway round the globe. Though the historic land which lies between the Mediterranean sea and the Asiatic deserts should be blotted from the surface of the earth to-morrow; though some strange miracle should roll the whole rough surface of the country smooth, and mix in indistinguishable confusion hill and valley, upland and river-bed, still there would be eternally a holy land. Still all over the world, wherever sacred associations had transfigured the old names, the Jordan would roll down its rocky bed to the Dead sea; still the hills would stand about Jerusalem; still the desert would open between Judea and Galilee; still Egypt must mean captivity, and the Red sea deliverance, and Gilgal providence, and Bethany domestic piety, and Calvary redeeming love, — although the visible places to which those names belong should cease to be forever. We little know how much we owe to this eternal picture drawn in the hearts of men, this mapped-out Palestine of the inner life.

Our text is one of the passages which have contributed to draw this picture. "Who passing through the vale of Baca use it for a well." Students have not been able to identify and locate the valley Baca, but it evidently refers either generally or specially to those difficult ravines which the people had to cross in coming up to Jerusalem to the feasts. The Psalm was probably written by David at some time when he was kept in exile and could not go up to Jerusalem. It is the yearning of a loving and devoted heart for the privilege of worship. "O how amiable are thy dwellings, thou Lord of hosts. My soul hath a desire and longing to enter into the courts of the Lord; my heart and my flesh rejoice in the living God. Yea, the sparrow hath found her an house and the swallow a nest where she may lay her young, even thy altars, O Lord of hosts, my King and my God." Then mounting up to the height of his sorrow (that height from which so often the best and widest visions come to men) a vision comes to him. He sees the multitude, whom he may not join, going up to worship. He watches their winding line from hill to hill as they draw nearer to Jerusalem. " Blessed is the man in whose heart are thy ways, who going through the vale of misery use it for a well; and the pools are filled with water. They will go from strength to strength," he cries, exulting in their progress, "and unto the God of gods appeareth every one of them in Zion." Then he falls back upon his own need, " O Lord God of hosts, hear my prayer, hearken, O God of Jacob. I had rather be a door-keeper in the house of my God than to dwell in the tents of ungodliness."

The lesson of the vale of Baca, the vale of misery, evidently is, the turning of sorrow into joy. Let us try to read the parable and understand it. Notice, then, it is the turning of sorrow into joy; the turning into, not merely the supplanting, the succeeding of sorrow by joy. There are two theories about this thing : One we may call the theory of compensation, the other the theory of transformation. The compensation theory is the commonest, the one most easily and so most generally understood. Even Christians are found continually confusing it with and so substituting it for the higher and better truth. Its idea is that the world is full of

evil and discomfort, and that discomfort is to be borne
only by the assurance that it is not universal or perpetual, that it is varied and mixed up with pleasure,
and that if we can only set our lips tight and walk on
over the sorrow we must come to the happiness by
and by. We are told that if it storms to-day the sun
will be out to-morrow; if this week's speculation
fails, the market is still open and to-morrow's investment or the next day's or the next day's may succeed; if our country is down in the depths of
trial, another somewhere else is sunning itself on the
summit of success. There is this poise and balance
and make-up all through life. This is a favorite doctrine of our philosophy. I do not find it anywhere
more strikingly stated than in these words of Emer-
son: "Polarity, or action and reaction," he declares,
" we meet in every part of nature, in darkness and
light; in heat and cold; in the ebb and flow of
waters; in male and female; in the inspiration and
expiration of plants and animals; in the systole
and diastole of the heart; in the undulations of
fluids and of sound; in the centrifugal and centrip-
etal gravity; in electricity, galvanism, and chemi-
cal affinity. If the south attracts, the north repels.
To empty here you must condense there. An inevitable dualism bisects nature so that each thing is a
half, and suggests another thing to make it whole;
as, spirit, matter; man, woman; odd, even; subjective,
objective; in, out; upper, under; motion, rest; yea,
nay." This endless up and down is the law which
this philosophy assumes to be the great consoler.

And far-sighted faith, hunted and tried by suffering, carries this philosophy out far beyond the limits of this world. To how many Christians Heaven and the eternal happiness present themselves under the guise of this compensation theory. This world is the great down. The next world is to be the great up which is to make it good. The bad prosper here, the good prosper there. The Christian suffers now to be rewarded then. This world is miserable, we must wait for our happiness, and struggle on with tight lips and torn feet to find it in the next. The deeper the misery, the more complete the future joy. It would be easy to point out passages in Scripture which seem to confirm this doctrine; passages in which the superior bliss of the perfect life casts the miniature experiences of this state of being into a darkened shade ; but he who accepts it as the general rule of existence has to do it against the general tone of the Bible and the general verdict of experience, both of which declare the possibility of happiness this side of the grave. It is the idea under whose strange tyranny some very earnest and conscientious souls have been made morbidly miserable because, forsooth, they could not help being happy. This would be the idea under which the pilgrim through the vale of Baca would not turn it into a well, but only be kept up through it by far-off visions of the waters of salvation which, when he got to Jerusalem, he should find flowing out of the mount of God. It would make earth not a foretaste, an earnest, but only a discipline of Heaven. Whatever truth there may be in it, it evidently is not the whole or the best truth. Such a faith, with all honor to its exaltedness and

nobleness, be it said, resembles that over far-sighted-
ness which is a disease, not because it sees things afar
off, but because it sees only things afar off and is
blind to the beauties and helps that lie about its feet.

Souls of less intense faith, who cannot carry the
doctrine of compensation into the next life, keep it
and try to use it in this. Nothing is more sad, as it
seems to me, than the way in which we comfort ourselves and one another for our sorrows, by vague,
unrealized promises that sorrow cannot last forever.

We conceive of life as a great swinging sphere
which must forever run a vast orbit, doomed to perpetual change, and so sure by and by to sweep into
the sunlight, if we can only keep alive and wait. It
is a forlorn and miserable comfort. It loses all the
certainty and personal graciousness of Christianity.
There is no *piety* about it. No man can get into
the habit of thus comforting himself every day and
seeming to be satisfied with this comfort, and yet
keep a real faith in a real, constant, unchanging, infinite, good God; and yet how common it is and how
pious we count it. We sing it into songs that sound
almost religious, and feel as if we were comforted and
resigned when their barren words fall on us.

> "Be still, sad heart, and cease repining,
> Behind the clouds is the sun still shining.
> Thy fate is the common fate of all,
> Into each life some rain must fall,
> Some days must be dark and dreary."

That means, (if it be not going too far to seek a
meaning in what is perhaps meant for mere sentimen-

tality,) that there is nothing to do on rainy days but to sit still and be drenched till it clears up. It is the theory of compensation. There is so much rain to fall, and if it did not fall to-day it would to-morrow; having fallen to-day, to-morrow we shall have the sun. There is so much suffering to suffer. If we get through with it this year, the more certainly next year will rise clear. I presume it is by no means certain that that is true in physics, it certainly is false in morals.

Nor can this barren consolation ever give anything that is worthy to be called patience or resignation. Patience and resignation are both calm and cheerful. This will be either the dogged and sullen yielding of a brute to a burden he cannot escape (losing cheerfulness), or else the reckless excitement of a gambler kept alive by the perpetual and unreliable alternation, losing calmness. These travellers through the vale of Baca have not even the distant vision of the holy city to inspire them. They can only plod along the dusty way in the vague hope that some oasis will appear where they can get a shadow and a drink. Such is the comfortless comfort that we give and take.

This is the theory of compensations. Now see how different it is from this other theory of transformations. David's pilgrims going through the vale of misery " use it " for a well. They were looking forward to Jerusalem. Their hearts leaped, as every traveller's must when any greener spot promised them a richer resting-place; but their life was not one altogether of the future, not kept distressed and anxious with uneasy alternations. They made the vale itself a well. It was not simply a sorrow that was succeeded by joy, not merely a peace promised and looked for and waited for, it was a peace found. When they grew thirsty they looked, not merely farther on into the heart of the future, but deeper down into the bosom of the present.

It seems to me the very drawing of this picture must describe to many a soul its own unspoken need, and make it recognize it. " Yes, that is what I want. Heaven is glorious, but it is far away. To-morrow may be all steeped in sunshine ; but meanwhile to-day is dark. There surely must be something better to do than to sit down and wait. What is it ?" We all feel that a religion which lives only on the future, dwells only in the future, is not a whole, cannot be a wholly efficient faith. What the world needs is present work, and what all men need are present working conditions, a present life. Hope is a splendid power, but I can hope fully, because I can hope intelligently, only as I already taste some intimation of the thing I hope for. I can strive after the streams of Zion only as I strengthen myself out of the wells of Baca.

If we look, then, to see if this doctrine of transformation be possible, it starts out of that word " use." Things are what they are used for. So it is all over nature. There stands a tree in the forest. What is it — a tree ? Yes, but a tree only as material. It is, in possibility, countless things. What it shall be, in reality, depends upon the superior will that uses it. The savage comes with his use, and the tree is a

canoe and floats upon the river. The builder comes
with his need, and the tree is a wall of planks and
shields a house. The physician comes with his use,
and the tree-bark becomes a medicine and cures the
sick. The farmer comes with his use, and the tree
turns into a roaring fire to keep the winter out at his
door. So of all things. The artist uses a stone,
and it is a statue; the mason uses a stone, and it is a
doorstep. And beyond mere nature. See how we use
men. We are each other's raw material. I make you
up in some shape into my life, and you in some way
make me up into yours. But what man is of so
fixed a character that he can be made up only into
one invariable thing? Each man makes of his
neighbor that for which he uses him. Why is it that
two men both know and use one other man of rich
and gracious nature, and one gathers and makes
out of him nothing but envy, and jealousy, and discontent, while the other shapes into his own life a
largeness, and sweetness, and fineness, like that with
which he has to deal? Why, except that the de-
termining power lies finally, not in the one identical
character of the man who is used, but in the two different natures of the men who use him? So of all influences and motives. The same educations wall and
press upon two lives. One rises on them into greatness, the other drags them down upon it and is
crushed beneath them into ruin. So, go to Heaven.
The same eternal glory feeds two heavenly spirits;
the same great throne looks down in loving authority on both. They tread together the same glassy
streets; they wait together for the same far-reaching

messages; they bend together, looking down into a wisdom they both crave to fathom. Why is it that Gabriel stands unstained out of all the glory, gathering strength and grace, while his brother Lucifer falls from his side, full of his hate, and treason, and revenge? We need not go to angels. How is it that men use God and make of him such different things grow by their use of him to saints or devils? How is it that the Pharisee and Publican came down the same temple steps, one cold, and proud, and bitter, and the other with his heart full of tenderness, and gratitude, and humblest charity?

As the world goes on and man becomes a more complete being, the truth that comes out more and more must be this of the regal importance of the using moral force. Man the savage is ruled by things, — rivers, hills, forests, — they make of him what their own tendencies suggest; and on the other hand, man the citizen, man civilized, rules things, makes of them what he pleases. Man the child is obedient and plastic; man the man is authoritative and decisive. Surely there is no picture in history so striking and sublime as that which is the one picture of all history : the soul of man which seemed at first so insignificant, so weak a thing among all these stupendous things and forces, slowly, surely, going up into its own place, taking its stand in the very central midst of all of them, moving them all, making them all be what it will, deciding their nature by their use.

Now, I said that in this truth lies the key to the difference between the doctrine of compensations and the doctrine of transformations. The mere compensation theory forgets this regal position of the human life. It puts humanity in the power of things. Man must be carried where things carry him, and trust to their continual changes to float him off to-morrow, if they ground him perchance to-day. "Nay," says the Christain doctrine of transformations, " things are in the power of man; as he uses them so they are." As God said to Adam about the beasts, " Whatsoever thou callest each, that is his name." In him, the user, rests the real nature of the things he uses. They have no invariable fixed nature apart from him.

Now, let this great user man, this one moral force, be called upon to go down into the valley of Baca, into the vale of misery. He finds there all the circumstances of suffering, poverty, sickness, bereavement, sin itself; what then, these are things and he is man. They are what he is. Let him rule them, not be ruled by them. Let him take down there a religious, trustful nature, a pious, cheerful heart, and there is more promised than just that his cheerful piety shall be able to support him through; he shall exercise his human right of ruling and of using these, and his cheerful, trustful heart shall come out with a more perfect joy and a more certain faith than he had carried in. He shall not come out half-dead with thirst, just able to drag himself up to the fountain at the end, but it shall be as David so beautifully says, " He shall drink of the brook in the way, therefore shall he lift up his head."

This, then, is the Christian economy of suffering; this is the high theory of transmutation. In a world full of sorrow and distress how noble, how benignant an economy it is! Our human instinct craves something like it. We cannot think complacently of this life or any part of this life as something just to be endured, to be got through with, as a preliminary to some unknown happiness in store beyond. We long for a present religion, a present strength, a present joy, a present God, and we find them all, not in any weak ignoring of the misery of life, but in the way in which that misery may become instinct with happiness, by the sublime mercy of "the vale of Baca."

If we go on, then, a little farther to try to find out something about the methods of this economy of transformation, how it is that suffering is not merely succeeded by but turned into joy, I suppose the one great answer that includes all others must be this: that suffering contains the elements of the highest happiness because it involves the condition of weakness, of helplessness, of dependence. If the condition for which man was made was a religious condition, that is to say a related, a bound up, a dependent condition, then the highest human happiness must always come with the most complete conformity to that first idea of human life. If dependence, then, be happiness, independence, (which if you take the word apart means just the same as irreligion,) independence of God, self-sufficiency, must be unhappiness. And then since suffering in all its various departments is the breaking up of self-sufficiency, of self-confidence, is it not evident at once that rightly used it may be the setting free of the human soul from an unnatural and forced condition, into its natural, regular, intended, and so happiest life ?   It is simply the conviction of weakness in one's self letting a man free to return to the strength in which he belongs.   It matters not what the weakness be, whether the breaking of a leg, so that the man who walked and earned his bread yesterday has to lie still and be fed to-day.   Or the death of a friend, so that he who used to lean on a strong shoulder as he walked feels for it now in vain.   Or the disproving of a favorite proposition, so that where we used to tread firm on what we thought was certainty, we now go cautiously and tiptoe over doubt.   Anything in body, brain, or heart that gets that idea of insufficiency home to us, may set us to digging beneath the self-surface of our vale of misery to find the God below for whom the thirsty soul was made.

There is something very beautiful to me in the truth that suffering, rightly used, is not a cramping, binding, restricting of the human soul, but a setting of it free.   It is not a violation of the natural order, it is only a more or less violent breaking open of some abnormal state that the natural order may be resumed.   It is the opening of a cage door.   It is the breaking in of a prison wall.   This is the thought of those fine old lines of an early English poet:

> " The soul's dark cottage, battered and decayed,
>   Lets in new light through chinks that time has made.
>   Stronger by weakness, wiser men become
>   As they draw near to their eternal home."

Oh, how many battered cottages have thus let in the light !   How many broken bodies have set their souls free, and how many shattered homes have let the men and women who sat in darkness in them see the great light of a present God! " Stronger by weakness !" " Who passing through the vale of misery use it for a well."

We have spoken thus of irresponsible suffering only; but in a far nobler way it is true of the responsible suffering which comes of sin. This is the hardest to believe; but yet, my dear friends, this is what we need to believe most of all. Beyond all suffering which comes by natural dispensation or by human weakness there is another which exceeds them all. A man loses his friend and he is sorry, he loses his property and he is crushed, he loses his health and he almost gives up; but there is a yet untasted woe of which that man knows nothing yet. With all his wading through deep waters, there is a suffering in which he has not yet dipped his foot. Let that same man find himself a sinner; let him wake up and see how his sin has set him far away from God; let him feel how antagonistic his whole life is to holiness; let him stand guilty, guilty, without a plea, without a hope, just with his stained and frightened soul naked before the eye of God, and then in the conviction of sin, then he has found what suffering is — sorrow ! The other sorrows of his life all fade back out of sight and this is left alone. He walks the valley of his misery and all is dark. And can this valley too break forth in wells ? Can these dry pools be filled with water ? Tell me, O Christians, you who out of the conviction of your sinfulness have found a Saviour from your sin,—tell me, all ye who, bowed down in the dust in the humiliation of your worthlessness, have heard there, with your face close to the ground, what you could never hear while you stood upright, the streams of pardon running sweet music down below,—tell me, is not the well of richest joy right here in the midst of the valley of completest sorrow; where sin abounded does not grace much more abound? O my dear brethren, if any of you now are going through that valley, may He who led you there teach you how to " use it for a well." Every step as you go through it may you hear a voice beside you crying, " Ho, every one that thirsteth, come ye to the fountain."

It would be interesting to trace out also, as an element in this economy of transmutation, the way in which a man may get joy out of suffering by being brought through suffering into a deeper knowledge of the nature and purpose of God. Prosperity, as we have seen, is unconscious of God. Suffering, whether it will or no, has to be conscious of him. And if there be a perfectly unselfish joy, one entirely and perfectly pure, one in which the human faculty of joyfulness reaches its highest exaltation, it must be the earnest delight with which a man who loves God puts himself aside and is utterly happy in watching and seeing what God is and how he works. I have seen a man whom the world called a fearful sufferer living delightful days in this high study of the ways of God. Day by day his Maker took some strength out of his life, unstrung some nerve, put some pain in; but the suffering of a decaying body was so far surpassed by the rare joy of feeling his Maker's hands busy on the body and the spirit he had made, and of studying his wondrous ways of working, that his hours of sickness were the happiest that he had ever lived. He saw God glorifying himself, and was abundantly content; that was the well of which he drank.

" Who passing through the vale of Baca make it a well; the rain also filleth the pools." How beautifully the two clauses tell of the responsive positions of God and the human soul in suffering! It is a meeting of water from below and water from above. The wells fill themselves out of the ground and the rain comes from the sky into the pools; yet both from the same original source. Never so much as in suffering does the divinity which God gave to man come out and show itself to meet the new divinity which he sends down to it out of Heaven. Have you never been struck by coming suddenly on the face of a man whom you had known long and well, but who since you knew him had been a sufferer either mentally or bodily; and seeing how his face had grown finer and nobler, so that you almost were awed before him at first? Something had come out from him and something had come into him. His grossness had grown delicate and his brutishness gentle by his sorrow. And as with faces, so with characters.

Here we must stop. The Bible calls the world a world of sorrow; but the same Bible tells us there is a way of making the vale of misery to laugh with springs and fountains. Remember, it is not just compensation, but transformation that you are to seek. Not Heaven yet. That looms before us always, tempting us on; but now the earth, with all its duties, sorrows, difficulties, doubts, and dangers. We want a faith, a truth, a grace to help us *now*, right here, where we are stumbling about, dizzied and fainting with our thirst. And we can have it. One who was man, yet mightier than man, has walked the vale before us. When he walked it, he turned it all into a well of living water. To them who are willing to walk in his footsteps, to keep in his light, the well he opened shall be forever flowing. Nay, it shall pass into him and fulfil there Christ's own words: " Whosoever drinketh of the water that I shall give him shall never thirst, but the water that I shall give him shall be in him a well of water springing up into everlasting life."

III.

HOMAGE AND DEDICATION.

" And the four and twenty elders fall down before Him that sat on the throne, and worship Him that liveth for ever and ever, and cast their crowns before the throne."— REVELATION iv. 10.

IT is impossible for the mind to conceive of a more majestic picture than is presented in this fourth chapter of the Book of Revelation. The Church of Christ, with all her labors done and all her warfare over, stands at length in heaven, before the throne of Him whose servant she has been, and renders up her trust and gives all the glory back to Him. When we hear such a scene described in the few words of John's poetic vision, I think we are met with a strange sort of difficulty. The great impression of the picture is so glorious that we are afraid to touch it with too curious fingers, to analyze its meaning and get at its truth. At the same time we feel sure that there is in it a precise and definitely shaped truth which is blurred to us by the very splendor of the poetry in which it is enveloped. We see on the one hand how often the whole significance of some of the noblest things in Scripture is lost and ruined by people who take hold of them with hard, prosaic hands. Their poetry is necessary to their truth. On the other hand, we see how many of the most sacred truths of revelation float always before many people's eyes in a mere vague halo of mystical splendor, because they never come boldly up to them as Moses went up to the burning bush, to see what they are, and what are the laws by which they act. Shall we interpret the poetry of Scripture into ordinary language or not? No one reads the commentaries without feeling that often it would be better not to do so; but no one sees how many of the false religious ideas and superstitions have come of an intense and dazzled, but blind, perception of Scripture poetry, without feeling how wisely it needs to be interpreted and studied. There is danger of mysticism and vagueness, if you leave the wonderful Bible images unexplained. There is danger of prosaic dulness and the loss of all their life and fire, if you elucidate them overmuch.

It is seen everywhere. The great New Testament image is the cross of Christ, and any one can see how on the one hand the cross has become a mere object of vague and feeble sentiment to multitudes who have been touched by its beauty without trying to understand its meaning; and how, on the other hand, it has become hard and shallow and commercial, all the mystery and depth and power of appeal passed out of it, as men have torn its sacred agony to pieces, and tried to account on mercantile principles for every pang that Jesus suffered and every mercy that His suffering offers to the world.

In view of all this difficulty, what shall we do? It is not hard to tell what we ought to do, by every Scripture image and poetic description, although it may be very hard to do it. We want to draw out its truth without forgetting that it is poetry; we want to get out of it a broad and clear idea, which shall still keep the glow with which it burned while it lay still in the fire of poetic inspiration. We want to leave it in heaven, and yet bring it down to earth. We want to understand it more, and yet feel it just as much. Something of this kind I want to try to do to-day, with reference to the great apocalyptic image of the four and twenty elders casting their crowns before the throne of God.

What is the broad idea, then, of this great spectacle? The four and twenty elders have been often considered to represent the Church in its two great series, the Jewish and the Christian orders. Twelve patriarchs and twelve apostles may be considered as representatively constituting that company who came, with all the fruits and honors of successful life, to offer them to Him by whose great strength they had been won. Such an interpretation seems very likely to be true; but in a yet broader way we have here crowned beings, those who had won some victory and possessed some kingship, giving the very badges and tokens of their victory and glory to another greater than themselves, casting their kingly crowns before the kingly throne of a royalty mightier than their own. I believe that the picture has that special reference to the relations of the Christian Church to its great Head; but does it not also suggest to us still broader ideas which are illustrated through all of human history, and which find their illustrations constantly in all our daily life? Those ideas seem to me to be two. The first is the necessary homage which the higher natures pay to those that are higher than themselves, and especially to the highest of all. The second is the way in which every great attainment gets its best value from being dedicated to somebody or some purpose that is greater still. These two ideas I see coming up out of this picture, as the soul of a man looks out upon you from his face. I want to dwell upon them with you for a while this morning. I think that they can suggest for us a good deal about the whole nature of reverence and worship.

Take, then, the first of these ideas — the. necessary homage that high natures pay to others which are higher than themselves, and especially to the highest of all. Here are crowned beings casting their crowns down at the feet of a dimly seen figure which sits upon a throne so much higher than they are that even their crowns can only reach his feet. Shall we take that idea and lay it down by the experience of ordinary life? Does reverence increase as men grow themselves to be more and more, greater and greater? Think of it first with reference to the homage that men come to pay to what is higher than themselves, but not the highest — not to God. Every strong young man starts in a true self-confidence. He is the master of everything. Everything is to be his servant. Centred in himself, he sees all other things revolving around him as if they were to be the ministers of his necessities. If he is going into politics, the country is an arena that has been spread abroad for the race he is to run. If

he is to be an artist, the laws of the materials of art
are but expedients to utter the beauty and sublimity
that is in his soul. If he is going into business, the
great adjustments of the business world are the machinery out of which is to be wrought his fortune.
There is no reverence in all that. Wrapped up in
himself, the eager young aspirant has not caught
sight of the true and regal dignity of these masters
whom he assumes to treat as servants. But what
comes later? Let our young man grow really great
in any one of these departments, and I take it to be
a universal truth, a truth which all will recognize,
that the greater he grows the more he will come to
know that those things, which he thought to make
servants of, are really masters, and by and by he
will pass into a region where he is able to pay them
the homage they deserve. The mere tyro in politics
thinks the country is made for his ambition; but the
great statesman sees his country a great and venerable
being for whom it is his privilege to work and live,
and perhaps die. The flippant beginner in art thinks
that all the laws of art are merely arrangements to
help his genius into expression; but the great artist
is sure that the noblest task his genius can attempt
is only to utter in visible material some of the everlasting laws of beauty. The confident young trader
thinks the whole market made for him; but the great
merchant has looked wide over all the earth, and is
proud to be a part in that great system of interlacing
work and mutual credit that covers all the continents.
Thus every man, the greater he grows, becomes capable of understanding the greatness of that with

which he has to deal, and so enters into the region of
a new homage. Newton could reverence the power
of gravitation more than the child who ignorantly
tosses his ball into the air and sees it fall. Morse
was more able to honor the subtle and mighty force
of electricity than is the mere telegraph operator
who knows nothing but the mere manipulation of his
machine. It is a universal rule that he is a poor
workman who does not honor and respect his work.
A man has no right to be doing any work which, as
he grows greater within it, does not offer him new
views of itself to call out an ever-increasing reverence and honor. And in all the good occupations of
life (one would like to impress it upon every young
merchant, young mechanic, and young student whom
he can speak to) a man's best proof of growing
greatness in himself is a growing perception of the
greatness and beauty of his work.

The same is true of men. The greater a man
grows, the more quick and ready he will be to recognize and honor another man who is his better. Here
again there is no test so certain of whether a man
has any greatness as whether he is able to pay intelligent and sincere respect to other men who have
more than he has. There seem to be certain states
of condition, as it were, with reference to this.
Down at the bottom an unenterprising mortal looks
with blank and stupid wonder at the really great
men who stand at the top of his race. Up a little
higher he is moved with envy and begins to dispar-
age them; but when he comes to be great himself, he
knows how to understand them, and yet recognizes

how much they are above him. He has become capable of truly venerating them. Only those who are kingly themselves can properly honor the kingliest.

And then think of the worship, not merely of that which is higher than a man's self, but of that which is the highest of all—the worship of God. There it is supremely true that men are capable of it only in virtue of and in proportion to something great, something divine in themselves. Only those who have crowns to cast can do true homage before His throne. This seems to me to be bound up with what I have already said. I claimed—and I think you agreed with me—that it was the man most proficient in any profession who saw the depth and range of that profession best, and so reverenced it most deeply. It is the mere smatterer in any profession who thinks it slight and is contemptuous about it. Now, just exactly this is true of life. The more completely a man lives, the more largely alive he is in every part of him,—in brain, and heart, and hands,—the more completely he will comprehend the magnitude of life, and stand in reverence before the Power that moves and governs it. The mere smatterer in life, the amateur in living, so to speak, with his half-vital movements, never realizes the immensity of existence, the vast variety of its complications, the infiniteness of its privileges and its dangers, the range upward and the range downward, and so he goes on satisfied within himself, and offering no tribute of adoration to the Power which moves in, and through, and under all this world of life, which

he has never fathomed deep enough to find adorable.
But this moving power of all things is God. His
nature is what the soul finds, when tired and bewildered, like a frightened bird which has escaped
from its own little cage, it flies through the vast ex-
panse of life and comes to the shadow that encloses
it. That follows then which I believe that we
continually see. The man most thoroughly alive, he
who lives most, will be most reverent to God. I do
not mean that he will always hold the correctest
ideas. The very fulness of the current of his living
may sweep out here and there strange eccentricities
and aberrations in his way of thinking, but he will
be most constantly conscious of a power over him,
from which he came, out of which streams of influence are always flowing into him, to which he is responsible, to which he must return. The more a
man loves, the more he realizes the limitations in
which all earthly affection labors, and the more
glorious appears to him the Infinite Love. The
more a man thinks, the more he sees how all human
thought is but a drop of water out of the illimitable
ocean of the thought of God. And when a true
man puts his hand to it and bravely does an honest
piece of work, he sees at once the beauty and the
littleness of the work he does, and comprehends the
glory of the perfect work of Him through whom are
all things, and by whom are all things. Some such
necessary connection there seems to be between the
largest living and the completest adoration. I have
known many scoffers, men who believed that there
was a God, but who did not in any way prostrate

themselves before Him, paid Him no homage; some of them were very bright men, some of them conscientious and dutiful, some of them affectionate and brave; but—I do not wholly know why—there was something imperfect in the development of their humanity, as it always seemed. They were the men of unsymmetrical culture; the men in whom some one power was overgrown and the rest were sluggish; the men who did not impress you with largeness of life, but with special, almost mechanical, dexterity of action; the men whom you might call upon for certain tasks which require certain skill, but whom you could not trust with that entire confidence which can only rest on character. In one word, they were not kingly men, not men who in any regal way, according to the old idea of a king, represented their race. Men with sharp, ingenious tools in their hands, but no crowns upon their heads. And almost every one of us knows, too, that in his own life there have been scoffing and scornful times, periods of irreverence, when the sacred was not sacred to us, and the venerable excited in us no veneration; times when if we did not scoff at God, it was not because we adored Him, but because the habits of decent, reverential behavior were strong enough to carry us through times of utter selfishness, when nothing seemed great to us beyond ourselves; times of utter demoralization, when nothing was mysterious, or inspiring, or sublime. And what is our impression of such times? Some of them were the smartest periods of all our life. They were perhaps the times when we worked our hardest—our keenest, wittiest, busiest days perhaps, but not our best, not those which we should choose even out of our poor, stained, sordid lives, if we were required to select some which should give a being of another race some notion of the best life of a man. Surely we have been our best at those times when we have most completely worshipped something far better than ourselves. It is when we have cast our crown most humbly before God that our crown has been most real, that we have known that there was indeed a spark of something kingly in our natures.

And then there is one other way of looking at this matter. Think what company you are in when you are most reverential and full of the spirit of worship. When a man is at his business on mere selfish principles, exercising his business shrewdness, providing for himself and for his family, far be it from me to speak with any slight of such practical good occupation; but yet he is not there about the highest labor, nor associating himself with the highest company in the long lines of history. So long as a man is living for himself and honoring himself, there is an association, however remote it may be, with all the lowest forms of selfishness in which men have lived; but the moment a man begins to live in genuine adoration of the absolute good, and worship God, he parts company from all these lower orders of human life and enters into the richest and best society that earth possesses or ever has possessed. Think who you are with in adoration. When you say to God, " O God, take me, for the highest thing that I can do with myself is to give myself to Thee," when you say that to

God, humbly, but with all your heart, kneeling all apart in your chamber, where no one can see you, it is bewildering to me to think into what company you are taken instantly by that prayer of devotion. You sweep into the current of the best, the holiest, and the most richly human of our humanity, which in every age has dedicated itself to God. The worshippers of all the world — the Jew, the Greek, the Hindu, the Christian in all his various cultures, take you for their brother. You have part in the offering of Abel's altar, in the worship of Solomon's temple, in the prison talk of Socrates, in the closet adoration of all the saints. You are never in such company as when you are before God's throne offering Him your brightest and most precious. Yes, men are measured by their reverences. All human life is like the annual procession of the Jews, marching up to Jerusalem, to the Holy City. The nearer we are to that place of supreme adoration, the nearer the purpose of our life is fulfilled. What do you adore, what do you really reverence and respect? is the real test question of your life. In- an age which makes too little of reverence, let us not dare to let drop the truth that only that which is high can worship the highest, and so covet as the best crown of our existence the power so to know and feel that we can genuinely worship God.

And now let us take the second idea which seemed to be in our text. That idea was, that our highest attainments always get their best value from being offered to others who are dearer to us and higher than ourselves. Go back to our picture again. The

four and twenty elders are casting their crowns before
the throne of Christ.   Those crowns are the attainments of their lives.   All that the work of grace had
done in them, all the fruit of their long education, —
they valued it only as they might offer it to Him who
was the object of their reverence and love.   How
clearly we are touching here upon one of the universal experiences of men.   Is it not true that we do
all things best, when out beyond the thing that we
are doing there stands some one whom we love and
admire for whom the task is done?   The scholar who
is working hard at his problem in order that some
day he may take his triumphant solution of it in his
hands and go to his master who gave him his first
lessons, and say to him, " Take this, this belongs to
you, for I never should have done it if you had not
taught me ; " the soldier who in the midst of battle
is inspired by the thought that if he is brave and
conquers he will give back life to the country that
gave life to him ; the school-boy, who, resisting a
school temptation, is strengthened by the thought of
father and mother at home, who have taught him to
be true and generous, and who comes home afterwards and says, " They wanted me to be mean and to
lie, and I did not because I remembered you, and so
it was your strength that resisted and not mine," —
all these seem to me to be younger brethren of the
elders casting their crowns down at the throne-steps
of their Master ; full of the same spirit, living the
same life.

Such influences are certainly stronger and more
frequent than we know.   We are often working in

this way, with a deep reverence for others, when it seems as if we were doing what we do wholly for ourselves. A ship captain sails out on a long voyage, and as he goes it seems as if he carried all his interests and impulses shut up with him in that little ship. He finds his plenteous enjoyment everywhere. He revels in the problems of navigation that his well-trained skill knows how to solve. He spends long nights on deck, and conquers the elements that seem to have marshalled all their fury to decree that the little ship shall not go through. He rules his crew. He feels the daily joy of difficulties overcome. At last he comes to the haven where he wants to be. There all his business crowds his days. He is full of intercourse with men. He accomplishes the purpose of his voyage. He sells his cargo, and with a new one shipped he sails back, through months of work and interest and danger, till he is at the wharf from which he sailed a year ago. And then — what then? Why, he goes up on shore and finds out a little house where a little child, a mere baby-child, is living in a nurse's care, and gives the treasure of his voyage, all that he has earned, into the little hands of his unknowing child, who really was the single cause and inspiration of his toilsome voyage, and really is the reason why he rejoices in its success. He has not seemed — not even to himself — to think of her, but really she has been there in the bottom of his heart all the long time. The whole success is valuable to him because he may make an offering of it to her. If you doubt it, think how it would be if he came back and found her dead — the house empty, and only a little grave for him to lavish his love on. Where would be the value of his treasures then? Who could wake him out of the bitterness of his sorrow by rustling the paper or rattling the money in his ears? How worthless it would seem when she, the little daughter for whom he earned it all, was gone!

Such consecrations of our life to others are very often not less real and powerful because they are unconscious. Often they are not revealed to us ourselves until some sorrow comes, such as I just described. How many of us have known what all this means! We have gone on with our work in life, thinking that the purpose of our work was centred in ourselves! It was our own work that we were doing. We were working for ourselves. But some day a friend died — one who was very near to us, one in whom our life was bound up in many ways. Who has not known sometimes in life the dreadful going out of all the interest of living at the time of such a death? It seemed as if there were nothing left to live for. You looked upon your money, and wondered how you ever could have cared to earn it. The commonest little duties that recurred after the death was over were weariness to you. You looked forward, and it seemed as if you never could live out the long, flat, dreary days that stretched between you and the grave. The days went by, each with its twenty-four hours, each with its sunset and its sunrise, but the zest of them was all gone for you. The public life, the social life, went on, but it called to your dead interest in vain. What did you care for it all? Then you found that you had indeed been working for that dear dead friend, that wife, child, brother, as you never knew. All that you did had taken its value, not from you, but from them. When you thought you were working for yourself, you really had been working for them. And so their death had taken all the spring and impulse from you. It was terrible. But it was blessed if you did not stop there, but, with persistent love that would not be satisfied until it found the object it had lost, you traced the precious life on as it left you, till you followed it into the very bosom of the God who took it, and poured out there the treasures of devotion which had no longer any one dear enough to tempt them on the earth.

One cannot help feeling as he looks at working-men that this more than anything else is what makes the difference between them — the presence or absence in their lives of some distinct superior purpose for their work, to which it is all dedicated. It may be the comfort of a family, it may be a good cause, the support of education, the fostering of the great work of the Church; whatever it is, so it be something greater than the work itself, so that the work is turned from an end into a means, it lightens the pressure of the work most wonderfully, it relieves the continual burden. Take two men working in the field together — they dig across the field side by side, but one is always longing for the end where he can lie down and rest. The other rejoices in every stroke of his spade as if it were one more stone laid in the home that he is trying to build, in the cause which he desires to strengthen. And there is no work so lofty in itself that it does not thus need something higher than itself to be done for, something to lift its heavy pressure from the sore and weary backs of men. Even the work of the Lord Jesus, that work in which His soul delighted, the work of telling men of God and saving the world of sin, — I think no one can read the Gospels and not see that He was always lifting the heavy pressure of that work by reminding Himself that He was doing it for His Father. Is it not very touching? He rests, beyond His own pleasure in His work, upon the consciousness that it is His Father's pleasure too. "I have finished the work that Thou gavest me to do." That was the perfect satisfaction with which the Saviour, as it were, folded His hands from His long task and went to hang upon the cross. That was the casting down, as it were, of His crown before His Father's throne.

We have been speaking of the smaller inspirations that come to men to lighten and redeem their labors, but they are all subordinate to this, the sense that the work that we are doing in the world is done for Christ and God. If a man or woman is able to get and keep that, there is no drudgery so mean and crushing that it cannot be lifted and made buoyant — absolutely none. It is good to think how many men and women that seemed to live in slavery have really lived the freest lives, lifted above their slavery by this continual consciousness of work for God. They realized another meaning of those wonderful words of David, — among the most wonderful in all the

Bible, I think, — " I will walk at liberty, for I keep thy commandments." They would know what those words that we used in this morning's service really mean, " O God, whose service is perfect freedom." This was the case with multitudes of the poor slaves who have toiled anywhere in their slavery upon the suffering earth. Flogged to their work, living in misery, torn from their families, stripped of all the sweetness of life that comes from having something, somebody, to work for, what was there to lift off the load of unthanked and unprofitable labor such as theirs? There could be nothing unless there came, as there did come to many a darkened soul among them, a conviction that their weary work, their weary lives, were tributes and offerings to Jesus — that He loved them so, and had so utterly taken them for His, that He was pleased and glorified when they were patient and submissive in the wretchedness from which they could find no escape. As soon as they saw this, all was completely changed. The cabin walls opened and it was a temple. The dreary cotton-field became already, by anticipation and faith, the field beside the river of life under the towers of the New Jerusalem, where they who have served Him faithfully and glorified His name are to walk forever with the Lamb.

We speak of them because their suffering stood out strong and picturesque. But the release that came to faithful Christian hearts among them was nothing different in kind from that which comes to hundreds of patient sufferers everywhere, always. When it enters like a flood of light into the soul of some wretched invalid or some victim of relentless misfortune, that by a faithful patience under his suffering he can glorify God and show forth the power of Christ, then what a change comes to him ! How all is transfigured ! How full of beauty the hated sick-room grows ! There is something behind the suffering for the suffering to rest and steady itself upon. The light has been kindled behind the dark window, and all its fair lines and bright colors shine out. In the purpose of the suffering the escape from the suffering is found ; as when Paul and Silas, in the book of Acts, sang praises to God by night in prison, when they turned their imprisonment into a tribute to their Master, then "the foundations of the prison were shaken, and . . . the doors were opened, and every one's bands were loosed."

I am sure that there are many among us who feel the need to have the labor of our life redeemed, — merchants, clerks, lawyers, laborers, teachers, house-keepers, one thing or another, — the chosen or fated task of our life so often seems to be mere drudgery, crowding us down, pressing the life out of us. It is strange how soon many young men get to feel this about the occupations to which they have given up their lives, and all their first enthusiasm dies away. Then come the dreary years of unrelieved and un-enthusiastic work, only enlivened by the unhealthy excitement of mere commercial rivalry or professional spite. How many men we have seen restless all their lives, forever changing their work because they could not stand the heavy pressure of mere heavy, hated toil ! Does not what we have been saying seem to show that the trouble lies not in the kind of work, but in this — in whether men have beyond their work a purpose to dedicate it to, which can make it light and buoyant? No doubt some works more easily find such a purpose than others do, but any work that is good and honest is capable of it. And this decides the ranks of works and their effects upon the men who do them. No work is necessarily sacred in its influence upon the man who does it, and no legitimate work is necessarily secular and secularizing. It is possible to sell goods for God's glory, and it is possible (as the Church knows only too well) to swing censers and preach sermons for our own; and then there is no doubt that the man who sells goods gets more blessing out of his work than the man who sways the censer or preaches the discourse.

One would wish to urge this very strongly upon every man, especially upon every young man who is just beginning his work in life, and to whom his work, it may be, has already begun to show that in time it may come to be a weariness and a burden. What you need is some purpose beyond. What shall it be? The possible purposes lie in circles stretching one beyond another. If you can do your work for a friend or for a family as well as for yourself, you have already redeemed much of its sordidness. If you can do it for a cause, for the progress of society and the improvement of business, for your country, for your church, then you have lifted it still more. If you can do it for God, in perfect, childlike, loving desire for His glory, then your work, be it as heavy in its nature as it may, leaps of itself from the low ground, and, instead of crushing you with it to the earth, carries you up every day into the presence of the God for whom you do it. That is the continual beauty of a consecrated life, possible under all sorts of circumstances, possible to every kind of man in every kind of task.

Need I tell you the only thing that remains to be told? Need I tell you that the only influence which can really make us consecrate our lives and works to Christ is the profound and joyous confidence that Christ has done that for us, which makes the utter consecration of ourselves only a feeble token of the gratitude we owe and want to give. It is the soul forgiven — the soul to which the cross is everything — the soul living every day in the richness of the new reconciliation to the Father — this is the soul that values all it has and does, only as a possible tribute to its Redeemer and its Lord. This is the soul that casts its Crown of life down at the feet of the Lord of life, and glories in its Crown's richness not for itself, but for the greater praise of Him. Is there a motive of work conceivable so pure, so strong, so joyous, so humbling, so exalting, as this? — that a man should first take Christ's free love and then try to live as full and bounteous a life as possible, that he might have as worthy a tribute as possible to offer to his Lord and Saviour?

IV.

THE EGYPTIANS DEAD UPON THE SEASHORE.

" And Israel saw the Egyptians dead upon the seashore." — Exodus xiv. 30.

IT was the Red sea which the children of Israel had crossed dry-shod, "which the Egyptians essaying to do were drowned." The parted waves had swept back upon the host of the pursuers. The tumult and terror, which had rent the air, had sunk into silence, and all that the escaped people saw was here and there a poor drowned body beaten up upon the bank, where they stood with the great flood between them and the land of their long captivity and oppression. It meant everything to the Israelites. It was not only a wonderful deliverance for them, but a terrible calamity for their enemies. It was the end of a frightful period in their history. These were the men under whose arrogant lordship they had chafed and wrestled. These hands had beaten them. These eyes they had seen burning with scorn and hate. A thousand desperate rebellions, which had not set them free, must have come up in their minds. Sometimes they had been successful for a moment; sometimes they had disabled or disarmed their tyrants: but always the old tyranny had closed back upon them more pitilessly than before. But now all that was over; whatever else they might have to meet, the Egyptian captivity was at an end. Each dead Egyptian face on which they looked was token and witness to them that the power of their masters over them had perished. They stood and gazed at the hard features, set and stern, but powerless in death, and then turned their faces to the desert, and to whatever new unknown experiences God might have in store for them.

It is a picture, I think, of the way in which experiences in this world become finished, and men pass on to other experiences which lie beyond. In some moods it seems to us as if nothing finally got done. When we are in the thick of an experience we find it hard to believe or to imagine that the time will ever come, when that experience shall be wholly a thing of the past and we shall have gone out beyond it into other fields. When we open our eyes morning after morning and find the old struggle on which we closed our eyes last night awaiting us; when we open our door each day only to find our old enemy upon the doorstep; when all our habits and thoughts and associations have become entwined and colored with some tyrannical necessity, which, however it may change the form of its tyranny, will never let us go, — it grows so hard as almost to appear impossible for us to anticipate that that dominion ever is to disappear, that we shall ever shake free our wings and leave behind the earth to which we have been chained so long. On the long sea-voyage the green earth becomes inconceivable. To the traveller in the mountains or the desert it becomes very difficult to believe that he shall some day reach the beach and sail upon the sea. But the day comes, nevertheless. Some morning we go out to meet the old struggle, and it is not there. Some day we listen for the old voice of our old tyrant, and the air is still. At last the day does come when our Egyptian, our old master, who has held our life in his hard hands, lies dead upon the seashore, and looking into his cold face we know that our life with him is over, and turn our eyes and our feet eastward to a journey in which he shall have no part. Things do get done, and when they do, when anything is really finished, then come serious and thoughtful moments in which we ask ourselves whether we have let that which we shall know no longer do for us all that it had the power to do, whether we are carrying out of the finished experience that which it has all along been trying to give to our characters and souls.

For while we leave everything behind in time, it is no less true that nothing is wholly left behind. All that we ever have been or done is with us in some power and consequence of it until the end. Is it not most significant that these children of Israel, whom we behold to-day looking the dead Egyptians in the face and then turning their backs on Egypt, are known and appealed to ever afterwards as the people whom the Lord their God had brought " out of the land of Egypt, out of the house of bondage" ? In every most critical and sacred moment of their history they are bidden to recall their old captivity. When God most wants them to know Him, it is as the God of their deliverance that He declares Himself. The unity of life is never lost. There must not be any waste. How great and gracious is the economy of life which it involves! Neither to dwell in any experience always, nor to count any experience as if it had not been, but to leave the forms of our experiences behind, and to go forth from them clothed in their spiritual power, which is infinitely free and capable of new activities, — this is what God is always teaching us is possible, and tempting us to do. To him who does it come the two great blessings of a growing life, — faithfulness and liberty: faithfulness in each moment's task, and liberty to enter through the gates beyond which lies the larger future. " Well done, good servant: thou hast been faithful over a few things. Enter thou into the joy of thy Lord."

All this is true, but it is very general. What I want to do this morning is to ask you to think about the special experience to which our text refers, and consider how one truth is true of that, and of what corresponds to it in all men's lives. It was the end of a struggle which had seemed interminable. The hostility of Hebrew and Egyptian had gone on for generations. However their enmity may be disguised or hidden, the tyrant and the slave are always foes. If hope had ever lived, it had died long ago. Patient endurance, grim submission, with desperate revolt whenever the tyranny grew most tyrannical, — these had seemed to be the only virtues left to the poor serfs. Not to be demoralized and ruined by their servitude, to keep their self-respect, to be sure still that they were Abraham's children and that Abraham's God still cared for them, patience and fortitude, — these must have been the exhortations which they addressed to their poor souls as they toiled on in the brickyard or by the river.

It does not prove anything, if you please, about our present life, but it certainly sets us to asking new questions about it, perhaps to believing greater things concerning it, when in our typical story we behold all this changed. Behold, the day came when the chains were broken and the slaves went free. Are, then, our slaveries as hopeless as they seem? Are we condemned only to struggle with our enemies in desperate fight, and shall we not hope to see them some day dead like the Egyptians on the seashore?

Surely it is good for us to ask that question, for nothing is more remarkable than the way in which, both in public and personal life, men accept the permanence of conditions which are certainly some day to disappear. The whole of history which teaches us that mankind does conquer its enemies and see its tyrants by and by lying dead on the seashore, often appears to have no influence with the minds of men, all absorbed as they are in what seems a hopeless struggle. But look around! Where are the Egyptians which used to hold the human body and the human soul in slavery? Have you ever counted? The divine right of rulers, the dominion of the priesthood over the intellect and conscience, the ownership of man by man, the accepted inequality of human lots, the complacent acquiescence in false social states, the use of torture to extort the needed lie, the praise of ignorance as the safeguard of order, the irresponsible possession of power without corresponding duty, the pure content in selfishness — do you realize, in the midst of the cynical and despairing talk by which we are surrounded, can you realize, how these bad tyrants of the human race have lost their power over large regions of human life? They are dead Egyptians. Abominable social theories which fifty years ago, in the old days of slavery, in the old days of accepted pauperism, men stated as melancholy, but hopeless, truisms are now the discarded rubbish of antiquity, kept as they keep the racks and thumb-screws in old castle-dungeons for a tourists' show.

Is there anything more wonderful than the way in which men to-day are daring to think of the abolition and disappearance of those things which they used to think were as truly a part of human life as the human body, or the ground on which it walks? Ah! my friends, you only show how you are living in the past, not in the present, when you see nothing but material for sport in the beliefs of ardent men and brave societies which set before themselves and human kind the abolition of poverty, the abolition of war, the abolition of ignorance, the abolition of disease, the sweeping away of mere money competition as the motive power of life, the dethronement of fear from the high place which it has held among, aye, almost above, all the ruling and shaping powers of the destiny of man. I recognize in many a frantic cry the great growing conviction of mankind that nothing which ought not to be need be. I hear in many

hoarse, ungracious tones man's utterance of his conviction that much which his fathers thought was
meant to cultivate their patience by submission, is
meant also to cultivate their courage by resistance
till it dies. " The Egyptian must die." That is the
assurance which is possessing the heart of man.

When any evil does finally perish, then there is
something infinitely pathetic in the remembrance of
the way in which mankind for generations accepted
it as inevitable and drew out of its submission to it
such blessing and education as pure submission to the
inevitable is able to bestow. The poor man, who
thinks his poverty, and the ignorance and servitude
which his poverty entails, all right, comforts himself
by saying that God made him poor in order that he
might be patient and learn to possess his soul in self-
respect. By and by when the iniquity of the system
under which he has lived gives way and he finds himself admitted to the full rights and duties of a man —
what then ? Infinitely pathetic, as it seems to me, is
the recognition that he wins of the great love and
wisdom with which God would not let even that
darkness be entirely fruitless of light; but while He
was making ready for the fuller life of which the
poor man never dreamed, at the same time fed him
in the wilderness with manna which the wilderness
alone could give, so that no delight of freedom to
which he afterwards should come need make him
wholly curse or utterly despise the regions of darkness and restraint through which he came to reach it.

Is it not thus that we may always explain at least
a part, the best part, of that strange longing with

which the world, when it has entered into any higher life, still finds itself looking back to the lower life out of which it has passed? It is not properly regret. It is not a desire to turn back into the darkness. The age of real faith does not covet again the chains of superstition. The world at peace does not ask to be shaken once more by the earthquakes of war. But faith does feel the beauty of complete surrender which superstition kept for its sole spiritual virtue; and peace, with its diffused responsibility, is kindled at the thought of heroic and unquestioning obedience which the education of war produced. Still let superstition and war lie dead. We will not call them back to life; but we will borrow their jewels of silver and jewels of gold as we go forth into the wilderness to worship our God with larger worship. Do you not feel this in all the best progress? Do you not see it in the eyes of mankind, in the depths of the eyes of mankind always, as it turns away from the dead forms of its old masters and goes forth into the years to be; the hoarded power of the past glowing beneath the satisfaction of the present and the fiery hope of the unknown future?

Ah, well, there is always something fascinating in thus dwelling on the fortunes of the world at large, peering, like fortune-telling gypsies, into the open palm which she holds out to all of us. It is fascinating, and is not without its profit. But just as, I suppose, the shrewdest gypsy may often be the most recklessly foolish in the government of her own life, so it is good for us always to turn speedily and ask how the principles which we have been wisely applying to the world, apply to that bit of the world which we are set to live.

Do we believe — you and I — in the death of our Egyptians? What is your Egyptian? Some passion of the flesh or of the mind? — for the mind has its tyrannical passions as well as the flesh. Years, years ago, you became its captive. Perhaps you cannot at all remember when. Perhaps, like these children of Israel, you were born into its captivity. It was your father, or your father's fathers, that first became its slaves. When you first came to know yourself, its chains were on your limbs. As you grew older you knew that it was slavery, but it was such a part of all you were and all you did that you accepted it. That has not made you cease to struggle with it, but it has made you accept struggle hopelessly, as something never to be outgrown and left behind. You have looked forward into the stretch of years, and in prophetic imagination you have seen yourself an old man, still wrestling with the tyranny of your covetousness, or your licentiousness, or your prejudice, getting it down, planting your foot upon its neck, even compelling it to render you, out of the unceasing struggle, new supplies of character; absolutely fixed and determined never to give up the fight until you die — to die fighting. All this is perfectly familiar. Countless noble and patient souls live in such self-knowledge and consecration. But there comes something vastly beyond all these, when the soul dares to believe that its enemy may die, that the lust, or the prejudice, or the covetousness may absolutely pass out of existence, and the nature be absolutely free —

sure no doubt to meet other enemies and to struggle till the end, but done with that enemy forever, with that Egyptian finally dead upon the seashore.

When that conviction takes possession of a man, his fight is a new thing. The courage not of desperation, but of certain hope, fills every limb and gives its force to every blow. The victory which the soul believes is coming is here already as a power for its own attainment.

Has a man a right to any such hope as that, or is it the mere dream of an optimistic sermon? I dare appeal to you and ask you whether, in your own experience, God has not sometimes given you the right to such a hope? Are there no foes of your youth which you have conquered and left dead, passing on to greater battles? I am not speaking of the vices which you have miserably left behind, merely because the taste is exhausted and the strength has failed — vices which you would take up again if you were once more twenty years old. Those are poor victories. Those are no victories at all. But I mean this: Whether you are a better or a worse man now than you were twenty years ago. Are there not at least some temptations to which you yielded then to which you know that you can never yield again? Are there not some meannesses which you once thought glorious which now you know are mean? Are there no places where you once stumbled where now you know you can walk firm? I pity you if there are not. Other enemies which you then never dreamed of you have since encountered, but those enemies are done with. The Moabites and Midianites are before you and around you, but the Egyptians are dead. And in their death your right and duty are to read the prophecy of the death of every power which stands up between you and the Promised Land!

The appeal is not only to experience. It is to the first Christian truth concerning man. I have preached it to you a thousand times. I will preach it again and again until the end. The great truth of Christianity, the great truth of Christ, is that sin is unnatural and has no business in a human life. The birth of Christ proclaimed that in one tone: His cross proclaimed it in another! And that which is unnatural is not by any necessity permanent. The struggle of all nature is against the unnatural — to dislodge it and cast it out. That beautiful struggle pervades the world. It is going on in every clod of earth, in every tree, in every star, and in the soul of man. First to declare and then to strengthen that struggle in the soul of man was the work of Christ. That work still lingers and fails of full completion, but its power is present in the world. When He takes possession of a nature He quickens that struggle into life. No longer can that nature think itself doomed to evil. Intensely sensitive to feel the presence of evil as he never felt it before, the Christian man instantly and intensely knows that evil is a stranger and an intruder in his life. The wonder is not that it should some day be cast out: the wonder is that it should ever have come in. The victory promised in the sinless Son of man is already potentially attained in the intense conception of its naturalness. This is Christianity.

F

Is not this the change which you can see coming in the faces of the sinners who meet Jesus and feel His power in the wonderful stories which fill the pages of the Gospels? The first thing which comes to them, the great thing which comes to them all, is a change in their whole conception of life. What used to seem natural comes to seem most unnatural. That which they called unnatural becomes so natural that they cannot see why it should not immediately come to pass. The rich young man's money begins to fade in his hand, and he feels its tyranny passing away. The Magdalen's face grows luminous with a new vision of purity as the only true human life. Bigotry looks to Nicodemus what it really is. The simple naturalness in the hope that the children of God should live the life of God comes and folds itself around each of them. And in that atmosphere of their new life the old life with its old bondages dies.

You see how positive all this is. And that, too, seems to me to be depicted in the old Hebrew story, which we are using for our parable. It was on the farther seashore of the Red sea that the Egyptian pursuers of the Israelites lay dead. It was when the people of God had genuinely undertaken the journey to the land which God had given them, that the grasp of their enemy gave way and the dead hands let them go. You may fight with your enemy on his own ground, only trying to get the immediate better of him, and win what he claims for yourself, and your fight will go on, more or less a failure, more or less a victory, forever. You must go forth into a new land, into the new ambition of a higher life, and then, when he tries to follow you there, he perishes.

O selfish man? not merely by trying not to be selfish, but by entering into the new joy of unselfish consecration, so only shall you kill your selfishness. When you are vigorously trying to serve your fellowmen, the last chance that you will be unjust or cruel to them will disappear. When you are full of enthusiasm for truth, the cold hands of falsehood will let you go. Get the Egyptian off his own ground, seek not the same low things by higher means; seek higher things, and the low means will know that they cannot hold you their slave. They will lie down and die. And then the pillar of fire and the pillar of cloud will have you for their own and lead you on in your free journey.

With regard, then, to a man's permanent escape from evil, may we not say these two things, — that it must come about as the natural privilege of his life, and it must be positive? To the soul which has finally escaped from sin into the full freedom of the perfect life, the soul which has entered into the celestial liberty, must not these two things be clear, — first, that his old dream of life was a delusion, that he was never meant to be the thing which he so long allowed himself to be; and, second, that the great interests of the celestial life, the service of God which has there claimed the child of God, makes sure forever that there shall be no return to the old servitude? And what we dare to believe shall there in heaven come perfectly, and with reference to all wickedness, why may we not believe that here and now it may come in its degree with reference to some special sin ? Know that it is not natural that you should steal, that you should lie ; get rid of the first awful assumption that it is bound up with your constitution, cease to be a weak fatalist about it. That is the first thing. And then launch bravely forth into brave works of positive honesty and truth. Insist that your life shall not merely deny some falsehood, but that it shall assert some truth. Then, not till then, shall the lie let you go, and your soul count it impossible ever again to do — wonderful, almost incredible, that it ever should have done — what once it used to do from day to day.

I think that there are few things about our human nature which are more constantly marvellous than its power of acclimating itself in moral and spiritual regions where it once seemed impossible that it should live at all. The tree upon the hillside says : "Here and here alone can I live. Here my fathers lived in all their generations. Into this hard soil they struck their roots, and drank their sustenance out of its rocky depths. Take me down to the plain and I shall die." The gardener knows better. He takes the doubting and despairing plant and carries it, even against its will, to the broad valley, and sets it where the cold winds shall not smite it, and where the rich ground feeds it with luxuriance. And almost as they touch each other the ground and the root claim one another, and rich revelations of its own possibility flood the poor plant and fill it full of marvel with itself.

Of less and less consequence and meaning seem

to me those easy things which men are always saying about their own natures and character. "I have no spiritual capacity," says one. "It is not in me to be a saint," another cries. "I have a covetous soul. I cannot live except in winning money." "I can make many sacrifices, but I cannot give up my drink." "I can do many things, but I cannot be reverent." So the man talks about himself. Poor creature, does he think that he knows, down to its centre, this wonderful humanity of his? It all sounds so plausible and is so untrue! "Surely the man must know himself and his own limitations." Why must he? How can he know what lurking power lies packed away within the never-opened folds of this inactive life? Has he ever dared to call himself the child of God, and for one moment felt what that involves? Has he ever attacked the task which demands those powers whose existence he denies, or tried to press on into the region where those evil things cannot breathe which he complacently declares are an inseparable portion of his life? There is nothing on earth more seemingly significant and more absolutely insignificant than men's judgment of their own moral and spiritual limitations.

When the fallacy has been exposed, when the man has become something which he used to go about declaring that it was absolutely impossible that he should ever be, or has cast finally away that which he has counted a very part and portion of his life, it is often very interesting to see how he thinks of his cast-off sin. He, if he is a true man, counts his escape complete, but he never forgets his old bondage. He is always one whom God has led " out of the land of Egypt." Egypt is still there, although he has escaped from it. Egypt did not cease to be when the Egyptians with whom he had to do fell dead. Men are still doing the sin which has now become impossible for him. He understands those men by his past, while he cannot imagine himself sharing their life to-day. He is full of sympathy with the sinner, which is one with, of the same substance as, his security against the sin. Pity and hopefulness and humility and strength all blend into the peaceful and settled composure of his life.

It is a noble attitude towards a dead sin. You look into its dead face and are almost grateful to it. Not with a gratitude which makes you any way more tolerant of its character. You hate it with your heart — but look! Has it not given you self-knowledge, and made you cry out to God and set your face towards the new life?

My friends, get something done! Get something done! Do not go on forever in idle skirmishing with the same foe. Realize, as you sit here, who your chief enemy is, what vice of mind or body, what false or foul habit. Cry out to God for strength. Set your face resolutely to a new life in which that vice shall have no part. Go out and leave it dead. Plenty of new battles and new foes, but no longer that battle and that foe! Get some-thing done! May He who overcame, not merely for Himself but for us all, give you courage and make you sharers in His victory and in the liberty which He attained.

V.

THE BATTLE OF LIFE.

" For we wrestle not against flesh and blood, but against principalities, against powers, against the rulers of the darkness of this world, against spiritual wickedness in high places."—EPHESIANS vi. 12.

" THE Battle of Life " is a metaphor which almost all men at some time in their lives realize and own as true. It suggests a picture which recalls to almost every man his own history, if his has been at all an earnest life. We may think that it has not been so with other men; we may look at some bright and smiling life, and say with something of envy, with something also almost like reproach in our tone, "Lo, life has no battle for him! Behold how smooth and easy all the world has been for him!" The man himself knows better. And we, if we come close to him, can see the scars, nay, we can hear the battle of his life still going on. But whether we come close enough to him to know the real truth of his life or not, we know the truth about our own. Life is a battle. Forever on the watch against our enemies, forever guarding our own lives, forever watching our chance for an attack upon the foe,—so we all live if we are earnest men.

And this universal consciousness of battle is true to the figure by which we illustrate it in this,—that it affects different fighters in different ways, it inspires them with most various emotions. To one man the fact of the struggle of life is a perpetual exhilaration: upon another it weighs with an almost intolerable oppressiveness. To one man the ever-sounding battle bugle calling men always to the fight, brings a dismay which paralyzes every power: another man it seems to distract into the wildest folly, and he rushes everywhere, striking at random at friend or foe. It has no uniform effect. It catches each man as it finds him, and inspires him according to his character.

But metaphors are delusive, and if we cling too long and closely to them they grow tiresome. They are very apt often to blind us to the need of careful definition and discrimination. This metaphor, for instance, — Life a Battle, — may seem so satisfactory that it may lead us to forget that there are all kinds of battles, that we do not know much about a battle until we understand who the enemy is and what the weapons are. Two tribes of savages hewing away at each other in the jungle, the host of crusaders contending with the soldiers of the prophet, on the great plain of Galilee, the Swiss peasants fighting for freedom in their mountain fastnesses, our soldiers struggling with rebellion, — all these are battles; but how different they are! Evidently, before the old metaphor, "the Battle of Life," can mean anything very definite or practical to us, we must open it with the sharp knife of a question. We must ask who is the enemy with whom the battle of life is being fought.

The answers which will come are very various, and more than one answer will be true. See what some of the many answers are. The men who are engaged in any of the hard elemental works by which the earth is subdued to the use of man will tell us that human life is one long fight with nature. The sailor on the sea, the farmer in the field, the miner in the bowels of the earth, the woodman in the forest, — all of these are wrestling with the outer forces of the earth, and their hard battle rings in the endless chorus of axe and hammer which sounds through every land. Then comes the merchant fighting with the competition of his brethren. Then comes the legislator fighting with the barbarous tendencies which still haunt the most civilized societies. Then come the philanthropists fighting with abuses and ignorance and cruelty. And everywhere there is the man, hopefully or hopelessly, fighting with what he calls his fate, — the general aggregate of things about him and behind him which seems set to keep him down and to impede his way. The world is full of all these ideas of battle. And then right into the midst of them steps Paul, with his clear, ringing Christian word, "What are you fighting with? Do you ask that?" he says. "Lo, I can tell you. You are fighting with great evil principles and powers. You are fighting with forces of wickedness which come into this world from depths beyond our human nature. Obstinate nature, the rivalry of men, imperfect institutions, cruel habits, all those are ugly enemies, but the real enemy is Badness itself. The real fight is with that." Surely there is something very sharp and ringing in his answer. To find out what he means by it, if we can, will be the purpose of my sermon.

There can be little doubt of what Paul meant when he first used the word. His thought is perfectly distinct and clear. He cries to his Ephesians, "You are fighting with principalities and powers, against the world rulers of this darkness, against spiritual wickedness in the heavenly regions, in the sky or air." They are lofty words, and they are very definite. He is thinking of evil spirits. He believes distinctly in a universe all full of unseen forces. The sky was full of them. They were about us all the time. As some of them were the friends, so others of them were the enemies, of our souls and our best life. How wide that faith has been among mankind! How deeply it is imprinted on the pages of the Bible! How it has been allowed to melt and fade away out of the belief of hosts of people, even of those who read the Bible! And the reason, it seems to me, why the belief in a world of unseen forces with which we have to do, which has to do with us, — the reason why the belief in good and evil spirits has so faded away out of men's thoughts, is not any essential unreasonableness in the belief itself. Nor is it merely the tyranny of the visible world over men's senses, and through them over men's minds. It is, in large part, the fact that very, very often the believers in a universe of unseen spirits have not had St. Paul's loftiness and wisdom, but have made this unseen world a field for witchcraft and magic and the play of influences which the common moral sense of mankind has not been able to understand. St. Paul believed in spirits good and bad. The beauty of his belief in them was that, different as they might be from us in the conditions of their life, they still belonged to the same great moral system to which he belonged. The good spirits were not to be propitiated, and the evil spirits were not to be disarmed by magic and incantations. He who did righteousness called to himself the most mysterious strength of the unseen worlds. He and he alone was safe against the assaults of the spirits of darkness. This appears, you know, in the very passage from which I take my text. "Because we wrestle against these invisible enemies, therefore take unto you the whole armor of God, having your loins girt about with truth, and having on the breastplate of righteousness." When we think how generally the believers in a world of spiritual forces have grown fantastic, and have tried to influence the forces of that unseen world by enchantments which had no moral meaning, we see how much more dignified and lofty is St. Paul's position. To him goodness, morality, was the first condition of all life. Here on this earth or anywhere beyond the stars, to be good must be the first condition of all strength. He who was good, he who was trying to be good, entered thereby into friendly confederation with all the noble forces of the universe, and bid defiance to all the evil powers of the sky and air. For him all good beings fought; against his simple righteousness all evil beings would beat themselves in vain, and ultimately must go down and fail, here or beyond the stars. That is a noble faith. In the simplicity and grandeur

of a faith like that, man will some day come once
more to the now almost lost belief in the connection
of his life with unseen spiritual powers. There is an
ineradicable disposition in the human soul to think
that this one little world is not apart from all the
rest. And Scripture finds its sanction in the best
human instincts when it says that he who is doing
righteousness is on the side of the great currents of
universal life, and has not only God but all good
spirits for his friends. I have wandered a little from
our subject, but yet it all leads on to this idea on
which we want to dwell, that whether we fully
realize St. Paul's description of the evil spirits with
whom the Christian has to fight, or whether his enemies present themselves to us rather as abstract principles to which we do not attach personality as clearly
as St. Paul did, still it is something invisible, something spiritual, something behind and deeper than
the mere outward forms of things, within which the
real difficulties of life lie, and with which the true
man must do battle.

In many ways men come to the discovery of this
truth, often in ways that are full of pain and disappointment. Some brave reformer has struggled
against a vicious institution, and by and by has
succeeded in breaking it down. The great re-
form is carried. Henceforth there is to be no
more traffic in slaves. Henceforth the sale of drink
shall be prohibited. Henceforth corruption is not
to make prizes out of public office. How often has
the successful reformer stood among the ruins of
the demolished institution, and there, just in the

first enthusiasm of his joy, been suddenly smitten
with dismay and felt the shout of triumph perish
on his lips; for lo! out of the ruins of the ruined
institution rose a spectre, which he saw was the
unkilled soul of the dead institution, and which,
even as he gazed upon it, began to put itself forth
in some new outward shape, to create for itself a
new body, and to look defiance on the poor discouraged fighter, who saw how all his work had to
be done over again from the beginning. Happy and
truly brave is the reformer who is not disheartened,
but enlightened, by that sight, and who does begin
again with unabated zeal, striking with ever new
vigor at each new abuse, but learning ever more
and more deeply that not in evil institutions, but
in evil principles, does the real evil lie; and so expecting to see slavery appear in one new form after
another until the soul of the community is free, and
intemperance revive in one new device after another
until the soul of the community is sober, and corruption reassert its power in one new shape after
another till the soul of the community is honest.
When he has come to that knowledge, then the
reformer settles down undiscouraged to the heart of
his battle, and summons the loftiest spiritual powers
to his aid, and perseveres to death. And when death
comes, and he goes, leaving his long work still
undone, the very sight of the reality of spiritual
forces which he wins as, dying, he comes nearer to
their home seems often to make him more sure of
the final victory just when his tired hands are drop-
ping their weapons; and he dies more than content.

The same truth comes in much the same way to the champion of sound doctrine and a true belief. "Break down this heresy and then men will have faith," so cries the lover of God's truth as he sits down in his calm study to show how destitute of reason is the last superstition of the day. Perhaps he perfectly succeeds. Perhaps he tears the poor flimsy argument to tatters, and leaves the fanatic or the blasphemer not a word to say for his poor fantasy. And then the weary controversialist goes to his well-earned rest, and wakes up in the morning to find the sun shining on a whole city full of new unbeliefs and misbeliefs, in which the spirit of faithlessness has embodied itself during the night, and which stand there facing the sunrise with their bright new pinnacles and spires, which have taken possession of the sky as if they meant to shine there forever. Happy and brave and wise the champion of the faith who is not discouraged, but enlightened, by that sight, and who goes out again, ready to strike down and disprove each new and special error as it rises, but who grows always more and more eager to change the deeper state, the heart and temper of the life about him, — to bring in faith for faithlessness, to give a true and deep, and true and healthy, tone to life, — so that this dreary work of ever disproving fantasy after fantasy need not go on forever; but some day, — however far away, — some day the time shall come when out of the heart of a healthily believing humanity nothing but true and healthy faith can grow.

I turn back for an instant here to what I said about Paul and his belief in good and evil spirits, and about the current disbelief in all such beings which prevails to-day. Is not the method of the true belief indicated by what I have just now been saying? How shall the field be swept clear of all the paraphernalia of ghost stories and the false supernatural which brings its double harm, degrading the souls that believe in it, and hardening into blank materialism the souls whom its absurdities or enormities drive into disbelief? You may prove one impostor after another to be false. You may demonstrate beyond all question that this or that phenomenon has nothing supernatural about it, but you will work in vain until you strike right at the root of all the folly by taking Paul's ground, and insisting that whatever unseen presences there may be about us, we and they and all the universe must be subject to the eternal, universal sway of moral law; that therefore the only way to really win the good and to really disarm the evil, from whatever region of the universe they make attacks upon us, is to live nobly, truly, purely. When men have been led to think thus of the world of spirits, then I do believe that we shall see a great restoral of healthy belief in spiritual presences. The fantastic and fitful, unreal and immoral, way of thinking and feeling about them will disappear, and calmly, quietly, without fright, without fanaticism, with a great deepening of the sense of the moral criticalness of living, men will know that the universe is larger than this little earth, and that for a human creature to be good or bad means something out into unknown, unknowable regions of spiritual life.

I have spoken of the way in which the knowledge of one truth, that the real struggle of life is not with institutions or creeds, but with moral and spiritual dispositions, of which institutions and creeds are only the expressions, — the way in which this knowledge comes to the reformer when his work against a bad institution or a false creed has succeeded and he has conquered it. Not less important is the power which that knowledge may have in him while his hot fight is still going on. I hope that I speak to some men and women who count it their duty and their right to set themselves against the wrongs and evils of the world, and to do everything they can to set them right. They cannot be unaware of what the dangers of the agitation against evil are. To let the battle against wickedness and cruelty pass over into a personal hatred of the wicked and cruel man, and exhaust itself in personal attacks on him for other things besides his wickedness, — that is the constant peril. How often does the hot agitator need these calm, strong words: "Not against flesh and blood, but against principalities and powers, and the world-spirit of darkness, and the evil that is in the air." I know the answer that will come : "Evil incorporates itself in men. How can you strike out the evil without beating down the men in whom it is embodied?" But surely no such statement as that, which is most absolutely true, can be stretched wide enough to cover the personal hatred, the wilful or careless misrepresentation, the petty spite, with which the earnest advocate of some cause which he thought indubitably right has very often followed up the man upon the other side whom he believed of course to be indubitably wrong. Just see what some of the personal disadvantages of such a disposition are. First, it puts it absolutely out of the angry partisan's power, in case he is not wholly right, to get any advantage or correction from the opposite light in which his opponent sees the same transaction which he thinks so wrong; second, it robs the furious hater of the chance to learn charity and personal consideration, for of course the chance to think tolerantly of a man who differs from us comes to us when we differ from him, and if, the moment that we differ from him, we begin to hate him, it is as if we shut up the door of one of our best school-rooms and turned the key of prejudice upon it; and, third, yet again it makes turbid and heavy and dull that stream of simple indignation against evil and love for righteousness which, when it is absolutely fresh and pure, is the most strong and persistent power in the world. These are the reasons why it is a sad loss when the fighter with wickedness turns his struggle against wickedness into angry attacks on men against whom perhaps their wickedness has first provoked him, but whom he has come now to hate for themselves. This was the spirit of our Lord's disciples when they wanted to call down fire on the village of Samaria. This was Luther's spirit when at Marburg he lost sight of the simple fight with error and plunged into a personal attack on Zwingle. It is the danger of all earnest men. It seems sometimes to be so inseparable from earnestness that the world thinks that it must not call it a vice or take any note of it in the earnest man. But no really earnest man can be so self-indulgent. Ever he must struggle to know who his true enemy is, and to fight finally with him alone. With wickedness we may be unmitigatedly indignant. We may hate it with all our hearts. Towards it there is no chance, there is no right, of indulgence or consideration. But with the wicked man, because he is both man and wickedness, we may be at once full of anger and full of love, and out of the spirit of the highest justice, both to him and to ourselves, insist always that it shall be the wickedness and not the man that we hate!

Now let me turn away from words which may appear to be addressed only to certain classes of my hearers, and let me try to speak of things which must concern us all. Inside of all the other battles we are fighting, there is the battle with ourselves. Inside of the battle with the world for the world, which the great champions of righteousness are fighting in their great way, and which you and I, I hope, are fighting in our little way, there lies the battle which every true man is always fighting with himself for himself —himself the hostile enemy, himself the precious prize. Oh, how real sometimes all that must become to the great workers for mankind! While Howard is travelling all over Europe, from prison to prison, while Clarkson has his hand upon the fetters of the slave, while Francke is gathering his orphans around him and struggling with their ignorance, while Garrison is striving to free the slave, sometimes the heart of each of them must have grown sick and

faint with the freshly heard sound of its own inner
conflict; sometimes each of them must have turned
aside and shut the door upon all the tumult of the
world and left the great cause for an hour to take
care of itself, while he fought with himself for himself, — with himself his own enemy, for himself his
own prize. There are verses enough, you know, in
St. Paul's Epistles which let us see that struggle with
himself going on all the time underneath the other
struggle with the men of Jerusalem and Athens.
While the foreign war was raging, the home country
also was all up in arms. How such men must have
thought often within themselves that the foreign war
would be as nothing, would be a very easy thing,
if only there were peace at home. "I could convert
the world easily," the missionary must often find
himself saying, "if only I had a solid ground to
stand upon, if only my own life were not all soft and
weak with sin and doubt." And sometimes, too, the
other thought must come, "What right have I to be
busying myself with the world's miseries while all
this unrest is tumultuous within me? Why is it not
best to shut in myself upon myself and fight my own
battle out before I meddle with the bigger battle?"

Such thoughts come naturally; but really it is
good, no doubt, that the two strifes, the outer and
the inner, the strife with self and the strife with the
world's sin, should go on together. The man who
knew no enemy within himself, who was so absorbed
in fighting with the world's sin that he grew uncon
scious of his own inner life, by and by would become
arrogant and superficial. Such men the world has

often seen among its philanthropists. The man who is totally wrapped up in the war within him, the war with himself for his own life, grows selfish and grows morbid. The two must go on together. Each keeps the other healthy and true. Fight with your own sin, and let that fight keep you humble and full of sympathy when you go out into the world and strike at the sin of which the world is full. Fight with the world's sin, and let the needs of that fight make you aware of how much is wrong, and make you eager that everything shall be right within yourself. Here is the balance and mutual ministry of self-care and world-care which makes the truest man the healthiest philanthropist.

Surely it always must be full of meaning, that Christ Himself, before He began his struggles with the Pharisees and Scribes, went out into the desert and struggled with Himself. It must have been present with Him ever afterwards, that wrestling with the evil spirit and all the knowledge of Himself which it called out. Many a time the wilfulness, and narrowness, and selfishness which He saw in the faces which surrounded Him in some crowd in the temple must have been clearer to Him and easier to understand, because they were just the passions which had tried to take possession of His own heart, and failed, during those long terrible days in the dark wilderness. And oh! my friends, there is no way in which whatever personal struggles with faithlessness and sin we may have gone through can be made to keep their freshness and power, and at the same time be kept from becoming a source of morbid wretchedness, no way that is half so efficient as that they should constantly be called on to light up for us the same sort of struggles in other men, and give us the power to help them with intelligence and sympathy. Demand that lofty service of every deep experience through which you pass. Demand that it shall help you understand and aid the battles of your brethren, and then the devils of memory which haunt your life may be turned into strong angels, by whose help you may do the will of God, and be in some small way the saviour of mankind.

Our allusion to the conflict of Jesus in the desert reminds us of how, to this internal strife which a man carries on with his own nature, St. Paul's description of the nature of all spiritual conflict especially applies. " Not against flesh and blood " was the wrestling of Jesus always. It was with the sin of Caiaphas and Herod, not with Caiaphas and Herod, that He strove. But here especially in the desert, it was directly with the spirit of evil, and not with any of its outward forms or symbols, that He struggled. And is it not true that just in proportion as all men's strifes with their own selves grow serious and earnest, they are always pressing in and in, and growing to be less and less struggles with the mere forms and symbols of wrong-doing, more and more profound contests with our own true selves and with our sins? Some young man here begins the noble work of trying to be a better man. He knows that it is no mere hoisting of holiday sails and idly slipping under pleasant breezes into another life. He knows that he has got to fight. But fight with what — with whom?

Where is his enemy? And then see how he begins on the outside and works inward as the combat deepens. First the enemy seems to be in the circumstances and conditions of his life. He fights with those. He gives up the business that is always full of temptation. He breaks off the acquaintance that keeps him in the low atmosphere. He moves out of the house where the wicked people live. He abandons the reading which kept certain bad thoughts before his mind. All that is good; but when he stands with all that done, the sense comes over him that his enemy is not conquered yet. He has only stripped himself for the fight. The real fight has not yet begun.

Then he goes farther in. More personal, more a part of himself than his associations and his circumstances, are his habits. If a man's circumstances are like his clothes, his habits are like his very body. With these habits he begins to wrestle next. He will not drink; he will not swear; he will not lie. All that is very good again. Most good. But once more, when all this is accomplished and the bad habits are all cast away, still the man stands aware that his self is not conquered. That mysterious centre of his being which is the He that thinks and feels and not merely does good or bad, but is good or bad, is the man; that still is in deep conflict with itself. The sin which is internal strife is not yet cast out there.

And then comes very often something else, with which in these days we are most familiar. The man who has found that the real struggle of his life is not with his associations and is not with his habits, often looks back to his hereditation, as he calls it. How familiar that long word has grown with certain very estimable kinds of people! "I have inherited all these bad dispositions. I have to fight with all that my forefathers have been. Pity me! pity me! for my dead ancestors are too much for my living will." So the poor victim cries as he feebly settles himself down to what he holds beforehand is a losing fight. It has its own despair already in itself, this hopeless struggle with hereditation which, as so many of our teachers now depict it, is so peculiarly, so literally, a wrestling against flesh and blood.

These are the several outer circles. The fight in them comes to seem either useless or hopeless. And then at last, if the man is thoroughly in earnest, then at last the man gets into the heart and centre of it all. Not in his circumstances, not in his habits, not in his hereditations, but in himself, in a heart ready to give itself up to the worse instead of to the better powers of the world, in a soul that loves baseness, frivolity, and falseness, there lies the real enemy. Oh, the great strength which comes when that discovery is made! And, feeling that now at last the real battle has begun, the man solemnly, solidly settles himself down to the conquest of himself. The army which has carried by storm one fortification after another and found that it has only gained possession of an outpost, more or less insignificant, now sits down before the central citadel and the real siege begins. Then comes the true calling up of all the powers. Then comes humility, and by humility self-understanding,

and in self-understanding strength. Then comes
that earnest cry for God's help which always brings
its answer. Then comes the giving of the soul's own
weakness into the abundant strength of Christ.
Then comes the great reality of prayer. All of
these, when the man has at last got to the centre of
his sin, and is at last fighting with himself for his own
soul.

My friends, do you know the meaning of all that?
Are you fighting that battle for self-conquest? If
you are, you know with what a true exhilaration that
which seems such a cruel and unnatural necessity of
life may occupy and inspire the soul. Almost with a
shout the man exclaims, " I will subdue myself for
goodness and for God!" And though no shout is
heard, though men beside him do not hear a sound,
though the battlefield is in some inmost secret chamber of his most secluded life, though the fairest
flowers of his own self-content are being torn to
pieces by the wrestler's feet, yet still there is — do not
you know it, many of you? — a deep, strong, solemn
joy as the night draws nearer to the day, and the self
with which we fight grows weaker, and the self for
which we fight grows freer, — a joy deep and strong
and solemn with which no other pleasure in human
living can compare.

And also there grows up a great charity and hope
for every other man who is fighting the good fight
with his sins — a charity and hope which is alone
reward enough for all our pain!

May God lead all of us speedily in, through all the
outer struggles, to this inmost fight of all! May we

begin it now, and never end it till our sin is dead!
May the Captain of our salvation be our leader and
our strength! May we be full of courage, because the
battle which we fight is not our own alone, but God's,
and at the last may we be conquerors in Him!

VI.

THE DIGNITY AND GREATNESS OF FAITH.

"No man can say that Jesus is the Lord but by the Holy Ghost."
— I. Cor. xii. 3.

These words must mean their deepest, or else they cannot mean anything for us. They were written long ago when Christianity was new. To say, then, that Jesus Christ was the divine Lord of the world was something different in the demand it made upon a man's powers and character from what it is to-day. In some respects it must have been much harder then than now: in some respects much easier. We cannot tell wholly, I suppose, what Paul's verse meant in the ears of the Corinthians who heard it first. But when we bring his words over to our own time and try to realize them now, it is evident that they mean nothing unless they mean their deepest. "No man can say that Jesus is the Lord but by the Holy Ghost." Evidently it is not true that a divine help is needed simply to declare as an article of one's creed, a conviction of one's mind, that Jesus Christ is Master of the world. Thousands of people are doing that all the time, and doing it evidently by themselves, not "by the Holy Ghost" at all, often saying the great words wilfully, obstinately, controversially, with a spirit and an impulse so essentially earthly that we know they did not come from heaven; with a vehemence so unholy and unspiritual that we know it is not the work of the Holy Spirit.   Evidently it cannot be the mere saying of the words or the mere acceptance of the fact that proves a divine influence.   It must be the saying of the words, "Jesus is the Lord," filled with the most earnest faith and the richest experience; the saying of them by a man to whom they represent the deepest fact and the most powerful impulse of his life.   It must mean this, and, if it does, then it involves one of the greatest and most urgent subjects of which we can think or speak.   That subject is the dignity and greatness of a faith in Christ. It is only, so says St. Paul, it is only by an action which outgoes his own powers and shares the strength of God that a man is able to own Christ as the master of his life.

The Dignity and Greatness of faith!   There are two classes of people, very different from one another, both of whom deny the proposition which I have announced and of which I wish to speak.   The first denier is the ordinary flippant church-member or partisan controversialist, who treats faith as if it were one of the easiest and most casual functions of a human life, and a confession of faith as if it were an indifferent sort of action to be slipped in almost anywhere, between two other acts of wholly other kinds. Such a man dishonors faith by the trivialness with which he treats it.   His denial of its dignity and greatness is a practical one, and while he makes it he may be all the time talking the grandest talk about the faith which all his life discredits.   The

other denier is more serious, and his denial deals with
the whole idea and theory of faith. Many and many
men there are to-day who most deliberately hold and
teach that the idea of man's depending upon a loftier
power than himself is a delusion of human immaturity, that it belongs to the infancy of the human mind,
that for the world or for any man to give it up and
count the human life sufficient for itself is a distinct
advance, that faith is fetich-worship gradually passing
out into the light, slowly becoming that full enlightenment of man in which, when it becomes complete,
there shall be no longer any such thing possible
as faith. In protest against both denials, the practical denial of the frivolous communicant in our
churches, and the dogmatic denial of the positivist
philosopher, we want to assert the dignity and greatness of faith. I would like to think that as I speak
I see two faces before me — one the easy, careless
face of the commonplace professor of religion. Looking into his trifling eyes I would like to say: "Poor
soul, this earthly, uninspired thing of yours is not
real faith. No man can have real faith but by the
Holy Spirit." The other face shall be the earnest,
puzzled, eager face of the young man who is trying,
as he has been taught, to despise and pity the victims
of the supernatural. To him one wants to say: "Do
not dare to despise what is the noblest act that man
has ever tried to do. You degrade yourself when
you do that. It is only by a divine, Holy Spirit that
any man can have faith."

Begin with this, then: that the greatness of any
act is to be estimated by the faculties of man which it

employs. It is a greater act for a man to write a book than for him to build a fence, because the writing of the book demands the use of deeper powers. The man must think, — at least a little, — and arrange his thought, and give it utterance in language. To govern a State requires still nobler faculties, faculties rarer, finer, more profound, faculties that must be summoned for their work out of yet deeper chambers of our human nature. When I know what faculties any man's work requires, at once I know where that work stands in comparative dignity among the works of men. When a new act of man is offered to me which I have not been called upon to estimate before, I ask myself what powers the man will have to use who does that act, and when I know that, then I am sure that I can judge it rightly.

This is the test that we must apply here: What faculties are needed in an act of faith? What powers must a man use who says with all his heart of an unseen Jesus, "He is my Lord and Master"? Let us see — and first of all there is the power of dealing with the unseen at all. Back from the visible to the invisible which lies behind it, the mind of man is always pressing; and as it presses back, there are new powers coming out into consciousness and use. The first man in his immaturity deals with things. Man as he grows maturer deals also with ideas. The things are visible and tangible. The ideas no eye has seen, no hand has ever touched. Subtle, elusive, and yet growing to be more real to the mind of the man who truly deals with them than are the bricks of which his house is built, or the iron tool with which he does his work, the great ideas of justice, of beauty, of sublimity, become at once the witnesses and the educators of man's deeper powers which must come out to do their work.   The birth of the power of recognizing and dealing with ideas, the birth of ideality, is an epoch in the history of the world or of a man.   Or, again, you know your friend by the seeing of the eye; all the distinct intercourses of the senses introduce your life to his; and then your friend goes away from you, out of your sight, to China or Peru; and as your power of friendship reaches out to follow him, as the thought of him takes the place of the sight of him, as association, and memory, and hope, and imagination come out at your need to bind your life with his, — is not your friendship growing greater with the new faculties it requires, has not your love for your unseen friend become a nobler exercise than any delight in his visible presence possibly could be?   These are instances and illustrations of the glories of the faculty in man by which he has to do with things which he cannot see.   And when the unseen one is Christ, a being whom the man never has seen, whom yet he is compelled to realize, not as an idea, but as a living person capable of being loved, and trusted, and obeyed, there surely is a noble demand there for one of the loftiest of human faculties; and the loftiness of the faculty which must be used in doing it bears testimony to the loftiness of the act which the man does who says of the unseen Jesus Christ, "He is my Lord."

Another of the faculties which is involved in faith,

and whose necessity is a sign that a true act of faith
is one of the completest acts which man can do, is
the faculty of personal admiration and trust. In
its fullest exercise faith is personal. We speak indeed of faith in principles, and that is a noble and
ennobling thing; but the fullest trust comes with the
perception of trustworthy character, and the entire
reliance of one nature on another. Is it a great
power or a great weakness in a man's life that makes
him capable of doing that? I am tempted, in answer
to that question, to point you simply to that which I
am sure that you have all seen and felt, the strange
and sometimes terrible deterioration which so often
comes in men's characters as they grow up from
boyhood into manhood, leaving the years of docility
behind them, pass into the years of self-reliance and
independence. The poetry and beauty and richness
of a boy's life lie in his power of admiration for,
and trust in, something greater than himself. If you
fathers make your homes what they ought to be, the
boys will find the object of that admiration and trust
in you. If you will not let them find it there, they will
find it somewhere else. Somewhere they will surely
find it. And in their admiration and their trust, the
outreaching and uplifting of their life will come.
What does it mean when men as they grow older
become narrow, sordid, and machine-like, when a
vulgar self-content comes over them, and all the
limitations of a finished life that hopes for and
expects no more than what it is makes the sad
picture which we see in hosts of men's middle life?
Is it not certainly that those men have ceased to

admire and ceased to trust? The objects of their childhood's trust and admiration they have outgrown, and like young scholars who imagine that the story-books of infancy are the only books in the world, and so, when those books cease to interest the maturing mind, lay by their power of reading as if there were no further use for it, so these men, when they can no longer admire and trust their fellow-men completely, as they used to do when they were boys, think that the faculty of perfect trust and admiration has no further use. The blight that falls upon their admiring and trusting natures is the token of what a lofty and life-giving faculty it is which they have put out of use. It was this faculty which made them at every moment greater than themselves, which kept them in communion with the riches of a higher life, which preserved all the enthusiasm of active energy, and yet preserved humility which held all the other faculties to their best work. This is the faculty whose disuse makes the mature life of so many men barren and dreary, and whose regeneration, when the man is lifted up into the new admiration and the new trust, the admiration for and trust in God, makes a large part of the glory of the full-grown life of faith.

One other quality I mention which must be in the man who sends his faith out into the unseen and fastens it in trust and admiration on a divine person. I know not what to call it except a hopeful sense of need, — not only a sense of need, for that, if it be not hopeful, may merely grovel and despair, — but a sense of personal deficiency, filled and lighted up all

through and through with the conviction that somewhere in the world, in some place not desperately
beyond its reach, there lies, waiting for its finding,
the strength and the supply that it requires. This is
the faculty in which has lain the coiled mainspring
of all human progress. Barbarism, filled with the
hopeful sense of need, has pressed onward and onward into civilization. Ignorance, hopefully knowing its need, has scaled the heavens and fathomed
the seas and cleft the rocks for knowledge. Man, in
all ages, has struggled and achieved, has wrestled
with his present condition and laid his daring hand
on higher things, under the power of this faculty in
which were met the power of his clear perception of
his deficiencies and his deep conviction that his deficiencies might be supplied. Is this a noble faculty
or not? I would be willing to appeal again to your
own consciousness. There are times when this faculty is very sluggish and dull within you, and there
are other times when it seems full of life. Some
days there are when the story of your need falls on
your ears like an unmeaning tale; when either you
are self-contented and feel no lack in heart or brain
or character, or, feeling it, have no hope but that you
must go on forever the poor, half-developed, crippled
thing you are. Then there are other days when you
look through and through yourself, and any thought
of keeping on constantly just as you see yourself
now is terrible. You know your sin and sordidness.
But at the same time voices are calling you to come
and get the things that you require. The whole
great voice of all the world seems to be promising

H

you escape and supply. As deep and strong as the sense of need is the hope. Of those two days, which is the greater? On which of them are you the stronger man? Is this faculty, which on the second of these days is awake in you, a degradation or an exaltation of your life? There can be but one answer, only one. You know you never are so great, never so thoroughly a man, as when with manly honesty you see yourself through and through, and, filled with shame, are yet inspired and held up by hope. But all that must come to pass, this faculty of hopeful neediness must wake and live, before a man can with true faith call Jesus Christ, the Saviour of the world, his Lord.

And now once more I say, it is the faculties which any act demands which indicate the degree of dignity and greatness in that act. Behold, then, what we have reached. In the act of faith, by which you or I trust ourselves to the keeping and make ourselves the servants of Christ, there must meet these faculties, or else the act cannot be done: the power of dealing with the unseen, the power of personal loyalty and trust, the power of a hopeful sense of need. Those three great powers in their aggregate meet in the man who is Christ's servant. Now what I claim is this, that the belief and personal devotion for whose attainment that aggregate of qualities must meet is a most great and glorious action. I do not say now that it is an action possible or impossible, or whether the man who thinks with all his soul that he is doing it is congratulating himself upon the great fact of his life, or hugging to

his heart the most shadowy of all delusions.   I only
say that the description of the act involves a picture
of the most complete and lofty and thoroughly
human action which a man can be conceived of as
doing; and that if man, having thought himself
capable of such an action, should be completely
proved to be incapable of it, his whole life would
have suffered an incalculable loss.   The world of
human existence would have been robbed of its sunlight and its sky.   On this I am sure that we ought
to insist.   There are bold, trenchant writers and
talkers to-day who are congratulating the world that
the days of faith are over, that the glorious liberty
of unbelief has come.   That certainly will never
do.   You must not pluck the jewel off of the fore-
head of the man who has counted himself a king and
then ask him to thank you as if you had broken fetters from his wrists.   You must not pull down the
sun out of the sky and then bid men rejoice that they
have escaped from the slavery of sunlight.   If there
is no God whom I can come to and obey and trust,
I want to know the dreadful fact, and not to go on
thinking that there is; for it is better for every man to
know the fact, however dreary and dreadful it may
be, than to believe a lie, however sweet and gracious.
But that is something utterly different from saying
that it would not be better for us all if faith were
possible, and that to be robbed of the possibility of
faith is the desolation and ruin of human life.

One wants to say the same thing to men who do
believe with all their hearts, men who believe with
all the strength of an experience which no man can

disturb, in the possibility and the reality of faith. I seem to hear a certain sort of apologetic tone among men of faith, which is not good. They sometimes seem to plead that their faith may be left to them, much as a baby pleads that he may keep his toys, or a lame man that he may keep his crutches. It is the appeal of weakness. The man who trusts God sometimes seems almost to say to his unbelieving brother, " Forgive me. I am not as strong as you are. I cannot do without this help. You are more strong and do not need it. But let me keep it still." No open foe of faith can do faith so much harm as that kind of believer. Shall the disciple be ashamed of that which is the glory of his manhood, its highest reach, requiring the combination of its noblest powers? The only thing to be said about such feeble-hearted faith as that is that it is not faithful enough to know the essential dignity of faith. It is a sick man apologizing to death because he is not quite ready yet to die. It is the meagreness of health in him that prompts his poor apology. Let him grow healthier and he begins to look not down to death with apologies, but up to life with hopes and aspirations. So let the weak disciple grow more strong in faith, and he will have no longer feeble words of shame and self-excuse to say about his trust in Christ ; only his whole life will grow one earnest prayer for an increase of faith, as the child's life is one continued hope and prayer for manhood.

O young disciples, whatever other kind of falseness to your faith you may fall into, may you be saved at least from ever being ashamed of it. It is the noblest, the divinest, thing on earth. You may have only got hold of the very borders of it, but if in any true sense you can say, "Jesus is the Lord," you have set foot into the region wherein man lives his completest life. Go on, without one thought or dream of turning back, and with no shamefaced hiding of the new mastery under which you are trying to live. If your Christian service is too small in its degree for you to boast of, it is too precious in its kind for you to be ashamed of. Go on forever craving and forever winning more faith and obedience, and so learning more and more forever that faith and obedience are the glory and crown of human life.

But now let us return to our text. We have been talking about the dignity and greatness of faith. But St. Paul says something else about it. It is the gift and inspiration of God. "No man can say that Jesus is the Lord but by the Holy Ghost." Not merely, it is a great and noble thing to feel through all life the grasp and influence of Jesus, but this great and noble thing no man can do unless God the Holy Ghost inspires and helps him to do it. This statement of St. Paul seems to me to have at its heart the profoundest and most beautiful conception of the relation between God and man. Suppose that it were not true. Suppose that faith in Christ being, as I have tried to show it, the crowning act of man, it were yet an act which man could do without any inspiration or help of God; suppose that in this, or any other of the greatest actions of his life, man could first conceive the wish to do it all by and of himself, and then could quietly gather up his powers and go and do it all by and of himself, — have you not in such a supposition broken the absoluteness, the essentialness, the permanency, of the whole relation between our life and God's? The true idea of that relationship involves the presence of God in every highest activity of man. It often seems to me as if men had got such a low and inadequate conception of all this! Men talk, very religious men, as if God were a sort of reserve force to be called in when He was needed — a sort of last resort when man's strength failed. And so I sometimes think that the whole Christian thought of man's being dependent upon God continually seems to a good many people like something cowardly, unmanly, a miserable calling up of the reserve when we ought to be fighting out the battle for ourselves. The thought of God which Christ came to reveal, the thought of God of which all Christ's own life was full, is something totally different from that. To Christ's thought God and man are part of one system — one structure, one working-force. To separate them is not simply to deny man a power that he needs : it is to break a unity, and to set a part of the power to the attempt to do what the whole power ought to do as one. The strength, the force, which is appointed to lift your burden, to run your race, to find your truth, to hold the canopy of faithfulness over your life, is not you. It is you and God. For you to try to do it alone is unnatural. It is almost as if the engine tried to run without its steam, or as if the chisel tried to carve without the artist. It is engine and steam that are to make the running-power. It is artist and chisel that are to carve the statue. It is God and you that live your life. For you to try to live it alone is to try to do all the work with one part of the power. God is not a crutch coming in to help your lameness, unnecessary to you if you had all your strength. He is the breath in your lungs. The stronger you are, the more thoroughly you are yourself, the more you need of it, the more you need of Him.

How clear this became in the life of Jesus Himself! There was humanity at its best. Could it do without those supplies of God which the lower humanity required? Did it throw away its crutch and walk in its own self-sufficient strength? Oh, no! It breathed deeper than any other human life has ever breathed of the breath of God. It filled itself with His Spirit. It did nothing by itself, but everything with, in, by Him. Oh, my dear friends, there is the everlasting testimony that utter dependence on God is no accident of man's sin or misfortune, but is the intrinsic and eternal necessity and glory of man's nature.

And so when man comes to that which I have claimed to be his completing act, when he says that Jesus is the Lord, it is not strange that he cannot do that alone, not by himself, a poor half-life, crippled and broken. It needs the whole of him — and he is not the whole of himself unless God is in him. He cannot do it "but by the Holy Ghost." The man with a duty says, "Jesus is the Lord," and he is brave. The man with a temptation says, " Jesus is the Lord," and he is firm. The man with a suffering says, "Jesus is the Lord," and he is patient. The man with a bewilderment says, "Jesus is the Lord," and he sees light. Is it not a true and precious part of the value of those great experiences, that in each of them there is both the struggle of the human soul up to God, and also the uprising of the divine soul carrying the man deeper into itself — that neither of those men says "Jesus is the Lord" but by the Holy Ghost?

There is one other point of which I wish to speak before I close. I have been magnifying faith. I have been painting it as what I know it is, the consummate action of the human soul, requiring the soul's best faculties working at their best. I can imagine while I speak thus that some hearts here may be asking themselves, "What then? If faith be such a supreme act, must it not be the privilege of a few, must it not be within the power only of the supreme souls? Can I, one of the weakest and worldliest of men, can I do such an act, an act that needs such powers?" And so perhaps I may seem to have lifted the very thing which all men ought to do out of the possibility of many men. I would not leave any such doubt in any soul. God forbid that in trying to make faith seem glorious I should make it seem impossible! But it is true of God's gifts always that the most complete of them are also the most possibly universal. Is it not so? Think of this illustration: wealth is a lower gift than health, and wealth is evidently limited in its possibility; all men are not intended to be rich — but health is for all men. It is unnatural for any man to be sick. And so of admiration and of love. To be loved is better than to be admired — and admiration is the privilege of a few brilliant natures, while love is within the reach of any pure and loving heart. And so of the subtler beauties of art and the simpler beauties of nature. Art is the privilege of the few, but nature opens her treasures wide. "There is no price set on the lavish summer, and June may be had by the poorest comer." But nature is as much more beautiful as she is more free than art. It is a splendid law. of all God's world, a law that makes the whole world shine with the splendor of His love, that everywhere the finest is the freest. The lower blessings are often the exceptions, but the higher blessings are meant to be not the exception, but the rule. If this be so, then how must it be with that blessing which outgoes all others, the blessing of faith, the blessing of living under the perpetually recognized lordship of Christ? The finest of all gifts of God — may we not look for it to be the freest too? Free as the air, which is the most precious thing the world contains, and yet struggles as nothing else in all the world struggles to give itself away — crowds itself in wherever it can go, and moves whatever will let itself be moved by its elastic pressure.

And this grows clearer and surer still when we remember that the part of us to which the pressure of God, the power of his Holy Ghost asking to be admitted to govern our lives, applies for its admission is the part which is most universally open and active in all the degrees of mankind; namely, the moral part. Think how often you are ready to listen to a poor ignorant creature's judgment of right and wrong, and pay the deepest reverence to it, when you would not care in the least for that same creature's judgment of any question of the intellect. Think how a little child can look you in the eye with his pure, clear glance, as you are telling your well-disguised falsehood, and say, "That is not true," and make you quail. Think how you can touch a child's conscience long before you can waken his brain. All these are illustrations and signs of the universalness of moral life. It is in all men and in all times of each man's life. And so a blessing which must enter by that door can find in every nature a door to enter by. A Holy Spirit, having its power in its holiness, need not be shut out of any heart that is capable of knowing holiness and being holy. Therefore no soul of dunce or boor or little child is too low to be brought by the Holy Spirit to the place where, answering back by the divine within it to the divine above it, it may say that " Jesus is the Lord." I have claimed already that no soul is too high to find in that announcement of its faith the consummation of its life. Here, then, is where the highest and the lowest meet. Here is where they have met through all the ages. Glorious thinkers, great strong workers, sufferers whose lives were miracles of patience, all of these singing as they went their ways, "Jesus is Lord, Jesus is Lord." And all around them, and in among them, dull, plodding souls, and minds whose thought was all confused and bewildered with emotion, and little children, with their crude clear pictures in their simple brains, all these too singing, in their several

tones and with their several clearness, " Jesus is Lord,
Jesus is Lord."

Would you be able to say that, to join that great
human chorus, to claim Christ for your Lord with
some especial claim of your own which shall make
the great human chorus which claims Him for the
world a little more complete ? You can do it. But
you can do it only " by the Holy Ghost." Only by
letting God enter into you can you go up to God,
and own with joy and thankfulness the mastery of
his Son. And oh, my friends, remember that the
owning of Christ's mastery here is but the beginning
of the participation in Christ's glory in heaven.

Into that may we all come at last by His great
love !

VII.

THE SANCTUARY OF GOD.

" Then thought I to understand this, but it was too hard for me;
Until I went into the Sanctuary of God; then understood I the
end of these men."—PSALMS lxxiii. 16, 17.

THIS is called one of the psalms of Asaph. About
Asaph nobody knows very much : only that he was
a friend of David, the master of his music, and evidently, from his writings, a man of very beautiful
religious and poetic spirit. If we can distinguish
between his psalms and those of his mightier friend,
we should say that Asaph's were more calm and even
and tranquil, more pensive and placid, with less of
triumphant exultation or of profound depression than
David's.

But in this psalm Asaph is sorely perplexed and
troubled. How old the bewilderments of the world
are ! I think it makes our own difficulties harder and
easier at once to bear when we think how many long-
forgotten souls have struggled in them too in the
years that are past. Here almost three thousand years
ago is a poor man who can make nothing out of the
same fact, precisely, which has kept thousands of
people wondering and questioning this last week.
You recognize it the moment that you open the psalm.
" I was envious at the foolish," he says, " when I saw
the prosperity of the wicked." The prosperity of the

wicked! that critical puzzle of all times, the apparent absence of justice in this life of ours. "They are not in trouble like other folk, neither are they plagued like other men." And they say, "How doth God know, and is there knowledge in the Most High? Behold, these are the ungodly; these prosper in the world; they increase in riches. Verily, I have cleansed my heart in vain and washed my hands in innocency." That is the puzzle; as old as Asaph, as young as some struggling child of God who knows that his uprightness is keeping him poor and that his unscrupulous neighbor is growing rich by his side to-day.

And then comes Asaph's escape from the puzzle: "I thought to understand this," he says, "but it was too hard for me; until I went into the Sanctuary of God; then understood I the end of these men." The escape perhaps is not so familiar as the puzzle. He goes into the sanctuary of God, he goes to church, and there he finds a light that makes the dark things clear, and the cloud scatters, and he understands it all. At once we feel that we are talking with the Hebrew. Here is the man to whom the temple was the centre of everything. There, not merely in burning shekinah, but in the deep-felt spiritual sympathy, his God abode, and there with his deep, strong, trustful love, and fear for his God, he was used to go to find Him. It was different from the way we go to church. There was nothing hard, dull, or routinelike in it. We cannot read the Psalms without seeing what a spring and life and freshness, what a holy curiosity and eagerness and affection there was in the hearts of the men who went up to the temple. "I was glad when they said unto me, Let us go up to the house of the Lord. Our feet shall stand in thy courts, O Jerusalem." Nobody can read the Old Testament without seeing something very beautiful and grand, almost awful. In the midst of all the pettiness and wickedness, the small intrigues and quarrels that show us the littleness of that wonderful Hebrew people, one sight never loses its sublimity. It is the yearly gathering of the people from every corner of the land to the sacred festival meeting at Jerusalem. The land swarms and hums with movement. The men of the seashore and the desert and the hills; they are all stirring. Judah among his peaceful hills, the wild Simeonites from their home in the desert, Zebulon and Issachar from the rich plain-country, Asher from his abode along the bays and creeks, the Reubenites and Gadites from beyond the Jordan, and the sons of Naphtali from the far north, about the very roots of Lebanon, — they are all coming to appear before God. Every pass is full, every hill-side is alive. I think we cannot estimate the power in a nation's life of such a great annual symbolic pilgrimage. Every man brought his own burden, his own sorrow, his own sin. The problems of the year, the things that had perplexed them as they worked in the fields alone, or debated with their brethren, or met the troubles of the household — all these they brought to offer to the Lord, to seek solution for them in the higher, calmer atmosphere of the temple. There was the place where their darkened and frightened understandings would find light and peace.

It is an old-time picture. We do not go to church so now. Indeed it is not well that we should, altogether. There is a certain amount of localizing and narrowing of the idea of Deity about it which is not good. But there is much in it which it is good to keep, — at any rate impossible to make light of or despise. It is the longing for some sacred and secluded place in this low beset world. Luther dreamed of it when as a young monk he went up to Rome as if he were going up to heaven. As you go through the old cities of Europe or the East to-day, you see the weary man or woman turn aside into the cool, deep door of the great cathedral to say a prayer, or the more ab- stracted Oriental drop his shoes from his feet and fall prostrate, with the crowd all around him, before the city shrine as if he were far off in the desert or on some lonely hill. I am sure we cannot help being glad for all the good it surely does them, for all the light they get, however dim, upon the hard questions of their lives. Woe to us if our more rational belief, instead of lifting all the earth up to heaven, only crowds down the hill-tops and leaves no heaven, and makes our whole earth earthly. It is sad indeed if our churches have no light to give to the problems that perplex our houses and our stores.

But having said thus much, I want to speak of the subject that these verses will suggest this morning, not in the ancient Hebrew, but in the modern Chris- tian way. What made Asaph see clearer in the temple was that he met God there. We have been taught that not alone in temples made with hands, but everywhere in this great world of God the devout and loving soul may meet with God. We have been taught to see already in the distance that world where there shall be no temple except the present God. "God Almighty and the Lamb the temple of it." Not only to the temple, then, but to the present God, everywhere and always ; not only to the church, but to the divine presence by our side the problems of life may be carried. I want to speak of the new clearness that comes into many difficult questions, and especially into this question of the unequal lots of men when we survey them in connection with the thought of God. How does the bringing of life into God's presence make it intelligible ?

There are, then, two persons I think to whom life seems pretty clear : the man who does not think or feel at all, and the man who thinks and feels very deeply. It is just like any complicated piece of machinery. The factory girl who sits at her loom and feeds it day by day learns just how the machine takes up the thread she offers it and seems to understand the whole. The engineer who has the plans of all the engineering, from the boiler out to the thinnest and subtlest steel finger that it moves ; he, too, is troubled by no problems, but has grasped the working of the whole. Between the two come all the different degrees of intelligence and knowledge which see the mysteries more than the work-girl so as to be puzzled by them, but do not see them as much as the engineer so as to understand them. Just so it is with this world. The sluggish creature who just runs his little fragment of the universe and asks no questions further is troubled by no doubts. The finished soul who sees with God's eyes the great moral laws which govern all God's worlds, he, too, may rest in peace. Between the two the great mass of men, seeing the difficulties, but not seeing their solutions, live in disquietude and questionings. And when one has once outgrown the first repose of ignorance and thoughtlessness, he never can go back to it — there is no hope for him except to go on to the higher repose of faith and knowledge and sympathy with God.

It is the moral difficulties that give men most disquietude. It is not the riddles that try the intellect, but those that perplex the conscience. When we know that a certain thing is right, and that righteousness seems to be ignored in the working of the world, that is the sort of puzzle that haunts men and makes them really miserable. And of all moral riddles none is more perfect a perplexity than this, — that with a righteous God the Giver of every good gift, those good gifts should be bestowed upon unrighteousness. Not here and there as if by accident, or as if an occasional exception was necessary in the working of a general law, but so generally as to seem sometimes universal. Unscrupulousness grows rich. Selfishness lives in luxury. We cannot open our eyes without seeing it. It requires no abstruse proof. The bewildering fact flashes itself into the poor man's eyes in the glitter of rich men's windows and flings itself as if in scorn upon him, as their carriages spatter him with mud as he stands waiting and chafing on the crossing to let them pass.

And first of all, if we feel the puzzle, we are sure that it is not one that comes to us out of any wantonness of God. It is one that we could not be spared. Let us always be much afraid of making our Heavenly Father a cruel monster who plays with the joy and misery of His poor children, and mocks them with questions for which they have no answers. The ancients in their fable of the sphinx who asked her riddles and destroyed those who tried but could not solve them, had just exactly this idea. They got it from the same experience of the mystery and contradictoriness of life of which our later days are full. Let us keep clear of any such thought of God. If there are riddles in life, He does not set them wantonly. He is always leading us towards their solution as fast as we are able to go. We are cheated by our weakness and our ignorance. He is always trying to make us strong and wise, and so to save us from delusion. "God is light, and in Him is no darkness at all." That is the first certainty about Him, which we must never lose; for when that is gone, there is nothing left.

After all, for every trouble and doubt of this life, except those which come directly from our own sinfulness, the only consolation that we really need is explanation. It is a great thing to know that. A really manly man will ask no other consolation. This world is not full of blunders of government that need to be reformed; but it is full of obscurities that we long to have enlightened. The fire comes, and the consolation for the loss of your burnt store that you need is merely to see something of the purpose for which God permitted it to go, something of the spiritual blessing that may come to you out of its loss. Your child dies, and you do not ask for the child to come back again, but your heart does ache to know what it all means, to see something of what it is to die, to trace the dear life that is gone into the bosom of the Eternal Love that has taken it. Everywhere the devout and manly soul asks for explanation, and is sure that if it could reach that it would find all the consolation that it needs. Such trust it has in God.

And now take the special bewilderment that puzzled Asaph. Put yourself in his place. It ought not to be hard to do it, for unless you are either more or less than man you have been in his place many a time. You see a man whom you know to be wicked prospering. Everything he touches turns to gold. When the city is on fire, his house does not burn. When the pestilence goes stalking about, his household is unbroken. A brighter life than any other house can show seems to flash through his glowing windows, in mockery of the starving honesty without. Health, honor, happiness, everything is there. That is what you and Asaph see. And now here, too, the consolation that your heart asks for is explanation. You believe in a God so sincerely that you do not say this state of things is wrong, but you do crave to see some glimpse of how it can be right. Then you go into the sanctuary of God; somehow you come into the presence of the Everlasting Father.

You fill yourself with the sense of His immensity and goodness. You see perfect happiness and perfect holiness brought to their absolute consistency, nay their absolute identity in Him. Do you not begin to feel it already? Is there not coming a calm over the tumult, a light into the darkness? Is not the promise being fulfilled, "In thy light shall we see light?" Already you are beginning with Asaph, in the sanctuary, to understand "the end of these men."

And what does this mean? Is it a mere expression of Asaph's triumph? Is it merely that he sees that by and by these prosperous men will have their troubles too, and hugs himself in the comfortable assurance that if they are the richest, he is the safest, that he has made the best investment? Is he merely encouraged to live out his present misery in the anticipation of the certain time when things will be reversed, when they will be down and he will be up? By and by their stores will burn. By and by their children will be taken too. That were a poor consolation to gloat over. Some vision of such a spirit does sometimes appear in some of those imprecatory psalms, which I hope that we all understand, that we read in church not as patterns of Christian temper, but as parts of the complete spiritual biography of a great but very imperfect man. But I do not think that the half-savage mood of some of those psalms is present here. When Asaph says that in the sanctuary of God he "understands the end of these men," he means that there became apparent to him the limits, the essential limits, of the life that they live. He has fallen into a low way of envying them their wealth, as if wealth was everything. He has been puzzled, because not being good they were rich, as if riches were the appropriate premium of goodness; but when he comes to stand with God all that is altered. He comes in sight of larger circles of bliss. He sees that God has other rewards to give His chosen besides these little trinkets. Absorbed in the newly realized beauty of these higher things, he sees the worthlessness of the lower, and easily leaves them to the souls they satisfy. "Verily I say unto you they have their reward." So long as he knows no higher happiness than prosperity, it puzzles him that the bad should have it. So soon as he comes to know the infinitely higher joy of company with God, and sees that that can be given only to the good, — " without holiness no man can see the Lord," — it no more troubles him that bad men should have the poor counterfeit of happiness, than it troubles the solid merchant, sitting in his houseful of plain and solid comfort, to see a miserable fop strut by in cheap and gaudy finery making believe and perhaps thinking that he is rich.

I think we can illustrate what I mean. Two young students start out together. One is conscientious and thorough ; the other is showy and superficial. In a little while the patient, thorough worker is surprised to find all the world staring at and talking about his showy friend. He himself passes unnoticed, but wherever the flimsy scholarship of his friend goes men clap their hands and stare with wonder. It puzzles him. It seems all wrong. Does flippant show, then, win the prize that ought to fall to honest knowledge? But as he goes deeper, as he comes nearer to the court where the personal majesty of Truth herself abides, it all becomes clear. The joy of knowing Truth and being near to her out-shines all those lower glories. He sees that the popular applause and admiration is just the appropriate reward of those lower devotions that have won them. He sees the end, the limit, of his brother student's life and gladly leaves him the honor he has won, pressing on himself into the sanctuary of the Truth, which is his own great reward, far above all honor and praise of men.

Is not this, then, the explanation which is consolation? As we rise higher the larger circles of life open to us their value, and the smaller circles show their limits. Abraham is summoned out of his fatherland, Ur of the Chaldees, and to every man of Ur who stays at home it seems doubtless very hard. They settle down on their snug farms, and are glad they have not to go. Perhaps to Abraham himself, although he goes, it seems hard too and very strange. But, then, the wider circles open. The Canaanite life appears. The Jewish life is born. Out of Jewry comes Christ. From Christ goes forth the Gospel; Christendom is born. All modern life, all promise of the millennial earth appears. How small beside this widening life of Abraham looks the limited life of Terah and Nahor and Haran, who were left behind at Ur! Who that stands high enough to see it all, who that has entered into the sanctuary of God, does not see the limit, the end of those men?

This puts in their true place, I think, all the lower

aims and purposes of life. Because the heart's beating is not the whole of life, it does not make the heart's beating unimportant. Because the outer life, the life of business and society, is but the smallest circle of existence, it is not therefore to be disregarded. To use it, yet always to use it with reference to its limits, always to understand its end, not to try to make it satisfy needs for which it has no satisfaction, this is the true life. The difference between living in order to make money, and making money in order to live, to live the fullest, most cultured, most religious life, this is the difference that the dullest perception can feel at once between two business men. We outgrow our lower occupations not as we outgrow playthings which we come to cast aside altogether, but only as we outgrow our first childish slavery to food and come to count it not an end in itself, magnifying our appetites, but the mere minister and material of thought and action and emotion. Thus things fall into their natural orders and get their true values for us ; we see their limits, we understand their ends, as soon as we look at them from a high enough standpoint, as soon as we go into the sanctuary of God.

I seem to see illustrations of this truth everywhere. Look at the nations, or at the periods of history, which may be said to have been fullest of the consciousness of a divine rulership. Some ages seem to be so worldly, so down to the human level as we look back upon them ; others seem to be trembling and heaving and rising with the very presence of God. In some, men have seemed to feel as if God was very far off from them. In others, all kinds of men, high or low, have been haunted in their several ways with the certainty that God was very near. Some nations and times seem to be wholly of the earth, earthy. Others truly have entered into and live in the very sanctuary of God, a solemn knowledge of His mercy, a solemn fear of His law. Of nations that seem thus full of a special sense of God the Jews stand out in old times; and of ages that have been most aware of Him the Puritan times in the history of our own English race are the most prominent. And no one, I think, studies the history of either without feeling that there was in them, roughly marked, because their character was very imperfect, but yet very real, a clearer insight into the relative values of things, a juster estimate of what was little and what was great, a truer judgment of the necessary limitations of wealth, honors, fame, success, than the nations and the times around them could claim. This is what made the one the most heroic and truthful nation of its time, and the other the most heroic and truthful period of our English history.

But men are better illustrations than nations or ages, and when we think of men we turn at once to the perfect man, and think of Jesus Christ. He dwelt with, dwelt in, God continually. He was all ways in the sanctuary of His Father, and as we turn the pages of His story what a clear sense we have that He was always "seeing the end of these men." Can you picture to yourself that Jesus could possibly have walked through the richest streets of Capernaum or Jerusalem, and had it for an instant suggested to His mind that it was a hardship to Him that all those low-minded traders should have been so rich and He so poor? Can you fancy Him looking into pleasant home-windows as He passed, and thinking that His Father had wronged Him because He had no home? Oh what a shielded and protected life He always carried! What false judgment or repining bitterness could find a weak spot to break in? He saw the end of Chorazin and Bethsaida, and it was as impossible for Him to envy those foolish cities their weak folly as it would be for you, familiar with gold and silver, to begrudge your child the chips and stones with which he plays at keeping shop; nay, as impossible as it would be for God, with the realities of eternity about Him, to want these toys and trifles with which we amuse ourself here in this world of time.

Such was the life of Jesus. And Jesus said, "No man cometh unto the Father but by Me." "By Him we all have access unto the Father;" and so by the power of Christ we may all come near to God too, and have from out the open door of His sanctuary to which we have fled, His view of mortal life and all its interests. For us, too, this world's existence may subside into its clearly marked circles, and we may see as God sees where each circle ends; see how the selfishnesses soon die out; see how the affections sweep out into wider lines; see how nothing but the highest loves reach out into infinity and sent life forward into eternity. These times, when we are nearest to God, are the times when this world's things show their true values to us. Do you not know that?   Do you remember how it all looked to you when you came home from the funeral, not morbid with hopeless sorrow, but seeming to be above the world, and to be standing with the friend who had gone, in the presence of the throne of God?   Do you remember how things changed their relative importance to you then, how the last were first and the first were last, as they shall be on the judgment day?   Could any one have made you wretched then by coming and telling you of a broken bank?   You were above complaints and small trials.   You had entered into the sanctuary of God, and you saw the end of these things.

Some of us who have thought about it must have sometimes been puzzled just what to think about the great men who are called the Hebrew prophets, —Isaiah, Jeremiah, Amos.   Sometimes they are the foretellers of future events; but sometimes they are apparently only the proclaimers of present duty, preaching with fearful earnestness and eloquence the righteousness of God to an unrighteous people. Which was their office?   Are they preachers to a present or foretellers of a future?   Does not what we have said seem to show that the two offices are really one?   To see the present deeply enough is to see the future.   Tell me perfectly what a man is, and I will tell you what he will be, such is the fearful logical continuity that runs through our life. These were men full of the spirit of God, in intensest sympathy with Him.   They abode in His sanctuary, and so they saw, as He saw, what Jerusalem and Samaria and·Babylon were worth.   They saw what sort of life was in those places and the men who ruled them. So they knew how long their life could last. They understood the end of these men. So they were prophets; and all prophecy that is more than mere jugglery must be of this sort. All true foresight must be insight first.

We hear of the men who have the care of the Atlantic cable, standing with this end of it when it is broken, and telling just where the interruption is. They can tell how long the piece is that they hold in their hands; just in what unseen spot under the sea the broken end of it will be found. They say, "It has broken here, or here, or here." And so there are some people of acute spiritual perception who can accurately tell the worth and promise of the men they meet. Can tell by a sense of touch which they cannot define themselves, how much real vitality there is in them, how long they will last. You come to such a person with your latest idol, the new sensation who has started your enthusiasm, and you say eagerly, "Here, the coming man has come. Here is the first bit of the millennium. Here is a man who will have long influence, and change the current of things to the end." But he takes your idol's life into his hands, and feels instantly that it is not what you think it. He understands its end. He says sadly, "No, this man is bright and energetic, but he is narrow, he is selfish, he is false; his end will be there," placing his finger on the limit of the man's selfhood, which is the farthest that such a character as his can reach. Another sends back its record from a little more distant point. Only when he touches the character of a thoroughly unselfish and true soul, given up to God, does he feel the thrill of a life that has no end, but runs around the whole circle of duty, within and parallel to the life of God himself. Such men there are. Such tests and judges of their brothers' lives, — not arrogant and self-asserting, but humble and meek. Such a man's thoughts will not be like our thoughts. He will know how to estimate the worth of men's lives. He will know whom to help. He will leave a man crying for his lost fortune, and go to a sinner who is struggling not to lose his soul, sure that his is the deeper need. He will devote himself to a little insignificant-looking shoot, that just peeps above the ground, and keeps the burning sun off of it carefully, leaving the great tall weed by its side to scorch as the sun pleases. Men may call him foolish, but wisdom will be justified of this one of her children by and by, when the weed has fallen and rotted, and the little shoot is grown to the great tree, with the fowls of the air among its branches and tired men resting under its shade. These are the men who keep alive true standards in the world. The men who live in the sanctuary of God, and so understand the end of these men.

The great question after all is this: Shall we judge man by God or God by man? Does light and understanding flow upward or downward? If we judge man by God, at once we have these true and discriminating thoughts of human life. We have absolute standards. We have a test of the worth of all we do or see. But if we judge God by man, we only have over again what the world has been so full of, —

the persuasions of self-interest, the disbelief in absolute righteousness, the changing standards of the changing times. Men have gone into the sanctuary of their own selfishness, the sanctuary of themselves, and straightway they have seemed to see an end of God. All sense of a supreme and awful Fatherhood on which all men depended, to which all action must go back for judgment, has been lost. No higher power than the human has seemed to be moving under and giving meaning to the events of ordinary life. All spiritual study of the world's course became impossible. A low and dreary economy became the main-spring of the universe. How much we have seen of that spirit just now in relation to this fire in Boston! Revolting from the irreverent and repulsive spirit of religious competency which undertakes to say just why the fire came, just why it destroyed this man's business and spared that other's, just what God meant to teach men by it, another school has been very loud in saying that there was no spiritual teaching in it, that it contained no higher lessons than those of more careful building and a better government. That it contained those lessons no wise man can doubt. God grant that we may heed them! We shall surely suffer if we do not heed them. But if there be a God who cares more for His children's souls than for their bodies, to whom the body is always manifestly temporal and the soul eternal, then for soul as well as body there must be a meaning in what we still call such a visitation of God as this. No man may read his brother's lessons and say, "This is what God meant for you;" but every man must read his own, his lessons of patience, spirituality, charity, and believe with all his heart that God has lessons for his brethren too, and pray that in what ought to be such a Pentecostal time, his brethren, too, may hear God speak His wonderful things, each in his own tongue.

But now let us gather and keep the meanings of this verse of Asaph for ourselves.   I am sure that we need them.   I am speaking to men and women who are in the midst of the pressing moral problems that cannot be escaped.   You see wicked men prosperous, and you say, "How can I believe in God?"   Only, my dear friend, only by coming close to God, and learning by deep and sweet experience that He has better things to give to His beloved than what men call prosperity.   The peace that passeth understanding, the calm rest of forgiven sin, and of a soul trusted away from itself into its Saviour's hands.   To one who knows what those high blessings mean, how little does it seem that other hands should fill themselves with the shining trifles which its hands are too full to hold.   Think how it will seem in heaven! Standing before the throne, filled with the unspeakable vision, conscious through all the glory of the culture that suffering has brought, hurrying with joy on the high missions of the Lord, who will look back then and be troubled an instant at the recollection of how a wicked man sat at a little richer table, or had a little higher seat in the market-place when we were here on earth?

Ah, but, you say, that is not my trouble.   It goes deeper than that.   It does not merely trouble me that others have these things. I cannot keep my-self from seeking them. How shall I overcome the temptation that is always driving me to let my religion go, and to plunge into this chase after wealth and comfort? Again the answer is the same: Enter into the sanctuary of God. You cannot let the lower go until the higher first has wholly filled and occupied you. Come with your sins, and find the peace and bliss of being forgiven. Come with your lonely heart, lonely in all its deepest wants, in spite of all the tenderest companionships of life, and find the perfect happiness of Christ's communion; then, filled with this new strength, when you turn round and say, "Now, let me see if I can fight down my enemies, can conquer my temptations," behold your enemies will be away down there beneath your feet, you will have passed out above your temptations, and will only see them raging and tossing impotently, as one who stands upon the sunlit peak sees the vain fury of the thunderstorm beautiful and not terrible below him.

That cannot come in this life, you say. But I do not know. There have been men and women with lives so calm and high that they seemed to have reached it, even on this tumultuous earth. Hardly a flake of spray from the storm below them ever seemed to dash up and wet their steadfast and placid feet. But whether it can come in this life or not, the struggle for it makes the two lives one. Already to him who is working towards it, part of its peace is given. The rock runs out under the sea, and your feet may be firm upon it even while the waves are still breast high.

Such be the peace in Christ which shall make all of our lives strong through all their struggle, until at last we enter into that rest which remaineth for the people of God.

VIII.

COME AND SEE.

"Philip saith unto him, ' Come and See.' " JOHN i. 46.

TWICE in the same chapter these same words, "Come and See," are spoken. Once they are the reply of Jesus to two of John's disciples, who having heard John speak of Him, are following Him, and when He turns and sees them ask Him, "Rabbi, where dwellest thou?" Again, they are the words of Philip, who having himself become the disciple of Jesus, findeth Nathanael, and saith unto him, "We have found Him of whom Moses in the law and the prophets did write, Jesus of Nazareth, the son of Joseph. And Nathanael said, Can there any good thing come out of Nazareth? Then Philip saith unto him, Come and see." And these words, thus twice repeated, are characteristic words of Christianity. They have a ring about them that belongs to all our religion. "Come and see!" They invite inquiry. They proclaim a religion which is to have its own clear tests, which it invites every one to use. It is an open faith. It will do nothing in a corner. It will be recognizable in its workings by men's ordinary perceptions. I need not remind you, if you know your Bibles, how common such appeals are everywhere. "Try the spirits whether they be

K

of God." "Prove all things." "Go and tell what things ye see and hear." "He that hath ears to hear, let him hear." There are institutions that shut their doors and windows, and say to the world of ordinary men, "You can know nothing of what goes on in here. If you come in you must come in blindfold, and let yourself be led, and examine nothing. There are no tests within your power — you must just be blind and obey." Christianity, however she may have been misrepresented sometimes, has no such tone as that; but everywhere she throws the doors of her secret places, of her most sacred doctrine and her holiest character, wide open, and cries to all men as to beings who in the healthy use of their human faculties are capable of judging, "Come and see." In that call she strikes the keynote of intelligent, and so of truly devout religion.

It is the necessity of Christianity thus to appeal to the observation of men. She openly declares that she seeks certain moral results of which men are able to judge. Think how Christ came into the world bringing the mysterious life of a higher world with Him! He told plainly what He came for. It was to renew men's spiritual life. It was to make men better. It was to save His people from their sins. There were profounder and more mystic aspects of salvation, subtle and exalted experiences, serene and sacred emotions, into which He offered to lead His followers, where the ordinary eyes of men were not prepared to follow them; but every statement of His purpose involved this as preliminary to everything beside. That His disciples should first of all become different men in those things which other men could see and understand, that they should be braver, truer, humbler, purer. A pure philosophy or a pure mysticism, dealing only in abstract thought or feeling, has no test for ordinary men. They cannot tell whether it is true or false. But a religion which must make men's lives different, must change characters, or be a failure, has to be always open to men's judgment. It has to work its <u>miracles in the light</u>. It has to take its man or its generation, and standing out on a platform where there can be no concealment and no jugglery and to say, "See, I <u>will make this man into this different man</u>. I will make this bad man into this good man;" and all the world knows whether the experiment succeeds or fails. The test is in the hands of every man who knows the difference between good living and bad living. She cannot fall back upon certain unintelligible experiences, certain unseen changes which she says have taken place in her subject but do not show themselves upon the outside. If they do not show themselves on the outside they are unreal. They are such in their very nature that if they are real they must show themselves on the outside. If the magician stands before me on the stage and points to a lion or a dog and says, "I will change this brute into a man," I have the test in my own eyes. It will not do for him to say while I see the brute still standing brutishly there, "Oh, but the substance is changed too deep for you to see, and that the old form remains the same is nothing." A changed form must betoken the changed substance. I must see the upright figure and watch the intelligent eye, and hear the articulate voice of manhood, or it is no man — there is no miracle. So Christianity by its very necessity is compelled to be judged of men.

I should like to speak to-night of some of the general principles of truth-seeking and truth-getting, first in themselves, and then in their relation to Christianity. It is the subject that is suggested by this invitation to observation and experiment, — this " Come and see " of the convinced disciple, Philip.

There are, then, two great methods by which men arrive at the knowledge of truth. One is the method of authority and the other the method of experience. I know what I know either because some one has told me of it, or because I have observed it for myself. To say nothing of the comparative trustworthiness of the two methods, everybody can feel the superior vividness of the second. What I see for myself is so much more real and vital than what I hear from another. The best teacher is always he who says, " Come and see." The brilliant lecturer on the laws of light stands at his desk, and in the choicest and clearest English describes to me the action or the composition of the ray, and I think I know all about it ; but suddenly he turns to his instrument and makes me see the ray of light doing its action or unfolding into its constituents, and my knowledge is of a new sort. The method of authority has been changed for the method of experience. We are like the Samaritans who said to the woman, " Now we believe, not because of thy saying, for we have heard Him ourselves."

There is always this distinction ; but yet remember that where truth seems to be received by the method of authority, still the method of experience must have preceded or else the other could not legitimately have been used. There must have been a previous conviction of the trustworthiness of the teacher got by our experience either of him or of some who have told us about him, or else we should have no right to believe what he says. So all comes back at last to the method of experience. The invitation, "Come and see," is the invitation into all truth. When Jesus had risen from the dead, you remember, His disciple refused to believe till with his own hand he had felt the wounds in the hands and feet and side. And Jesus gently rebuking him, compares, as it were, the methods of authority and experience, of faith and science, so to speak, to the advantage of the former when He says, " Thomas, because thou hast seen thou hast believed. Blessed are they that have not seen and yet have believed." And yet when we come to think of it, is not His rebuke really that Thomas had not used the method of experience enough, not that he demands it too much? He rebukes him that in all the years that they had been together he had not observed Him deeply enough to learn His character and understand His words. Is He not pleading, not against science, but for a higher science? Must it not be always so? Must not all truth come to us through the faculties that God has given to us, faithfully employed. Jesus always asked the people to believe what He told them of heaven, of the judgment day, of His own mysterious nature, in virtue of what they saw, — the sick man made well and the poor made rich. "If I do not the works of my Father believe me not," a direct appeal to experience. "Come and see, and according to what you see believe, or disbelieve in the awful unsearchable truths of God and the celestial life."

What follows, then? Having this method of truth we have no right to expect the attainment of truth except in the use of this method. We have no right to count that as truth which has come to us without its use, without some steady application of our faculties to the matter which is in question. But how much people do hold to be true or not true which they have reached in no such way. Men are prejudiced, we say, and prejudice means simply this: "A judging before;" a forming an opinion before you have any grounds for an opinion; a judgment before evidence; a making up your mind before you have come and seen. Do we not recognize our old vexatious friends? A man is unwilling to say of any subject that he has no opinion about it because he has had no chance to examine it (as any sensible man must say of a hundred subjects), and so he makes up an opinion without examination, and it is only a prejudice that he flaunts in the world's eyes. A man would like a certain thing to be true, and so he says over and over again, "This is true." He would like his house to be just so high; he would like the Bible to be verbally inspired; he would like that there should be no future punishment, and so he says over and over again, "This is so," and never comes squarely and fully up to the facts to see whether it is so or not, or if he does meet the facts some day he meets them so encased in his armor of prejudice that they are powerless to break it. A good man — and this is one of the commonest of things — thinks that in order to keep the world sound and good and healthy such and such a statement ought to be true; thinks that the world will go to ruin if it is not true, and so he says, "It must be true," and there is his prejudice full made. He may be right or may be wrong, but either way he is prejudiced, and so feeble. He has never got up to the facts where strength lies. Indeed, I think this last is one of the hardest cases to make perfectly clear either to ourselves or others. It is no doubt a certain presumption for the truth of an idea that the world would be wiser and better if it were true. If we could be perfectly sure that the world would be wiser and better for it, it would be a very strong presumption of its truth ; but, after all, it could be no more than a presumption. Finally, we must go and see whether it be true; we must face facts, and our presumption could only send us with more interest and earnestness to the facts which alone could give us an answer.

These are some forms of prejudice as concerns our estimates of truth. The same is true concerning also our estimate of persons. Indeed, to this last the term "prejudice" is perhaps more commonly applied; at any rate, it was a case of personal prejudice that drew out the invitation of our text. Personal prejudice is the formation of an opinion of a person's character before we have the ground for an opinion. Here was Nathanael who heard Philip tell of Jesus.

All he knew of him was that he came from the town
of Nazareth. At once he formed an opinion of Him;
He could not be great or good and come from such a
place. "Can any good thing come out of Nazareth?"
The answer is wisdom itself: "Come and see the
man whom you dislike. Get your evidence and then
make your judgment." I know some one thing about
a man, some one act that he did when he was a boy,
perhaps not even that, something about his parents
or his relatives, something about his birthplace, or
the school he went to, or his place of business, or his
business partnerships. Now, it is almost impossible,
as we are made, that such things should not influence
us, that they should not give us some first impression
of what kind of a man we shall find him when we
come to know him; but to let such first impressions
magnify and harden themselves into opinions, to let
them influence our action, to let them decide us not
to know the man whom we so rashly judge, this is
personal prejudice. And yet who of us is not guilty
of it? Who of us does not know of some man against
whom he has taken a dislike, whom he would avoid
or depreciate, or perhaps harm to-morrow if he were
brought in contact with him, whom yet he must hon-
estly own that he does not know, that he has no real
ground for thinking ill of, a man whose character he
has never "come to and seen," by any such experience of him as can justify him in having any real
opinion about him whatever? How many men will
go up to the polls and vote for a President of the
United States, some on one side, some on the other,
making believe that they have judgments about the

men, when they have really nothing but prejudices? They will vote for and against phantoms of their own fancy, and not clearly understood characters. Why, take away our prejudices about each other, and how much do we know of one another's life? How much solid judgment is there that is really full of intelligent experience? I think that when we die and go together to the world of perfect light, we shall have to begin almost all our knowledge of one another entirely afresh. We shall see that these ill-considered fancies that we have about each other are good for nothing. They will all be swept away out of the clear atmosphere of that celestial life. Our deep affections, our real loves and hates, we shall keep, our trivial fondnesses, our foolish likes and dislikes, will go together. We shall find by our side upon the sea of glass — if God's mercy bring us there — some saint whom an inconsistent habit or a scandalous report has made us think that we dislike, and find, as we look him through and through with the insight of that perfect world, and know him for the first time, that we cannot hate, but must completely love, so noble, true, and pure a soul as his. We shall leave these clouds behind, as we get higher up the mountain. And this freedom from personal prejudice, this really sympathetic knowledge of one another, may begin here, and will be one of the purest earthly foretastes of heaven.

You see, then, whither we are always being tempted if we could only hear the invitation. It is to trustworthy knowledge of the facts of life, away from phantoms and fancies and our mere imaginations.

You think that work is disgraceful and degrading, and that taste and true culture ripen only in idle leisure. "Come and see." Set yourself to work. You know nothing about it. Try it, and see what a good life it brings. You think that serious thought is stupid, that nothing but trifling dissipation is interesting and exciting. "Come and see." Try it, and find that there is an exhilaration about a high pursuit of ideas that is as far beyond all mere frivolity as climbing a mountain peak is better than running races in the valley. This appeal to experiment and fact is the great hope of mankind. This is the very soul of modern science. Philosophers had been making theories about what the world ought to be and what nature ought to do. "Come and see," said Bacon. That was the watchword of the inductive philosophy, and to-day the world is full of men just patiently seeing what Nature is doing, learning her by the humble wisdom of experimental science. And in religion, bigotry and superstition are the result of men's theorizing and speculating about what God ought to be. "Come and see; come and see what God is," cries the reassuring voice of Him who would not hide Himself from, but show Himself to, His children, and out of a devout and humble study of His words and works, out of a readiness to take whatever He shall show it, there comes the large, earnest, true religion which really elevates and saves the soul.

So everywhere this invitation rings through the world. True, the sight which we send out in answer to the invitation must be the large use of all our faculties. Not merely the outward eye must see, the mind must see as well. It is not answering the whole invitation unless the whole man goes and sees with all his powers of vision. The eye sees phenomena; the soul sees causes underlying and connecting the phenomena. We must not stop merely with what the eye sees, and, having written down the facts we have discovered, call that the all of science, and brand all beyond as superstition. It is not superstition, not prejudice, but science still, spiritual science, when the mind sees a causal will, out of which all phenomena proceed, and the heart feels a mighty love beating through all the ordered system. It is not well to live and see only from the eyes and brain outward.

To every man there is a fundamental division of this universe that the oldest philosophies have recognized. It is not conceit, it is the mere law of his personality that makes it. He is on one side, and all the rest of the universe is on the other. I is one division. All the rest, all that is not I, is on the other. Out of that rest of the universe comes the endless call to knowledge. "Come and see" whispers in every wind, seems written in the mystery of every sunset and starlight, cries pathetically to him out of every strange movement of this human nature that his heart hears when to the ear all is still. To every man it is as if the rest of the universe were made for him to use his faculties upon, to learn, to know, to love, to hate, as, stand where he will, the horizon forms a circle about every man. To say that we know that world, before our faculties have met and grappled it, is prejudice and folly. To be at work really learning it, in any part of it, however small, is noble and makes us noble. That is the everlasting and unspeakable superiority of any work in life, however small, that is true, over every work in life, however great, that is false.

So far I have been speaking of the duty of the learner, but the duty of every teacher becomes plain, also, from what we have been saying. And every man is a teacher, or wants to be sometimes. Every man sometimes knows and believes something which he desires to make his neighbor also know and believe. How shall he do it? If he is wise he will try to take his friend to the same facts that enlightened him, and make him see them. He will not merely try to get assent, but to get conviction. He will say, "Come and see," if it is possible. This was the admirable wisdom of Philip. What had converted him was the personal sight of Jesus. He had no other religion but that. He meant to follow Him because he had seen Him, and was satisfied in seeing Him. He might have gone to work to argue with Nathanael a multitude of side questions, to show that Nazareth was not such a bad place after all; that Jesus had escaped its contamination, or that, indeed, He was born in Bethlehem, and not in Nazareth at all. But he was too wise and too eager for that. Jesus Himself was His own evidence. To get his friend face to face with Jesus — to make the guileless Nathanael see with spiritual sympathy the spiritual Christ. This was his object. This was what he did. And oh, if every preacher could only do it too! If, instead of arguing a hundred half-relevant questions, the apostles who fill our pulpits were all crying like this wise, honest apostle of Bethsaida, " We have found the Messiah, come and see ;" and when men hesitated and objected, crying still, " Come and see," merely laboring to bring the souls of men into the presence of the personal Christ, to make them look upon His face, and hear His voice, and feel His heart beating, I am sure that our pulpits would change weakness for power, and our churches be full of life. The really strong and effective preaching that the world has seen always has been just this. Men who had seen Jesus, wise or ignorant, strong or weak, crying to their brethren to come and see Him, too.

And so of all teaching. A man insults me if he tries to force himself on me merely repeating his opinion and expecting me to receive it because it is his. But a man honors me if he takes me back to the source where he found his truth, and bids me drink where he drank. I cannot take another man's truth, but he can show me where he got his, and I will get my own and thank him. A man trying to make you take his opinion just because he has thoroughly adopted it and likes it, is like a man who had been cured of his palsy, thinking that therefore he can cure yours if he touches you. All that he can do, evidently, is to take you to the doctor or give you the medicine that cured him. And yet the land rings with mere positiveness. On every platform men are shouting over and over their loud persuasions, and deafening us into assent. How powerful it seems at first! How powerless it is in the long run ! Mere assertion may force assent, but it never creates belief. Of all the causes and theories and political and social parties that are vociferating in our land to-day, it is comfortable to know that none will finally establish itself by mere vociferation. All must die out in noise, except the one or two that shall prove strong enough and wise enough to take men calmly by the hand, and lead them down to the foundations that they rest on, and say, " Look for yourselves," and so finally convince men's minds as well as deafen their bewildered ears.

And now I want to apply what I have been saying to Christianity more distinctly. I think it is a question that many Christians are not wholly clear about. Are there any clear reasons, capable of statement to other people, why we are Christians? There are people who know that they are Christians, and always mean to be. But does our religion stand frankly before the world and say to the doubter, " Come and see ; " and having something really to point to which can convince his reason and change his heart? Has she got just to stand, with her creed in her hand, saying, " Believe this or die," threatening the penalties of unbelief ; or can she do what any honest man would like to do, — call other men to see what she sees, and so believe her belief, not because they will suffer if they refuse, but because they cannot help it. I believe, indeed, that no man ever loses any truth, whether through his own fault or not, without suffering for it. It may not be in the way of punishment, but he suffers. If every truth gained makes a man richer, any truth lost must make him poorer. I believe that the fear of such suffering for disbelief may be rightly used to break up men's sluggishness, and compel them to inquire; but that is a different thing from attempting to compel belief by fear. Philip may say to Nathanael, "You will suffer if you do not believe in my Messiah; therefore, 'Come and see;'" but he cannot say, "You will suffer if you do not believe; therefore believe without seeing." It is a perfectly simple distinction, but one that men are always forgetting. Fear can induce inquiry, but cannot create belief. In a frivolous age, before frivolous minds, one may well stand and portray the terrible effects of rejecting truth. But when the age is serious, and when the minds to which he speaks have lost their frivolity and really are in earnest, then he must be ready to throw aside his terrors and to lead them to the reasons of the faith he thinks they ought to hold. Can our faith thus utter her invitation? Men almost fancy to-day that she cannot; that she must hide herself behind vague terrors. If that were so, not merely we could not make other men believe, but we could not believe ourselves. Let us see what the invitation is that Christianity gives to earnest men really looking for the truth.

1. It is the Bible first that she is holding as she stands there saying, "Come and see." The Bible as the word of God — as the true story of His dealings with the world. Christianity holds that out and frankly bids men come and examine it for themselves. She cannot escape that, and she does not want to. The Bible as a book of history and teaching, to be examined like other books, first as to its

truth and authority, then as to its meaning, this must always be the first principle of a reasonable Christianity. That in the four Gospels we have the story told by His own contemporaries and disciples of how Jesus the Saviour lived and taught, and died; that is the truth which Christianity lays first before men's eyes. She calls them to examine for themselves whether the book from which the warrant of her life proceeds is genuine and true. Men come to it, and by every trial they can make of it, of critical study or of spiritual experience, they test this spring out of which the whole stream flows.

2. And then, secondly, Christianity offers to the world her historic Christ. Again she says, " Come and see." Back in the centuries, yet set so clearly in the light of authentic history that all attempts to melt His life into a cloudy myth have always failed, there stands this figure. She claims that this Being to whom she points is the power and wisdom of God present upon the earth. You hesitate and doubt. Then "Come and see," she says. Put yourself in the presence of this Being. See how He lives. He is a man surely. In suffering and joy alike, the identifying proof-marks of our humanity are all here. But ennoble humanity as completely as you will, and it will not explain this phenomenal character and life. There is a simplicity, a largeness of purpose, which is divine. Explain this phenomenon of human history, how can you? She says it is God manifest in the flesh. Come and find another explanation, if you can. Come, and if there is no

other to be found, take this and own the divine Christ.

3. And thirdly, Christianity calls us to see her Christian history. She claims that the Christ, forever present in human life, is a renewing and comforting and strengthening power everywhere. You doubt and hesitate. Again, frank as Philip, she cries, "Come and see." Then the great books are opened; the birth and growth of modern history is shown; the larger reign of conscience; the gradual advance of freedom; the ever-moving spiritual element in life; the refreshed, invigorated world of modern times. Then here and there a veil more sacred is lifted from the hearts of single men. The record of the saints is shown, — men, women, little children, borne up over their sorrows so that their voices ring still to us out of the fires where they burned, — made giants in their weakness, to do the work of God so that the hard world still bears the pressures where their feeble fingers laid hold of it, as if it had been seized with some grasp of iron. These are the phenomena. Come and see them! Come and see them! Other religions can show you some of the same sort, no doubt. We rejoice to recognize the proof that in them too the divine Spirit has been at work. When the faith of Christ shows her marks of the divine Power, let our voices gladly rejoice to acknowledge the divine Presence.

The Bible, the historic Christ, the Christian history, — these, then, are what the religion we believe in lays before men who are really willing to come and see whether what she claims is true or not. But is this all? Is there not another region of evidence from which the Christian draws his deepest assurance, but which seems less open to him who is looking at the faith from its outside. I mean the region of personal experience. Christ says to the Christian, "I can bless you with spiritual blessings, with a loving, happy inner life." "Yes," the glad soul answers, recalling many a bright passage in its own career. "Yes, surely, Christ can do, will do, has done all that He says." And so it gladly looks forward and trusts Him for the things to come. But, then, when that soul turns to another by its side, and tells of the richer life, the trust, the hope, the peace, the courage, the gradual purity which the Saviour can give, and that stranger soul, weary of a search for these high things in which it never has succeeded, looks incredulous and hopeless, can you say to it simply, "Come and see," tempting it to an experience which lies wide open to any one, like these others I described? "How can I?" it replies. "To try these things implies already a sympathetic appreciation of them, which is the very faith I lack and cannot find." We stand apart. "I say I cannot believe, and your only answer is, Come and believe." This is the real difficulty that many people feel when they are asked to test the reality to its spiritual power by making themselves subjects of it. Their answer, often not captious, but very sad, is that they cannot make themselves subjects of it until they do believe in it. And so the weary circle runs around.

Is it a hopeless difficulty? Some people seriously believe that it is. They hold that the whole Christian experience is so foreign and so unintelligible to a soul that God has not called, that it is utterly unapproachable and unattractive to that soul, and they fix the calling of God at one definite recognizable point in a man's life. Until that moment comes, it is as impossible for that man to make his way into the charmed circle in which they live who live with God, as for Lucifer to gather up his own shattered strength and holiness, and go and stand again beside Gabriel and Michael before the throne of God. To invite the soul to such an experience is to invite to an impossibility — it is calling upon a corpse to live. There is nothing for it to do but to lie helpless and wait. The father may tell his child of the joy of the Christian, but the child cannot rise up and say, "I will go." Friend may cry to friend out of the fullness of his heart, "Oh, taste and see that the Lord is good!" but he is tempting only to a Tantalus feast. This test of Christianity which lies in the personal Christian experience can be nothing to you till first you are a Christian.

I cannot think that this is true. It does not sound to me like the New Testament. It does not sound to me like Christ. And its fault seems to me to be in this assumption, that there is one fixed moment in a man's life when the spirit of God comes to him for the first time — that before that moment he is an outsider, a foreigner, and an alien. If our first view is different — if we believe that all men are God's children, and that each of the children from his birth into this world, and how long before we cannot say, is on the Father's heart and mind; if we believe that every truth and goodness that the most benighted soul finds comes to him from the one only source of truth and goodness which the universe contains (and in order not to deny that, men have been compelled to deny that much which was evidently truth and goodness was either true or good); if the hour of conversion is the time when the soul comes to God, and not the time when God comes to the soul, that having happened so long before; if all this different idea be true, then the difficulty is not so great. I go to my friend and bid him test Christ by this experience of the inner life, and he answers me as I described, "I cannot come to Him till first He comes to me." The answer is, " He has come to you. All the truth and goodness that you have He brought you. Your coming to Him will be only coming into a consciousness, and so a complete service of the Saviour who was already with you." When I invite you, then, to the religious experience, I invite you not to something strange, but to something which in its rudiments you know already. You have already seen the opening of the paths that lead to Christ. You cannot see the depths they lead to, but they do lead finally to Him. When I urge you to come to Him, I am urging you to follow those paths out to the end. You cannot see their whole course, but you can see one step at least farther than you have done yet, and so test the steps beyond, so come nearer to the illumination and assurance that awaits you at the end.

I am sure that this is true: that when I take a man who says that he knows nothing of Christ, and yet who owns that he has instincts of duty and aspirations of reverence to God, and a longing for purity, that I believe were put into his heart by no other than Christ's Holy Spirit, and when I urge and beg that man to do the duty and to believe the truth which he has had made known to him, I am leading toward that Christ who is the centre of all duty and all truth. If I found a man who believed in a God, but not in any self-manifestation of that God in human life, what would I do? I would do all that I could to make that God whom he did believe in more and more real to him. I would waken his conscience till it cried out with the sense of disobedience. He should see that God awful in His righteousness, more awful in His love, close to his daily life. New needs should start out of his deepening religion, until only an Emmanuel, a fatherhood made manifest in brotherhood, a God in Christ, could satisfy him. So I would try to get him to "come and see" Christ, where He is most mighty, — in His work in the soul of man. Only when I found a man who owned no duty which was yet undone, before whom there opened no vista of spiritual aspiration that was yet unfollowed, — only when I found the man perfectly bounded and contented with this earthly life, should I feel that I had found one before whom there opened no way to the Saviour of us all.

This seems to be reasonable, surely. If you knew that the benefactor of your life was living now in Europe, though you did not know just where or how to reach him, or what he would do for you, or even thoroughly and certainly who he was and what he was, only that he was and that he was there, you would go to Europe and live there yourself, if you had any way of getting there, that you might be in the same land with him and certainly somewhere near him. If a soul has many doubts and bewilderments about Christ, and yet knows that there is a Saviour, and that that Saviour's home is in the land of righteousness and truth, then to that land of righteousness and truth that soul will go by any road that it can find, eager to get there, seeking a road, pressing through difficulties, that it may be in the same country with, and somewhere near, its unfound Lord. It may be that the clouds that for us mortals haunt that land of righteousness and truth may long hang so thick and low that living close to Him the soul may still fail to see Him, but some day certainly the fog shall rise, the cloud shall scatter, and in the perfect enlightenment of the other life the soul shall see its Lord, and be thankful for every darkest step that it took towards Him here.

And is this what it means, then, that " Coming to Jesus "? That phrase that is so old, so vague, whatever it means, means for you, first of all, just this doing the duty which lies next to you, and following out whatever spiritual conviction you have to its next result, being true to the light you have, and waiting, hoping, praying for more. Yes, simply, just exactly that. If you have any duty that you know you ought to do, and are cowardly and dishonest about and will not do it, then to go, and do it, if

you have any spiritual aspiration that you are keep·
ing down under a weight of business and selfishness,
then to set it free, that is what it means for you
now to come to Christ. It may be that Nathanael's
first step when he started with Philip was into the
dark shadow of some Capernaum alley or up the
steep rocky path that led from town to town. Afterward Christ clothed in light upon the lake at midnight, Christ at the table in the chamber of the
supper, Christ in the room where the disciples were
assembled after the resurrection when the door was
shut. And so for you hereafter, Christ in the highest experiences, the purest raptures of this life and
the other, Christ in forgiveness, in communion, in
fellowship of work, in fellowship of glory; but now
Christ in these first steps that lead you towards Him,
in the truthfulness and purity and unselfishness and
humility, in the struggle to do right, and the sorrow
when you have done wrong, which are possible for
you right away.

I am well pleased that our long journey of this
evening has brought us out at last upon this clear
and open ground of immediate duty, — the duty for
to-morrow, the duty for to-day. You are in doubt of
Christ. "How can He be this that you claim? How
can He be, indeed, at all?" The answer is, "Come
and see." You say, "I cannot." Say it sadly or
bitterly, "I cannot." I do not know what your impossibility may be, but I am sure of one absolute
impossibility that may be yours. You cannot see the
highest and the best so long as you are neglecting a
known duty or stifling a known truth. I am well

pleased to leave it here. Go home and search your heart. Let it speak out. Be brave and honest. Take up your wronged duties and do them. Take up your wronged truths and really believe them. Enter into that region of sincerity and faithfulness where Christ abides, and then surely some day you will find Him there. Then not merely the lowest but the highest evidences of our faith shall become clear to you, even that highest of all its evidences, the Spirit itself bearing with your spirit that you are the child of God and joint heir with Christ.

IX.

THE PRINCIPLE OF THE CRUST.

" Let no man deceive himself. If any man thinketh that he is
wise among you in this world, let him become a fool, that he may be
wise." — I. Cor. iii. 18.

THERE must have been plenty of people in Corinth to whom these words came home. The conceit
of Greece was wisdom, and Corinth was one of the
eyes of Greece. There were the scholars of the
schools. There, in that bright transparent air, everything quivering and blazing in the sunshine, the
passion of knowing was the great dominant emotion ;
the pride of knowing was the complacent satisfaction
of men's lives.

And there is no satisfaction so subtle and insidi-
ous as the conceit of knowledge — no other possession so becomes a very part of the possessor. The
money which you hold in your hand, the laurel
which men wreathe around your brow, both of these
may disappear and you are still the same, but the
thing you know is part of you. No man can take it
from you. Its subtle essence is in your heart and
character. You are something different because of
it. And so, as a man loves what he is more than
what he has, self-love lends all its intensity to the
pride of learning, and no man is so proud as he who
" thinketh that he is wise " among men in the world.

To such men writes St. Paul. St. Paul, himself the wise man, the lover of wisdom, and he says that there come times when the great need of life is to put aside what seems our wisdom, to give it no value, to make no account of it, to seem to ourselves to know nothing, and in his strong words, to "become a fool," and this with the distinct purpose that we may really get the wisdom which we have thought ourselves to possess. Surely there is enough of strangeness in such exhortation to excite our curiosity, and set us to studying to see what the great apostle, who always means something weighty and timely and interesting, means here.

And at the very outset we cannot help feeling how his words have the same tone with which a good many other words in the New Testament, and especially in the Gospels, make us familiar. We think about those words of Jesus when He said, " Whosoever loseth his life shall save it; " or those other words to the young rich man, " Go and sell all that thou hast ; " or yet those others, " Except ye be converted and become as little children." And of a general spirit which runs through all His teaching, that very much which the world has been elaborately building up must be pulled down, before the true city of God, the new Jerusalem, can be established in the earth. No one can read the New Testament and not catch that spirit, and whoever catches it, sees the far-off hope of a perfected humanity only through falling systems and the ruin of the vicious and imperfect conditions which must take place first. Whoever has thoroughly accepted and been filled ·

with that spirit, is ready to feel how like it is to what Paul teaches in this text, and that the man who calls himself wise must become a fool to gain true wisdom.

It is no mere abuse of earthly wisdom, such as religious teachers sometimes have allowed themselves. It goes more deep. It comes more down to fundamental principles than that. Let me try to state the principle which seems to me to be involved in it. If I gave it a name I should almost venture to call it the Principle of the Crust. What I mean is this: There are two sorts of hindrance or obstacle which may settle around any object and prevent a power from outside from reaching it. One of them is a purely external obstacle, built round it like a wall, of stuff and nature different from the object itself. The other is simply its own substance, hardened upon the surface and shutting up the body of the object, as it were, behind and within itself. This latter is the Crust. The river freezes, and it is the river's self, grown hard and stiff, which shuts the river's water out from the sunshine and the rain. The ground is trodden hard, and it is the very substance of the ground that lies rigid and impenetrable and catches the seed, and will not let it enter in and claim the soil and do its fruitful work. The loaf hardens its surface, and the Crust which confines the bread is bread itself. This is the notion of the Crust. It is of the very substance of the thing which it imprisons. It is not a foreign material; but the thing itself, grown hard and rigid, shuts the soft and tender and receptive portions of the thing away. The in-

fluences from outside are powerless to reach it. Not
until the Crust is broken, and the ice melts once
more into the stream, and the hardened ground is
crumbled into the general system of the soil again.
Not until then can power and influence easily find
their way in and permeate the whole.

Is not the parable plain? Can we not recognize
how that which takes place in the lake or on the
road-side takes place also in the ordinary intellectual
and moral life of man. Out of the very substance
of a man's life, out of the very stuff of what he is
and does, comes the hindrance which binds itself
about his being, and will not let the better influences
out. His occupations, his acquirements, his habits,
his standards of action and of thoughts, make Crusts
out of their own material, so that, beside whatever
foreign barrier may stand between them and the
higher food they need, there is this barrier which
they have made out of themselves. That self-made
barrier must be broken up, must be restored to its
first condition and become again part of the substance out of which it was evolved, before the life can
be fed with the dews of first principles and the rain
of the immediate descent of God.

Let us see what all this means in special illustrations. What is it that we mean by Prejudice?
Simply the premature hardening of opinion. A man
is thinking and studying, seeking after truth. He
is open to all light and influence. He is ready to
be taught on every side. Knowledge is welcome
whencesoever it may come. The surface of his life is
free. ·But suddenly or gradually the man stops.

As if a cold wind touched the stream and froze it, the water turns itself into a wall of ice. The degree of thought and truth which has been reached becomes a stopping-place. It is no longer a promise and prophecy of more beyond. It is an end — hard, stiff, impenetrable, nothing can break through it. What is it but a Crust? It is itself made of the thought which it imprisons. It is the toughened surface of the student's study, making it impossible for any further light to enter in and play upon the thought imprisoned in itself.

This is the essence of all prejudice : my tyrant says to me, " You shall not learn," and shuts me up behind a wall of brass or iron. My own nature says to me, "You shall not learn," and throws out its armor of prejudice, made of its own crude conceptions and half-mastered learning, and within that I am as helpless as behind the iron or the brass. Those crude conceptions must be broken up and turned again into good truth-learning capability before I can once more lie open to the light.

Another kind of crust is formalism. Truth utters itself in outward symbols. Belief and resolution declare themselves in forms. It is the natural law of expression, and so long as the form remains soft and pliant, full of the spirit of the belief or resolution it expresses, all is right. Form and belief are like body and soul to one another. But when form hardens into formalism, when the real substance of belief, instead of remaining soft and pliant, grows stiff, and will not let belief grow and enlarge, will not let the food of belief which is new truth come pouring in, then you have got the most crusted and impenetrable armor that can be imagined. Forms ought to be the medium through which truth comes to the inner nature, as the surface ground furnishes the channels through which the warm sunshine reaches the deeper soil. When forms do not do that, but shut truth out, and make the inner nature starve on the stale remnant of what it already has, keeping no free and open communication with the perpetual source, then forms have hardened into formalism. Beware of formalism, — not by discarding forms, but by keeping them soft, by refusing to let them grow hard; and that can only be by keeping them in true connection with the faiths which they express. When they cease to express faith, break them up, return them to the ground again, and ask God to feed you directly with the ministrations of His truth.

What is a great reformation, a great fresh start and new departure in the world's religion, but just the breaking up of a formalism which has become a crust? The ways of the church have grown hard. They are imprisoning, instead of cultivating or expressing, the church's life. A great explosion comes. The traditions and habits are all broken to pieces. The fragments of the crust are swallowed up and stirred in, and become again part of the mass of true faith and healthy feeling, which lies once more open without hindrance to the sunlight of God. That is what took place in Luther's day. That is what, in many ways, is taking place in ours.

Another sort of crust is the conceit of knowing the world. Have you not all known men who, sooner or later, came to the conclusion that they knew mankind. They found some stiff, tight, narrow conception of what human life amounted to. It was sceptical of any good. It was cynical and bitter. It disparaged the good in man which it could not deny. It was largely the echo of the man's own selfhood; the image of his own nature, accepted as the type and picture of universal humanity. However it was formed, there it stood, this man's knowledge of man. And he was very proud of it. He thought it was a miracle of insight. It stood to him as the result of wonderful observation. He went about the world reading his fellow-creatures by this key which he applied indiscriminately and stupidly to them all. And what was the result? Was that man ready or able to see and own a new, fresh, singular specimen of manhood when it appeared? Could the mystery of human life, its pathos, its wonderful variety, its suggestion of undeveloped power, get any chance of play upon his imprisoned perception? Surely not. There is no blinder bat in all the heavens than this conceited man of the world who goes about saying, " Oh, I know man!" and is perfectly incapable of forming just judgments, or seeing the finest shades and distinctions of men and women. His crust must be broken up. His crude conceit must be dispelled. Some experience must teach him how much richer is the nature of man, how much harder to know than he has guessed. Then, perhaps, when he had ceased saying, " You can't teach me anything," he may begin to learn.

Out of all these instances does there not issue to our sight a truth or principle which we recognize at once? It is that all life tends to encrust itself, to imprison itself within itself, and that its crust needs to be constantly broken and returned into the general mass out of which it was formed, in order that the best influences may be received. Ever there must be a return to a primitive simplicity, to a condition of first principles, in which the power to receive may be freshened and renewed. Do you not recognize that? It is part of the old craving to begin the game of life again. It is not that life has been miserable, or has wholly failed, but it has lost simplicity. We long for that openness in which all things seem possible. A greater and greater number of things seem to have become impossible. "I shall never do this; I shall never do that," we have come to say of one thing after another, till the things which there is any chance of our doing seem to have become very few indeed. Then youth, with its unlimited possibilities, seems bright to you, as it never did when you possessed it. You cry out hopelessly for its return:

" Make me feel the wild pulsation that I felt before the strife,
When I heard my days before me and the tumult of my life."

The same is felt about some special department of life, or some special kind of knowledge. Have not you men in your professions often thought whether you would not gladly give up all the knowledge and experience which you have gained, precious as you know it is, if only you could get again the freshness and eagerness and enthusiasm, the sense of how much there was to know, and of what a capacity there was in you for knowing it, which filled the first years of your life in your vocation ? Have not you readers of the Bible sometimes wished that you could rise up some morning and find your Bible a new book, fresh and strange to you as if you had never seen it before ? Have you not almost envied the heathen to whom the story of Jesus came unstaled by countless repetitions, with no hardness on its surface from the thoughts and theories which have pressed and handled it for all these thousand years ?

Oh that I could go back and know nothing, with my power of knowing and my eagerness to know, set free from under the weight of helpless knowledge and unused experience which are pressing on them now !

And, now, do you not see ? Is not that craving for a return to simplicity just what St. Paul has in his mind when he says of the man whom he wants to see made wise, " Let him become a fool." Is it not just this getting rid of the crust of life, in order that life itself may be open to the sunshine. This is what he means by his strange word "fool," I think. It may have some reference to what the world will think of him who accepts the Gospel in its simpleness ; but more than that, I think it also must refer to that condition of simplicity to which the nature must return before Christ with all His great enlightenment can take possession of it.

There is an illustration and anticipation of this power of Christ to simplify the nature and break through its crusts, in the way in which all great experiences tend to do the same thing, which Paul says that Christ can do. Do you not know what I mean when I say, that under all strong emotions, and at all critical instants, men who have seemed to be wise among other men in the world, very often "become fools that they may be wise." Look at your accomplished man — which means your finished man. The man who has got every problem solved and every question answered; the ends of life all gathered up and folded in; the surfaces all smooth and hard and shining; everything neat and snug, and trim and wise. Suppose some great calamity comes upon him — some one of those terrible things which tear life up from the bottom and leave no stone or timber standing where it stood. What is the result? How the old settled questions burst to life again, and will not stay imprisoned under what seemed their sufficient answers. The adjustments are thrown all out of gear. The ends are all torn loose and sent flying out upon the wind. He who seemed to himself to know everything, seems to himself now to know nothing. The wise man has become a fool.

A great joy sometimes has the same result. I become happy beyond my highest dream of happiness, and what then? Again my theories of life give way. They will not hold this overwhelming pleasure. The sails are torn to tatters with this tempest of joy. I dare not try to account for it.

I take it in a dazzled ignorance. It is in a fool's hands that this new preciousness of life is tremulously held.

And yet in both these cases this foolishness of a great experience is only preliminary to and makes possible a higher wisdom. Into this heart, all torn and dismayed with sorrow, pours a new sense of the greatness of life and life's relationships. Into this soul, all turbulent with joy, there comes a knowledge of goodness and responsibility, that was impossible before the great disturbance came. You needed larger theories, more profound and spiritual thoughts of things, than those which you had lost. You must have them. And lo! they came to you! Lo there they were; filling the depth which had been broken up. Was it not just the story which Paul tells. You had seemed to be wise. You became a fool. And then you were really wise.

And yet, to come back to our crust philosophy again. That which had shut the higher wisdom out of your soul was part and portion of the soul itself, and so when it was broken up and kneaded in, it became part of the substance which received the new illumination. Do you see what I mean? Your experience proved insufficient. Your life had to open itself again in primal simplicity to God. But the life, which opened itself, had the experience in it as an element, and through the presence of that experience in it, it was more fit to welcome the new wisdom. The new simplicity was not the old. It was a richer, a completer, a diviner simplicity. It was the man's simplicity, and not the child's.

It harmonized all the results of experience within itself. Your learning was not able to account for and to satisfy your life; but when the conceit of learning had been all destroyed, and the real power of knowing thrown open to the highest truth, then the discipline of the old thought and study made that power of knowing a richer thing, more able to receive its higher gift of truth. Nothing is lost. Conceit paralyzes even the highest attainments by making them inhuman. But humility humanizes them again and causes them to be receptive. It is the story which Tennyson has told so wonderfully in his great poem, " The Palace of Art." The spirit driven out from the home which its selfishness and vanity have built, then daring to hope that when it shall itself have grown larger and truer and better it may come back and find its palace grown large to receive it.

> " Yet tear not down my palace towers, that are
>   So lightly, beautifully built;
>   Perchance I may return with others there
>   When I have purged my guilt."

It is the wise man going out from his wisdom into foolishness, but yet believing that he shall some day come back and occupy the old wisdom in a nobler spirit.

Thus I have spoken of the power of a great experience to turn the wise man into the fool for whom the higher wisdom becomes possible. But now, to come to St. Paul's teaching, the greatest of all experiences is the access of a great mastery. Nothing means so much to a life as to be taken into the power of another life, and lovingly and sympathetically and firmly ruled by it. And beyond all comparisons, the greatest of all such masteries is Christ's. That which is true, then, of the effect of all great experiences, is truest of all about the mastery of the soul by Christ, of the beginning of the Christian life. Indeed Christ and His mastery of the soul seem in some strange way to have in themselves the power of all great experiences. To become Christ's servant does for us that which all great emotions and occurrences of very different characters can do. It sobers us like sorrow. It exalts us like joy. It calms us like satisfaction. It quickens us like suspense. It deepens us like doubt. It irradiates us like certainty. It warms us like friendship. It disciplines us like authority. It restrains us like fear. It inspires us like hope. It touches us with all the hands of all the influences which our nature can receive.

If this is true, then it is not strange that the power which, we saw, belonged to all great experiences should also belong supremely to the mastery of the soul by Christ. A man transfers the whole thought of life to Christ. That great, that mighty alteration comes. The man is born again. New principles, new standards occupy him. The life which he now lives in the flesh he lives by the faith of the Son of God. There never was a nobler instance of it all than St. Paul who wrote those words. And in the man's doing of that, all the selfish and self-satisfied conceptions of life go to pieces. The plans which the man has made and elaborated and provided with the means for their execution no longer seem to be worthy or sufficient ambitions of a human soul. The higher, holier, manlier ambitions of glorifying God and helping brother-man possess the life. The purposes of life grow personal. They lose their definiteness and trimness. " What are you living for? " you ask the new Christian with his glowing face. " Is it to get rich? " — " Oh, no! " — "Is it to enjoy yourself? " — " Oh, no! " — " Is it to make men praise you and get fame? " — " Oh, no." — " Is it to heap up learning? " — " No." — " What, then? " " It is to follow Christ and do His will and grow like Him by obedience." What a bewilderment that answer brings! How he who asked the question cannot understand it! Has the man then "become a fool"? Yes; in the higher sense, surely he has. He has found all the ordinary standards of life insufficient, and cast them away. He has gone back to the elements of things. He has thought of himself once more, not as the millionaire, not as the scholar, not as the politician, but as the man — Nicodemus, Matthew, Pilate, Paul, these are the men in the New Testament whom Jesus thus dissolved out of their artificialnesses, and brought down to their essential manhood. Wonderful was His power, then ! Wonderful is the power, now and always, with which He says to everybody with whom He comes face to face, " If any man thinketh that he is wise let him become a fool."

And why? For what? If this were all it would be most bewildering. Sometimes it has been made to seem as if it were all. Sometimes pious men have talked as if the breaking up of worldly wisdom were everything, as if a sort of celestial folly, a sanctified babyhood, were the consummate achievement of our Christianity. Not so talks Paul : " Your wise man must become a fool," he says ; but why ? " That he may become wise." Behold wisdom is the end of all ! No less in the Bible and in the church than in the schools. It would be indeed a dreadful world in which that was not so. A dreadful world in which ignorance and foolishness should be the conditions of the most approved and rewarded life. The end of all is wisdom. If the Gospel discredits any of man's achievements, declaring them to be incompetent to satisfy the soul and educate the nature, it is always only that it may insist upon a higher knowledge. Christ was a teacher. Christ is a teacher forever. If He declares, as He certainly does, that no scholastic culture, and no skill in the arts of life, and no acquaintance with the ways of men, can save a soul, it is only that He may insist upon another knowledge, only that He may insist that man must know his own soul, and the deep difference of right and wrong, and the infinite holiness of God. These are true knowledges. " That they might know Thee, the only true God, and Jesus Christ whom Thou hast sent." It is of all importance that we should know that the Christian life is a life of knowledge, not of ignorance. It is a separate, a higher region of knowledge than that to which we generally give the name ; but it is knowledge still. It is the apprehension of truths, of those vast truths which the senses cannot discover nor the intellect evolve, but which through the open avenues of the spirit enter in and occupy the life. Who can tell what knowledge of the earth, and of the history of man, and of the things the Rabbis taught in their solemn school, was in the mind of Jesus Christ, and yet who doubts His wisdom, who dares to call Him ignorant or foolish? In every age and every land, except the lightest and most superficial, this higher wisdom has been recognized and treasured. To the purest and most exalted souls it has seemed to be the one precious thing on earth; all other kinds of knowledge have seemed to be easy sacrifices, if by their loss it could be won. Let us beware that we do not despise this spiritual wisdom, which is the ultimate treasure of the human soul.

And yet I must not seem to talk as if this spiritual wisdom involved the final and perpetual sacrifice of all the other attainments of man. I must once more return to the Parable of the Crusted ground. You break up the hard hindering surface, and, as I pointed out, it becomes part of the soil on which the sunshine and the rain descend and out of which the flowers grow. So you break up the crusted conceit of human wisdom, and its fragments make part of the simplified and softened human nature into which pours the higher wisdom of the grace of God.

What is the crust upon your life, my friend, that keeps out holy influence? Is it the knowledge you have gained from books? Is it the multiplied complexity of your affairs? Is it the busyness of every day? Is it your complicated relations with your friend? Is it the richness of physical life satisfied with its abundance, health rejoicing in itself? It may be any one of these. What shall you pray to God for? Oh, pray to Him to break this crusted hindrance all to pieces. It need not be that the possession itself should be taken away. What you want to lose is the conceit in the possession. You want to learn that it cannot satisfy you. Then, when you have learnt that, the real satisfaction, the only real satisfaction, can come in. And then, when they have been put in their true place, these things, knowledge and wealth and health and the complexity of life, which once hindered the divine wisdom, may become the means by which it takes possession of and spreads itself through the life. This is the dream we dare to dream for ourselves and for our brethren. Now, it is your learning, your busyness, your physical health which keeps you from, which keeps from you, the inflow, the influence of God. Sometime it shall be through those very possessions — learning, busyness, physical strength, — broken out of their conceit and made capable by humble consecration of their true ministry, that God shall come to you.

What shall bring about so great a change? Nothing can do it but the overwhelming love of God taking possession of your soul and making you feel through and through that to know Him is the one only satisfactory attainment of a human life. Reach that, and, whatever else you miss, your life is rich. Lose that, and, whatever else you gain, your life is poor. Reach that, and then gain everything else you can, and your master, knowledge. Your knowledge of God shall dominate it all. Oh, be all the man that it is in you to be, only at the heart of all be God's man, and then it will be safe and good for you to be all the rest.

Such men may all of us be by the power of Christ. Give yourself to Him simply, totally, and then live as fully as you can, letting Him claim all your life and fill it with Himself.

X.

THE LEADERSHIP OF CHRIST.

"In my Father's house are many mansions. I go to prepare a place for you: and I will come again and receive you unto myself."—John xiv. 2.

The disciples of Jesus must often have felt a strange uneasiness while they were with Him. Close as He drew them to Him, well as they came to know Him, there must have always been a sense of how much greater He was than they were, and so a fear lest sometime He should leave them. Have we not all felt something of this sort when we have had a friend who was far nobler and larger than ourselves? We lived in closest intimacy with him; our power worked at the same tasks, but all the while we felt that there were other powers in him which we could not match. Sometime he certainly must outgo our sphere, begin to do wider tasks, enter fields where we could not follow him. Sometime, at least, when he put forth the wings of his immortality, and entered on the other life, our friend must leave us, completing himself in regions far beyond our powers. Such a feeling had added keenness and pathos to many a friendship. And we can see traces of it every now and then in the intercourse of Christ and His disciples. They cling to Him as to one whom they are afraid to lose. Whenever He foretells a separation from them, they receive it as if it fell in with some misgiving of their own. Every sensitive reader of the Gospels must have felt, it seems to me, that sort of fearfulness in all the love, and anxiety in the midst of satisfaction, in the companionship of Jesus and the twelve, which showed how they felt that they must some day lose Him, that there was something in Him which must complete and manifest itself outside of their sphere. "Whither I go, thither ye cannot come." When Jesus said those words, they were terrible to His disciples, just because they confirmed the unspoken fear which was lurking in their hearts before.

We must bear all this in mind, I think, or else we cannot wholly understand the feeling of our text. I want to speak to you this morning from these words of Jesus, which seem to me to tell the story of all His life with His disciples, and so indeed of all His life with those whom His disciples represented, — the Christendom and Christian souls that were to come. They are words which have in them the whole of Christianity. Think, then, of these disciples wondering whether they could keep Jesus, fearing that He must leave them, fearing that the time would come when His life would outgo theirs and go to regions of activity whither they could not follow it. To them, fearing thus, Jesus answers, "No. Let not your heart be troubled. I am going, indeed, but I am going for you, not away from you. I go to prepare a place for you. In my father's house to which I go are many mansions, and if I go and prepare a place for you, I will come again and receive you unto myself." See what He says: "There is a region where we both belong. You as much as I. I am going forward to enter there so that your entrance may be the easier. I am going to open the door, and then am coming back to take you into my power again and carry you on with myself, and the end shall be that we shall be together there." Now, forget that when Jesus said that He was just upon the point of leaving this world. Forget for the moment (we will come back to that before we close) that the first application of the words was to the transfer of Christ's life, and His disciples' life, from earth to heaven. Think of it as if it were a saying that belonged wholly to this world, and have we not in this utterance of Jesus an account, clear and intelligible, of the way in which He always led His disciples from one stage of life into a higher. This is no illegitimate use of the words. Christ could not lead His followers from earth to heaven except by the same means by which He had already led them from one spiritual stage of earth into another. We have, then, a clear and definite plan laid down. He says, when I would lead you forward I go forward first myself. I establish for myself a place in the new region where I want you to be. You and I belong together, so that establishing for myself a place there I really set up your right to be there too. Then I come back to you, and by the love that is between us I draw you on into the realm that I have opened. That is the way I bring the souls that belong to me from strength to strength, until before the God of gods appeareth every one of them in Zion.

I remember how once travelling in Syria the guide

upon whom we wholly depended disappeared. By and by he came back to us as we rode along and told us where he had been; that in the village which we were approaching and where we were to spend the night his family lived. That he had ridden on to see that they were ready to receive him and to prepare quarters in their house for us, the travellers under his charge, and now came back to conduct us thither, and by and by he had brought us where he belonged, and where through him provision had been made and a welcome was waiting for us.

Let us look, then, at this plan of Christ's culture. It is really the same by which any man leads another who believes in him on to loftier and loftier things. I spoke about the friend who seems to be perfectly one with you, yet whom you are always lurkingly afraid of losing because you feel that there is in him the capacity for being something which you are not, and cannot be. Suppose some day that your friend does leave you, not that his bodily presence is taken away. Still he walks by your side, perhaps lives in your house, but all of a sudden he begins some higher life, enters upon some self-sacrifice for which you are not ready. Have you ever had such an experience? It seems as if you had lost your friend. You reach out after him, but there he is away above you, walking on higher ground, doing diviner things. But gradually you find that you have not lost him. Your love for him, his love for you, continues. You become aware that he is drawing you upward into that new region where he has entered, and which through his entrance has come to seem familiar and not so far away to you. The self-sacrifice seems not so unnatural or hard now that he is living in it. Your love for him draws you on into his company, and makes you attempt unattempted things. He has outgone you with his goodness, but he comes back after you with his love. He has gone to prepare a place for you, and he has come again and received you to himself, that where he is there you may be also.

Or just reverse the case. Suppose that you are the more enterprising and ambitious soul. Your friend loves you, but he lags behind, appears unconscious of his higher powers, of the higher life that he might live. How can you start him? Evidently you must start yourself. You must go out yourself into the region where you know he ought to be. It will seem as if you were leaving him. You speak to him some morning and say, " This is all very pleasant, but I will live no longer in this easy, self-indulgent life. I am determined to be up and at work for other people." Your friend remonstrates. He begs you not to leave him. But you go on. And though at first you seem to have gone away from him, your higher life becomes a revelation to him. Your love is drawing him up. It seems less and less an impossibility that he too should live a noble and unselfish life, and by and by you two are living in a higher fellowship in the higher land. What is it that has happened? You went to prepare a place for him, and then you came again and received him unto yourself.

Ah! there is really no friendship worthy of the sacred name where each of the two friends is not thus always making ready places for the other in higher and higher mansions of the Father's house, where each is not always opening to the other some higher life. Do not dare to think that friendship is a mere pleasant amusement. Do not dare to take out of it the moral responsibility that makes its depth and sacredness.

Two merchants are partners in a selfish business. No thought of charity finds any entrance into their sordid shop. By and by one of them learns the duty and the joy of helping other people. It seems as if their sympathy was broken when one has this new taste, this new desire. But if the other be worthy of the partnership, the time comes when he wins it too, and the broken sympathy is reunited on a higher plane. Two boys are boon companions in each other's frolics. By and by one of them is touched with the desire of learning. But if his comrade is worthy of him, he, too, after a while is brought up by his friend's fellowship into the realm that he has entered. Husband and wife live together in perfect domestic sympathy. Not a thought of either that the other does not share. But when one of them enters into Christ and knows His peace and joy, it seems as if for the first time they had separated. But the soul that has found the Saviour comes back with its love, and tells the story of the Saviour it has found, and, Andrew-like, brings the other soul to the Christ in whose love it has found a place. Everywhere this ministry of life to life is finding its illustrations.

And now this is the way in which Jesus had been treating those disciples of His for the three years in which He had been with them. The purpose of His mission had demanded that He should first of all take those twelve men and introduce them into higher thoughts, new ways of living, new standards, new ideas which they had never known before. How could He do that? Several ways were open. He might read them long lessons, give them abstract teaching. He might put on His power, and, awing them with His miracles, make them obey Him as he pointed them to a new life. To one who reads the Gospels truly, it becomes evident, I think, that He deliberately chose another way, a way that involved His own personality and made all His disciples' progress consist in following Him. First He knit His life in with theirs. The cords were twisted together as they sat and as they walked together, as He shared their board and bed. He made them know that He was what they were, and they what He was. He did this devotedly, laboriously; and then when they were feeling this completely, some day He suddenly took a step across some border which they had thought impassable —He stood clothed in light in some new land which they had counted inaccessible. He did some act, He manifested some quality, to which they never had aspired, He put himself close to God; and then when they stood amazed and seemed to themselves to have lost Him He came back to them by His love without coming out of the new goodness which He had entered, and He said, "No, I am this new thing not for myself but for you. By all the oneness between us, you can be this as well as I, you can be holy as I am holy. Now by my holiness, come in. Be holy because I am holy. I have proved it possi-

N

ble for such as you and I am. I have prepared a place for you. Now I am come again to receive you unto myself."

It was no accidental habit. It was a deliberate specific culture. It will be well worth while to linger and point out two or three instances of its application. They are the old stories which we have known from childhood. Jesus was going up to Jerusalem, and He had to pass through Samaria. The Samaritans would not receive Him, because he was a Jew and going to the sacred city of the Jews. His disciples instantly were full of Jewish indignation. "A miracle, a miracle," they cried, "to destroy those enemies of the Lord!" "Wilt thou that we command fire to come down from heaven to consume them as Elijah did?" They looked round for Jesus to keep company with them in their rage. But where was He? Afar off, walking in the cool, serene heaven of Pity and Toleration. "Ye know not what manner of spirit ye are of," He said. "The Son of man is not come to destroy men's lives, but to save them." He had eluded them. He had gone where they could not follow Him. They seemed to have lost Him. But still His love was around them, and by and by He came to them and received them unto Himself; took them up into the tolerance where He Himself had entered. And the time came when Peter and John were laying hands on these Samaritans, welcoming them into the Christian churches. Or again, two disciples came to Jesus and said, "There is to be a kingdom here upon the earth, here in Judea. Let us sit, we pray thee, as thy Viziers, one on thy right hand, the other on thy left." It was all of the earth, earthy. They wanted to hear of the cabinet of the new kingdom. But where was Jesus ? " It shall be given to those for whom it is prepared of my Father which is in heaven." He was far away from earth. It was all heavenly, all spiritual to Him. They did not understand Him. They had lost Him. But He came back for them and took them up into His own spiritual conceptions, for the time came when a new ambition had swallowed up the old in John, and he was writing in his Epistle, " We know that when He shall appear we shall be like Him, for we shall see Him as He is." Or take one more. Jesus lived very near to His mother. They must have understood each other deeply. But one day He outwent her. He entered into a new consecration to His Father which she had not imagined. Her touching words we can hear still when she seemed to have lost Him. "Son, why hast thou dealt thus with us ? " But she had not lost Him. As she " kept all these things and pondered them in her heart," she saw that for her, too, there was a mansion of self-consecration in that Father's house where her Son had entered. And when His consecration at last completed itself at the cross, she was with Him there in a compliance as deep as her suffering.

This is Christ's way. Wherever he would have His disciples go, He goes first Himself, and through the door which He has opened He draws them by His love. That is the whole philosophy of Christian culture. And that is the meaning of the Incarnation. God entered into human life ; made Himself one with it as He only could have done with a nature that was originally one with His own. He became man as He could not have become brute or stone. Then in that human nature He outwent humanity. He opened yet unopened gates of human possibility. He showed what man might be, how great, how god-like! And by the love and oneness He has always been claiming man for the greatness whose possibility He showed. As we think of the Incarnation deeply, these three stages come in one thought. First, the God in Christ seems very near to us as we think of His love. Then He seems very far above us as we think of His holiness, and then again He seems to bring us very near to Himself as we feel His power. He is one with us. He goes beyond us, and He comes again and receives us unto Himself.

Thus we trace Christ's treatment of those first disciples. And what then? Here we live at this late day. Is any such method at work, any such culture possible now? My dear friend, one thing is certainly true about Christ. That all that He has ever been He must forever be. All that He was to those first disciples, He must be ready to be to any one, even the least of His disciples always. His power is nothing at any one point if it is not powerful at all points ; nothing, if not eternal. How is it possible, then, that Christ should do for you and me what He did for Peter and John, and Matthew and Nathanael? It is not hard to see, and to many people living just such lives as we live it has become the most real of experiences. Jesus, the Jesus of the Gospels, fastens His life to our life. By His life and death, bearing witness of His love, He twines Himself into our being. To love Him becomes a real thing. He is close by our side. He is right in our lot every + day. Then as we go on living thus with Him some crisis of our life occurs, some need of action. We are put to some test, and as we stand doubting, or as we go and do the act in our low way, Christ, right by our side, does it in His higher way. Not that His hands visibly touch our tools and do the work we have to do. But it becomes evident to us what He would do under our circumstances, what one only thing it would be possible for Him to do as we are situated. It is very different from what we are actually doing. We are truckling to men's opinion, compromising principle, telling a lie. And it is made manifest to us that Jesus in just those same circumstances would defy men's judgments and stand by principle and tell the truth. We are not up to that. We see Him leave us. He outgoes us. But if we really love Him, if our life has grown one with His, He does not leave us really. His going on into principle, honor, truth, and God is a pledge and promise that in those holy homes there is a place for us, too, and soon we are restless unless we follow Him, and the gates of that nobler life which He has opened shine before us, and His love draws us on to be with Him.

Look at the progress of Christendom. Christ first touched the world's heart, fastened Himself into the world's life. He did not begin with a lecture or a lesson. He began by coming Himself to the world; and the world took Him, as it has taken so many of

His choicest treasures, through suffering and death into her life. And then having come to her and fastened His love upon her, He went away from her. He set up impracticable standards. He lived an apparently impossible life. The world was full of war, and He preached peace. The world was full of pride, and He was humble. The world was false, and He by every word and action said, " Be true." The world, looking at Christ, said, " We never can be that," but more and more the world has become that ; Christ first touching it by His love has little by little drawn it on into His character ; and peace, humility, and truth are no longer vague dreams, but recognized ambitions, earnest hopes, here and there real attainments, among men.

And so I ask an earnest Christian how he began to pray, when it first came to seem possible to him that he should forgive his enemy or live in the realized companionship of God? And his answer must be, " Christ, my Lord, having bound my life to His life, went there first and then drew my life after His. I saw Him pray. I heard Him speak forgiveness from the cross. I watched His feet treading close to God, and because I must be where He was, I left the old life and went with Him into the new. My love to Him was first the revealer of the higher possibility, and then the power of entrance into it.

This is what I really understand by being saved by Christ's love. This is what it means, dear friend, when always you are urged to love Christ so that you may be saved. It is not that Christ stands jealously and arbitrarily and will not admit you to His privileges until you have certain feelings about Him. It is that only by loving Him can your life be so bound to His that where He goes you will go with Him, into holiness and peace. Alas! that men are so unambitious. Here is a man who in times of business trouble is distressed and anxious. He cannot help letting his troubles depress him. He is discouraged and disheartened. Is that necessary? Who is the noblest man that ever lived? Jesus Christ, you answer. And do you know what He would be if He were in your place? " Yes," you say; "brave, strong, hopeful, conscious always that there are better things than money — ready to lose the fortune if He could get nearer God, calm and serene and undismayed." Very well, that is what the highest man would do in your place. And why are you not doing it? " Because I am not Christ," you say; " I must not expect of myself what He would do." Ah! that is just your error. That is just where you lose the truth of the Incarnation. Whatever Christ is we can be. Wherever Christ goes we can go. Say that over and over to yourself. Read the assurance of that written on every page of the New Testament. He does go away from you. He leaves you in your lowness and enters into the higher lands of God, but only that He may take your soul afterwards and bring it there to Himself. You are a slave here to the world, to men, to business. Your only freedom is in intercourse with Christ. Bind your soul to His, and it must rise with Him into His liberty. You know that this is true. You know that you could not be such a slave of the world, so beaten by temptation, so trodden down by trouble, if you really loved Christ. In that love there must be freedom and power to go where He is, away from anxiety and sin into peace and holiness.

There is one feature about the truth which I have tried to preach to you this morning which is very beautiful. The truth is that every Christian enters into every higher spiritual condition not absolutely and by himself, but through Christ. But one consequence of that will be that every higher spiritual state will shine to the Christian soul that lives there, not merely with its own lustre, but with the personal dearness of the Christ through whom the soul has gained its entrance. Just as a delightful study, into which some dear friend first initiated you, has always over and above its own delightfulness a beauty that comes from your love to him; so the soul that Jesus has made holy lives always in the beauty of holiness, made more exquisite and dear by the loveliness of Christ. Of every earthly grace as well as of the heavenly glory it is true that " the Lamb is the light thereof." Every new attainment which the Christian makes is but an entrance into another mansion which his Saviour has made ready for him. He grows brave; but Christ was brave before him. He enters into self-sacrifice; but Christ leads him with His cross. He finds the home of his soul at last in perfect communion with God; but the Godhood is familiar and doubly dear to him because of the Christhood through which he enters it. All virtue, all holiness and truth throughout the universe loses the chill of abstractness and glows with the warmth of personal love.

This brings us around to say a few last words upon the first application of these words of Jesus to which I just alluded at the beginning of the sermon. He was just leaving this world for the other when He spoke them first. When Christ has led His disciple on and on from stage to stage of spiritual growth, at last He opens the door and gives him entrance into heaven. Remember always, what I have tried to insist upon this morning, that that new change is of the same sort as the others that have gone before it. Whatever other joy and Glory may be waiting for us in heaven, the Glory and the joy which will be most to us, and which we ought most of all to anticipate, is that there there will be new regions of spiritual life thrown open, new and deeper experiences of the soul made possible, deeper knowledge of God, deeper knowledge of ourselves, deeper delight in purity.

If that is really what we are looking forward to in heaven, then it is easy to realize that the same Christ who has been our leader in each spiritual advance which we have ever made here, will be the leader who will bring us there. Oh, the next life seems all so vague to us! We reach out after it. We believe in it, but how hard it is for us to take hold of it! How can we? Only by living here with Him who is to bring us there. Only by growing so familiar with Christ that when He outruns us and enters in behind the veil, when the strings of His influence outgo our mortal state and run into the darkness, we may still feel the tug upon them from beyond the darkness and know the reality of heaven because our Christ is there. By constant living with the Eternal, so only can you realize Eternity.

To one who believes that Christ, having led him on through this life, will lead him at last by the same culture to the other world, the supreme expectation of that other world is that there he will see Christ. It ceases to be dreadful and far off. When he sees his friend die, when he gives his little child to death, there is nothing cold or lonely or forlorn about it. He knows the Christ to whom they go; when he thinks of his own death, it is only of the opening of another door behind which the Hand, whose pressure he knows well already, shall clasp his hand a little more closely to lead him on into a little richer light and happiness. It is the same Christ who has been making a place in us for the Kingdom of Heaven who will at last make a place in the Kingdom of Heaven for us.

To welcome all His leadings now so cordially that we shall know our Leader when He opens the last great door; to be always following Him so obediently that we shall have faith to follow Him even when He leads us into the river and into darkness, — this, and only this, is readiness for death. May God grant it to us all!

XI.

PEACE IN BELIEVING.

"Now the God of hope fill you with all Joy and Peace in Believing, that ye may abound in Hope through the Power of the Holy Ghost."— ROMANS xv. 13.

ALTHOUGH I wish to speak this morning of only one phrase occurring in this verse, I quote the whole verse, because it will be good for us if we can catch its spirit and feel the enthusiasm that pervades it. See how the most glowing words are crowded into it: "The God of Hope," "Joy," "Peace," "Believing," then "Hope," again, and "Power," and "the Holy Ghost." Any short verse with words like these in it must have vitality and vigor. Out of the centre of it let us take one expression. St. Paul asks for these Roman Christians that they may be filled with "Peace in Believing." To see just what he is asking for them, what "Peace" is, and what "Believing' is, and how Peace everywhere comes by Believing, this will be our subject. We feel at once, I think, that we are dealing with large words, with words which have something of the manifoldness of life, and which like life it is hard to reduce to a clear definition. Take this word "Peace." We all have our ideas about it. To all of us it represents something very attractive and complete. But I suppose that to all men Peace means something different according to their different characters. And the main difference must be in the positiveness or negativeness with which it presents itself to them. To the sluggish man, peace must mean mere repose, the cessation of work. To the active man peace must mean merely the power and chance of work free from interference. "Leave me at Peace," says the lazy man, and as he says it he drops the tools which the world has thrust into his hands and lies down to go to sleep. "Leave me at Peace," says the busy man, and turns to his tools and his task, with the thought of how much he can do when he and his task are left to one another. The men of negatives and the men of positives are everywhere, — the men who describe things by what they are not, and the men who describe things by what they are. It seems to be one of the fundamental divisions of human character. And there is hardly any idea in relation to which this difference comes out more clearly than in relation to this idea of Peace. But evidently the positive man's notion of it must be the truest and highest. Peace must be in its essence something real in a man's life, and the exemptions and negations that it brings must be its incidents. And when we look carefully for a definition that shall be positive and that shall include the highest idea of peace, must it not be this? Peace is the entire harmony between the nature of anything and its circumstances. That is what every healthy aspiration after peace is really seeking for. Whether it be high in its sphere or low, whether it be the star moving calmly in its orbit, or the seed silently wedding itself to the rich ground in which it is buried, or whether it be the laborer at his plough or the statesman in the capitol, wherever there is a nature in harmony with its surroundings, so that they call out all its best activities and at the same time it is able to answer all their demands, there is Peace. All the disturbances of peace come from the breaking of this harmony. Sometimes on one side, and sometimes on the other. Sometimes the nature has powers and capacities for which the surroundings offer no employment. Sometimes the surroundings teem with demands for which the nature has no powers. In either case you have unrest and discontent. But when the two correspond, then everything moves smoothly. There is abundant motion. There is no sleep. But motion without fatigue, or waste, or need of refreshment or repair, that is the finished idea of Peace. We talk about the "Peace of God." Is not this really the conception which, carried to its highest, reaches that sublime idea? "My father worketh hitherto and I work," said Jesus. It is no Oriental apathy. The Christian thought of God is full of interest, zeal, emotion, action, only it is always perfectly balanced with its surroundings, since its surroundings are the utterance and creation of itself. God and the universe in their unbroken harmony. The universe never asking anything of God which God cannot do. God having no power or affection which the universe cannot utter. That is the Perfect Peace. To match that consummate Peace in our lower little sphere, to be to our world as God is to His, to work as perpetually and yet as calmly and so effectively as He works; that is the real thing that we pray for when we ask for one another the Peace of God.

With this idea of what Peace really is, we can see where the failures come in of the attempts at peace which men are always making. The secret of Peace is in perfectly harmonious relations between a nature and its surroundings. The loss of Peace, then, will come either in the abandonment or in the distortion of these relations. Wherever any being withdraws itself, and does not have anything to do with those objects and tasks to which it naturally belongs, it loses its true peace. Wherever it remains among them and deals with them, but uses them wrongly, it too has no peace. It will be clearer if we take an instance. Here is your nature, and here is its environment, its surrounding, which is the society in which you live. The result of your living with that society ought to be one large, quiet, healthy, active, restful condition which could be rightly named by the great name " Peace." You ought to help that society, to make it purer, wiser, happier; and you ought to feel it continually helping you, making you happier, wiser, purer. You lose all the richness of such a life in either of two ways. You may refuse to have anything to do with the society you live in, make yourself a recluse, or you may enter into false relationship with it, be arrogant, and overbearing, and selfish, and try to compel it to minister to your pride and luxury, or be servile and obsequious, and let it domineer over your conscience and self-respect. In either case, you are not at peace with it, and you live a peaceless life. A disused relation, or a misused relation, is fatal to the comfortable and healthy action of a life. It is as if you had to travel around the world or through a long stretch of woods with one companion. To ignore him, and act as if he were not walking by your side, or to quarrel with him, or to impose on him, or let him impose himself on you, either of these destroys the pleasure and profit of your journey. Only in mutual helpfulness and respect can you find peace. And what is true of going through the woods with a friend, is true also of going through the world with your wealth, with your conscience, with nature, with duty, with pleasure, and with the constant presence of God.

Let us count this, then, our definition of Peace. It is harmonious relation with our surroundings, and evidently, then, Peace will become a deeper and deeper word, a deeper and deeper thing to men as they become aware more and more of what their surroundings are, as they open their eyes to more and more intimate and sacred things with which they have to do. And so the opposite of Peace, namely, disquiet, unrest, will also become more and more real to a man as he comes to the knowledge of his circumstances, of the beings and powers which surround his life with which he ought to be in harmony, but which he is either ignoring altogether, or to which he is relating himself wrongly. Let us see a little what the deepening degrees of such disquiet in a man's life are. And, first, most patent of all, so that we often get no farther in our use of the word "Peace" than its application to that relationship, there is the position in which a man stands to the world about him and to his fellow-men. There is one, and only one, conception of the world in which a man necessarily assumes a right attitude and relationship to his fellow-men. It is that conception which thinks of the whole world as God's Family. The instant that that idea is presented and comprehended, peace looms up in the distance as a possibility. Just as fast and just as far as that idea is realized in a man's own life, he comes to be at peace — a high, pure, intelligent peace — with his fellow-men; not the peace of compromise nor of armed defiance, but the peace of clearly understood relationships and mutual love and mutual help. For just see how the lack of peace shows itself in you as it concerns your fellow-men. I take you for the average man, neither worse nor better. If you are like most men, what is your relation at this moment to other mortals? Well, there are probably a few, some three or four — perhaps, if you are usually offensive or unfortunate, a dozen — men with whom you have quarrels, you do not speak to them, and speech is the primary pledge of common human brotherhood. It may be you are all ready to do them an injury if the chance offers, or, if it is not as bad as that, you never count them in the number of those to whom you can do any good; and, if we think of it, it is a dreadful thing that almost all of us should have some such little fragment, reprobate from any grace of ours, cut out of the great bulk of the human race. And then, besides these men with whom you quarrel, there is the vast multitude to whom you are entirely indifferent, with whom you think that you have no concern whatever. And next to them, another company whom you are always trying to outstrip and get the better of, people whom you count your inferiors, on whom you impose your will, whom you domineer over if you can. And next to those, another company to whom you truckle, whose authority and domination you accept, before whom you are servile. And then, besides these, smaller groups towards whom you hold still other unworthy relations. There are children whom you treat as toys. There are good men whom you dread as bores. There are false men whom you admire as heroes. Now, sum all these up, and then remember that Peace consists in just and harmonious relations to our surroundings, and then ask yourself whether you are, in any true, high sense, at peace with your fellow-men. You see that it is not by any means the mere amount of declared war. Out of policy, or out of good-nature, you may have kept clear of that entirely. But it is the false adjustments, it is the untrue relationship, in which you stand to them that make the absence of peace between your life and theirs.

And all that I have said about our relations to other men might be said in a true sense of our relation to all the external world — to nature, to the physical forces, to the social laws, to everything not ourselves on which our lives act, and which acts on them.

But the next step takes us to ourselves. It is only the most superficial people that recognize merely their relations of peace or discord with the external world, and never ask whether they are at peace with themselves. To be at peace with a man's own self! We use the phrase; we think we understand it. There are certain comfortable and satisfied conditions in which we think we have attained the thing. But we do not really understand it till we have got this fundamental idea of what peace is, the harmony of a being with its surroundings. Now, every man has these two parts in him: a will encircled by its cabinet or council of affections, and a system of powers which that will governs. The true relation between the will and the powers constitutes the true peace of the life. Will using powers to their best capacity. Powers supplying will with all the instruments it needs. Now turn again, and look at your own life. Are you at peace with yourself? If your will is taking your powers, which were made to do noble and gentle and generous things, and forcing them to do sordid and brutal and mean things; if you are living a life of miserable drudgery, treating yourself like a machine; or if you are living a life of dissipation, treating yourself like a brute, then you are not at peace with yourself surely. Yourself is misusing, is abusing yourself. There is war between your will and your powers, as there is war between the harp and the hand that smites discord from its tortured strings. A man is both harp and harper. The harp may not complain, but all the time the music it was meant to make sleeps in its strings, and it cannot be at peace with the cruel fingers that make it unmusical. And in your powers sleeps the nobleness that they were made to do, in everlasting protest against the wickedness to which you compel them. O my dear friends, to be at peace with ourselves is not to loosely approve ourselves in what we are. It is to work with ourselves, that we may be all that God made us for.

Evidently it is a great deal deeper discord when a man is not at peace with himself than when he is not at peace with his brethren. But there is something deeper, something nearer to us even than our brethren or ourselves. And that is God. The will of God, which is the law of holiness, is the deepest and inmost thing of all this world. And the ultimate question of every human life is, whether he is at Peace with God. Once more remember what Peace is. It is the being rightly and harmoniously related with that with which we have to do. Now, the only right relation of man to the will of God is loving obedience, affectionate and happy loyalty. What then? If you are simply ignoring God altogether, living as if there were no God, you are not at peace with Him. Or if you are absolutely defying Him, doing what you know is wrong, what you know He hates, then certainly you are not at peace with Him. Or yet again, remember this, if you are serving Him in mere slavery, doing His will simply because you must, disliking it, disliking Him all the time you do it — in either case you are not at peace with God. Here we have reached the bottom of Peacelessness. Indeed, this discord must include all others. For this discord, in one word, is sin, and I think we can see at once how inclusive it makes sin. It compels it at once to be large enough to embrace the neglect of God ; not simply the violation of His commandments by positive disobedience, but the absence of any thought about Him, the absolutely worldly life which tries to satisfy itself without Him ; all this evidently is a discord which makes sin, if peace be really the completeness of harmonious relations. Are you at peace with God? The question comes to some man living his ordinary worldly life, and he looks up and answers, " Yes ; I pay Him reverence ; I never blaspheme His name ; sometimes I try to pray to Him a little, and I hope that He will take care of me when I die. Surely I am at peace with Him." But are you really, if peace means nothing less than the existence between your life and His of all the relations and affections which ought to be between the infinite Father and His child? Are you really at peace with Him, if peace means loving loyalty?

And then, add one thought more. Remember how no sin belongs entirely to the moment that commits it ; remember, what you will only need to look into your own history to know is true, how sin clings to the nature that has done it, and lays itself like a shadow between the soul that sinned and the God against whom the sin was done. Remember this, and then not only the sin which you are doing now measures the discord between your soul and God — all that you have ever done, all your past comes in. By all that you are shut out from peace with Him. Your relations to His life to-day are broken and distracted because of all that you have done, of neglect or disobedience, in all these accumulated years.

And now look over this account. Is there not something very terrible in seeing where we stand? A man, a soul, a will set here in the midst of forces which are touching it on every side, with all of which it might relate itself nobly and to beautiful results! And see what is the case! Out of our neighbors we are getting never the best, — often the very worst; ourselves we are dishonoring, misusing; the Will of God we are neglecting or disobeying. There, in those deep disturbances, lie the real discords, the real tragedies of life. Not in the mere discontent and chaffing, not in the querulousness and restlessness, the envying, the perpetual wish to be away from where we are, to be somewhere, something else. Not in these is the deepest, saddest essence of our lack of Peace. These are only the symptoms. The real wretchedness is in the essential wrong relations in which we have set ourselves to fellow-man and ourselves and God. The true picture of Peace is simply the restoral of true relations, so that each soul of us should give its full due to, and so get its full due from, the souls around it, and its own self, and the soul of God, its Father.

And now, with this conception of Peace clearly before us, let us go on to what is always the next question. How can this condition, so precious in itself, be won? How can all things be brought to such a state that they shall do their best and most harmonious work in the fulfilment of their truest relations to themselves and to each other? And one answer immediately suggests itself, which I think we shall find to fall in with St. Paul's verse which is our

text. As soon as we come to any thoughtful examination of the world we find that everything is finite
and limited, and lives at its best only in relation to
other things. Everything is a part, nothing is complete and absolutely a whole. And it is only in recognition of this fact, only in counting itself a part,
only by living along with the other parts, within the
embrace and envelopment of the whole, that everything does its best work and so attains its best peace.
This is a universal principle. Everything falls into
disorder, runs wild, loses its symmetry and its effectiveness, unless it feels around it, as it lives and
works, the embrace and restraint and protection of
the controlling whole of which it is a portion. And
peace for finite creatures only comes by such envelopment. The illustrations of this are numberless.
The peace of the family consists in the envelopment
of the household by the father's life. Each child's
life finds its place and plays its part within the girdle
of that authority and love. The father, in the old
Saxon phrase, is the " husband," the " houseband,"
that holds the parts in their places, and makes each
keep its true relation to itself and to the rest. And
so the work of all goes on, and Peace is within the
happy walls. And so a man's life grows peaceful
and effective when it has some great controlling idea
which is bound about it, as it were, to keep each action and thought in its place, in true subjection and
relation to other thoughts and actions. Within such
an enveloping idea no upstart action or thought
makes confusion by trying to lord it over the rest ;
each tries only to help fulfil that which is the great

purpose of the living, and so the Peace of the natural world is preserved by the harmonious working of all its laws within that one great mysterious enveloping whole which is so real to us that we give it a name and call it nature. All our science, finding unity and simplicity of force everywhere, is making that existence, that being nature, more and more real, continually. So everywhere. A picture has peace when all its details are harmonized and held within some dominant idea. A story has its prevalent purpose; a piece of music its controlling theme; a government its policy. Everything, in so far as it is a part, is held in safety and given the chance to do its best work only as it is included within some greater whole. That whole in its time becomes a part in some whole that is larger still; and so out to the infinite, which nothing can limit or contain, this system of envelopment goes on. I want to state it just as generally as I can, because I want to show that St. Paul's special statement of a special Christian truth is part of a universal law which runs everywhere. All Christian truth is in harmony with, is but one utterance, is the highest and fullest announcement of, the universal truth, the truth of the universe. And so the broadest statement of St. Paul's utterance here is this: that everything lives its full life and does its full work, or, in other words, completes that condition of absolutely perfect relationships which we saw was what Peace meant, only as it lives and works within the compass of something greater than itself, which holds each part into its place, and to which each part must be loyal, obedient, and true.

Just for one moment pause and think of that great idea of Peace by Envelopment. It has no end or limit until we come to God. The prerogative, the distinction of the divine life is this, that it, and it alone, is self-enveloping. There is nothing beyond it. It is held within nothing. It holds all things within itself. There is nothing to which God is bound to be true but God. " Because He could swear by no greater," the epistle says, " He sware by His own self." Included within His life there lie first the great primary ideas which are forever true in Him. Within these ideas, loyal to them, only powerful as they embody and enforce them, lie the laws which all men own. Within these laws, held into peace and power by obedience to them, are all the positive institutions of mankind, the family, the state, the church. Within these institutions live the lives of men, harmonious and effective just in proportion as they perceive and cordially acknowledge their envelopment. And then, these lives again envelop one another. Countless systems are formed and live within this great system. The larger the envelopment that each life is aware of, the more effectively it works. The greater its loyalty and trust, the more true it is to itself and to all the sharers of the same envelopment. Every harmonious and effective working, though it may be aware only of the envelopment that touches it most immediately, is really held within the great all-embracing envelopment of God. Every action is exalted to its highest self-consciousness when it feels, through all the intermediate envelopments, that outermost envelopment of all, the holding of God, and answers back to it, sending through all inferior loyalties a last consummate loyalty to Him. "In Him we live and move and have our being."

And now, what shall we call this law, — the law that every power comes to its best and most harmonious action only within a larger envelopment to which it trusts itself and to which it is loyal? This faithfulness to an enveloping principle and power — what is it really but belief? The child believes in its father. The life believes in its idea. The law believes in its principle. Everything lives and works by believing in something larger than itself, until you come to God. God believes in Himself. With Him alone, in all the universe, is self-belief, the condition of the highest life. And so the truth which I have been trying to state, a truth which in some form or other breaks out everywhere through all the world, is really, as you see, the truth which is wrapt up in St. Paul's phrase, — "Peace in Believing." And if the truth which I have tried to state is true, there is no peace anywhere in all the world save in believing. No high complete activity of anything, no fulfilment by anything of all its natural capacity, unless it is held in the hand of something greater than itself. Oh, the disjointed, distorted little bits of life that such a truth explains! All the world, all the society we study, is full of little fragments of activity, little restless bits of movement which vex us with their ceaseless action of brain and hand and heart which comes to nothing. Society and the world often come to seem to us, I think, like a watchmaker's shop where there are small pieces of unattached clock-work lying scattered about, each running by itself, accomplishing nothing because each is fastened to no weight, which it has to move, no purpose which it is trying to fulfil. Clicking and clattering, they keep the shop in a perpetual confusion. There is no peace. Mere motion with no work. Mere action with no unity. Each separated bit of machinery has no envelopment, belongs to nothing, believes in nothing. So is it with a multitude of lives among us. Active from mere irrepressible impulse, their action is all restlessness. They belong to nothing. They believe in nothing. No loyalty to principle or fellow-man or God envelops them. Their lives inspire us with continual dissatisfaction, and they are not satisfied with themselves. There is no better thing to see than that which comes when one of these bits of machinery is taken up and set into its true envelopment. When a man's activity is rescued from aimlessness by learning some devotion, and the man, beginning to believe in something, gains peace in believing.

This, then, is the general statement of our truth. And now turn and see what is St. Paul's peculiar Christian statement of it. His Peace in Believing is to be distinctly a Peace by Gospel Faith, by faith in the Incarnation and Atonement of Jesus Christ. Is this, then, something different entirely from what we have been speaking of? Surely not. It is simply the completion and consummation of them all. Around a man's life fold its various envelopments. The man's peace depends upon whether he is in

living and true relations to all of them. Now, the
Gospel of Christ is simply the perfect presentation
of all these envelopments to the soul of man ; and he
who is in the power of the Gospel, he who approaches
everything with which he has to do in Christ, finds
his true relation to everything. Shall we trace this
out? Shall we look one moment in this new light
at the different departments in which we saw that
the peace or the peacelessness of human lives resided?
Peace with our fellow-men. How will that come
about by faith in Jesus Christ? If Jesus Christ is
the perfect humanity, the consummation of all human
hopes and desires, the visible achievement of that
perfection to which all our brethren's lives are struggling, then must not he who sees his brethren not in
themselves, not as if this which they are now were
the end and crown of all that they could be, but in
Him, in Christ, reading their possibility in His complete attainment — must not such a man be filled
with Pity and with Hope and with Respect for the
greatest and for the most insignificant of men? And
these three are the elements of peace. Let me be a
thorough believer in Jesus Christ, let me, that is,
have taken Him with all the revelation of humanity
that there is in Him, and where is the fellow-man
with whom I shall not be at peace? Is it the man
who domineers over me and bullies me? The
supreme mastery of my Lord adjusts these lower
masteries and compels them to keep their proper
places. When I have learned really to "fear Him
who can cast both soul and body into hell," I am
able indeed not to "fear them that can kill the

body." The martyr seeing Christ standing at the right hand of God is at full peace with his murderers. Is it the man who vexes me with his stupidity, whose awkwardness and spiritual sloth seem even to be hindering the salvation of the world? If I believe in Christ, the possibility of that man opens before me. He is a child of God. Pity, enthusiastic desire to waken him and call him to the knowledge and use of his sonship. These may fill me, but I can have none of that petty personal irritation which is the destruction of peace. No; there is no one to whom a true faith in the divine humanity of the Redeemer does not adjust my life, calling out my best power of appreciation, and my best power of help, bringing me Peace.

And then, my discord with myself. It is as old as that wonderful story in the seventh chapter of the Epistle to the Romans. The way in which a Belief in Christ harmonizes that struggle of the two wills which makes our inner peacelessness. Deeper than every revelation that Christ gives me about these, my brother men being God's children, is His revelation to me that I am the Child of God. When He has shown me that, then I know which of these two wills in me is master. The other will is not killed out. It lives, but it is conquered. And just as there was peace in the land as soon as the Rebellion was crushed and the power of the rightful government everywhere established, even though still rebellious outbreaks here and there showed that the old fire was not totally extinguished, so there is peace in me when the divine Christ has become my master and is strengthening my love of right every day with His imparted righteousness; even though still the evil wishes haunt the dark places and break out from the outward thickets of my soul. The peace of a man with his own self when his sonship to God is perfectly established as the fact, and his return to his Father is perfectly established as the law of his life by faith in Christ the Son of God! Why, here in our country there has been a poor, unhappy father whose child was stolen from him years ago, as all the land has heard with a heart full of sympathy. Think of that child wherever he may be, if he is still alive to-day! Think of the restlessness in his young heart! Think of the dim and dying memories in conflict with the things that are around him day by day! Think how, while others can find perfect satisfaction in the life he leads, because they never have known any other, down at the bottom of his heart there is perpetual unrest! And now suppose the father finds his child. The house is open — the home-life folds itself around him. Where is the unrest then? Still this strange exile haunts him with its memories and its power. But the dominion of the life is fixed again where it belongs, and held in the hand of that dominion, the jarred and disordered activities of heart and mind and outward habit begin to beat again truly, and once more there is Peace.

I need not stop, as certainly I must not stop, to tell how the third element of perfect peace, peace with the law of God, comes by the faith in Jesus Christ. One of the words which we make far too little is that great word "forgiveness." It means more than the mere taking off of penalties. It means the putting of the soul where penalty cannot find it any longer, in the restored fatherhood of God. To the soul so brought back what is the relation between it and the law of that fatherhood, the law of the household of God which is to be his home henceforth? Hear David cry, " Oh, how I love thy law!" and as to the restored child the house is always tenfold dear because of the exile in which he used to live, so to the forgiven soul the law which he obeys is always more precious, and the joy of obeying it more deep, because of the exile of disobedience in which he lived, and from which he has been brought back by grace. " Oh, how I love thy law!" for to the soul which knows God in Christ the law of God is the utterance of God, is God, and obedience is not only duty — it is love.

I must not dwell on all this any longer. Let the great truth be clear to us to-day. Peace comes by belief; not by ourselves or our own strength, but by being held in the hand of Him who saved us, do these disturbed natures of ours come to their true selves and work harmoniously and to their best results. Doubt finds its only rest in personal confidence. Self-conceit, which is the most peace-destroying thing in all the world, is overwhelmed in consecration to the Master, and contrition starts from the dust, and turns into the very angel of hope and growth when once a soul believes in Jesus Christ.

Oh, then, that over us, perplexed and troubled and afraid, as over the disciples in the chamber long ago, the hand of Jesus might be stretched, and we, to-day, might hear Him saying, " Peace I leave with you ; My Peace I give unto you. Believe in Me." Oh that our souls may say, " Dear Lord, we do believe in Thee, and so we claim Thy Peace."

XII.

WHOLE VIEWS OF LIFE.

" And Balak said unto him, Come, I pray thee, with me unto another place, from whence thou mayest see them. Thou shalt see but the utmost part of them, and shalt not see them all : and curse me them from thence." — NUMBERS xxiii : 13.

MANY of you will recall the story from which these words are taken, and the striking picture which it draws. The Israelites are travelling through the desert. They are approaching the domain of Balak, King of Moab. Balak is frightened, and sends for the Mesopotamian wizard, Balaam, and bids him curse the dangerous intruders. But Balaam, filled with a higher spirit than he understands, blesses instead of cursing. Again the effort is made and the disappointment follows in another place. And then it is that there occurs to the monarch the idea which is recorded in the text. Perhaps if the prophet did not see the whole host in its multitude the curse would come more readily. " Let us stand where we can only see a part of them," he says. " Peradventure thou canst curse me them from thence."

It was a vain expedient. The blessing came still pouring forth more richly than before. Why should it not? It was not the quantity but the quality of Israel which drew the blessing. It was not because there were so many of them, but because they were set on lofty purposes and carried in their bosom mighty spiritual issues, that God took care of them and made them strong. It was a hopeless hope of Balak. And it was like a child. It was the transparent self-cheat of infancy. So children play with themselves and one another, saying, " Let us see only a part and make believe that that is all."

It is this childlikeness, this primitive simplicity about the incident, which makes it capable of being expanded and of applying to all life. The wisdoms and policies of childhood find their illustrations everywhere. They are so simple that they fit on every life. A child says a wise word, and the sage catches surprised sight in it of complications in his life of which the little head has never dreamed. A child does some act of transparent folly, and by it you easily understand the elaborate superstition or the intricate villany of the full-grown conspirator or bigot. The children go about with the keys of our conditions in their hands. They hold them up before us, and we take them and unlock our problems and give them back again, and the children know nothing of what they have done.

So is it with this childish act of the barbarian Balak — so fresh and simple is it that I feel sure I shall not fail to find the repetitions of it everywhere. And I do! It is about its repetitions that I want to talk this morning. I would speak about the modern Balaks, who think they can indulge their passions and scatter their curses as they please, by shutting their eyes to all but some small portion of that with which

they have to deal. They are the men who wilfully
take partial views, who will see nothing which will
interfere with that which they have already made up
their minds to think or do — especially the men who
have made up their minds to curse, and who refuse to
look at that part of a subject or a life which will
make cursing impossible, and compel a blessing upon
that which they choose to hate.

Of such a disposition — and I am sure that you recognize the disposition which I mean — the first thing
that impresses one is its lack of absoluteness. There
is an absolute truth about everything, something
which is certainly the fact about that thing, entirely
independent of what you or I or any man may think
about it. No man on earth may know that fact
correctly — but the fact exists. It lies behind all
blunders and all partial knowledges, a calm, sure, unfound certainty, like the great sea beneath its waves,
like the great sky behind its clouds. God knows it.
It and the possession of it makes the eternal difference between God's knowledge and man's.

It is a beautiful and noble faith when a man thus
believes in the absolute truth, unfound, unfindable
perhaps by man, and yet surely existent behind and
at the heart of everything. It is a terrible thing
when a man ceases to believe in it, and ceases to seek
for it. He sinks out of the highest delight and purity. For him the great glory of life is gone. Petty
and selfish economies sweep in and overwhelm him.
Not what is true, but what will tell for the advantage
of something which he thinks valuable, becomes the
object of his search. He questions everything, as

the lawyer questions a witness, in the interest of a
cause. Then comes the Balak folly. Then the man
shuts his eyes to everything which will not tell upon
his side. Then he refuses to look upon the whole of
things, and sees only the portion which will minister
to his passion or his spite. Oh, keep your faith in,
your love for, the absolute, my friends! Be sure that
it exists. To find it, to come a little nearer to finding it, — that, and not the gaining of a new argument
or the sustaining of an old prejudice, is what you
must be craving when you seek for truth.

In the loss of this faith lies the secret of all partisanship. The partisan always is a Balak. What is a
partisan? Is he not simply a man who will see only
a part of truth, lest he should be compelled to aban-
don a position which he loves, or to adopt a position
which he chooses to dislike? How many men are
there to-day — Republicans or Democrats or anything
beside — who are genuinely and really as ready to
give its full value to a fact when, if it is true, it tells
upon the other party's side as if it told on theirs?
"Behold," you say, "look at the total case. Take
in the entire situation, and then condemn this party
and its leaders and its policies as all foolish or all
false." Your friend looks, and, Balaam-like, to your
dismay he breaks out into telling of the good which
he sees even in this party you despise. What impulse is more natural than yours to say, "Come
I pray thee, unto another place. Thou shalt not
see them all. Thou shalt see only that which I
choose to let thee see of them, and thou shalt curse me
them from thence." This is not — he would com-

pletely misunderstand what I am saying who thought it was — a mere assertion that there is good and bad in everything, and the preaching of a feeble vacillation that could never come to any decisive action. There is just the difference between partisanship and reasonable choice. The reasonable man who has surveyed the whole condition, by and by strikes his balance and announces his result. He finds that which is genuinely and hopelessly bad, the base, the false, and the impure, and he denounces that unsparingly. Then, among honest and honorable differences, he judges what he thinks comes nearest to the absolute truth, and sustains that with all his strength. But he has no curse for the man upon the other side. He will not impute miserable motives. He is brave as well as bold. He must be just and generous as well as strong. And so the policy which he contends for is in the end not weaker, but stronger, for his breadth of view.

Away with cursing! Away with vehement denunciation which prevents right judgment with the intensity of personal passion and dislike! One man denounces civilization. He sees the wretchedness and misery of which its streets are full. He hears the cry of outraged natures and of ruined souls. He says it is an organized selfishness, and he curses it with all his heart. Another man denounces education. He says it is superficial and misplaced. He says that instead of fitting children, it unfits them, for the work of life. He says it makes cultivated villains and useless burdens on society ; and so he curses education very loudly. Another man denounces society. He tells us how selfish and narrow and corrupting is the intercourse of man with man. He shows us the social world all honeycombed with insincerity. He says, "Is that the way for the children of God to live with one another?" And so he curses society and turns ascetic. Another man curses the scientific spirit. "Behold, how hard it is," he says, "how unbelieving! How arrogant in its self-conceit! How it would reduce life to a desert and the world to a machine! How it despises the spontaneous affections! How it worships its idols!" And his curses fall upon it furious and fast.

Now notice that all these accusations have their truth. Each of these mighty and benignant interests is guilty of the sin with which it is charged. But it is only as one shuts out all except a little portion of it from his view that any man is able to see each of these interests absolutely given up to its sin, so that he can curse it. In each case if a man takes into view the whole of civilization or education or society or science, he sees its graciousness and beauty, and cannot curse, but bless. And so it is with life in general. There are parts of it and aspects of it which, if they were all, would make existence an accursed thing. "Come," says the pessimist, "you shall not see the whole. I will set you where you shall only see a part, and curse me it from thence." There is where pessimism is made. The man who sees the whole of life must be an optimist. I know dark points of view, grim gloomy crags of moral vision, hideous observatories on which if a man stands he can see nothing but the dreadful side of life, its wretchedness, its disappointment, its distress, its reckless, wanton, defiant sin. I can see gathered on those horrible observation points the despisers, the revilers, the cursers of our human life. I know that if I went up there and stood by their side, my tongue would curse like theirs. But there I will not go. If there be any point whence I can see it all, however dimly, through whatever clouds, there I will go. So will I keep my faith that life is good, and work with what strength I can against its evils, knowing that I work in hope.

Upon those dark places of partial vision I know that I should never find the great Seer of human life, who is Christ. Christ saw all life in God. That means that He saw life in its completeness. No being ever saw the evil and misery as He beheld it. He saw sin with all the intensity of holiness. But nobody ever has dared call Jesus Christ a pessimist. He saw the end from the beginning. He saw the depth from the surface. He saw the light from the darkness. He saw the whole from the parts. Therefore He could not despair. There was no curse of life upon His lips. Infinite pity! A pity that has folded itself around the world's torn and bleeding heart like a benediction ever since — but no curse! And who are we, with our little feeble rage and petulance, flinging our testy curses where the Lord's blessing descended like the love of God? Oh, if you ever find yourself cursing life, get your New Testament and read what Jesus said looking down on Jerusalem from the height of the Mount of Olives, looking down on man from the measureless height of the cross!

Do I talk too generally? Let me then illustrate and enforce all this with instances. A man's career— every man's career, we may truly say — is made up of struggles and victories or defeats. More defeats than victories there are in most men's lives, we think. But, however that may be, at least the defeats, the weak and wretched failures, the troublesome, exasperating, disappointing incompetency for the work of life, force themselves most upon the eyes of those who watch their fellow-men. And to a very great many people there is a continual temptation to ignore the fact of struggle and remember only the fact of defeat. It is so satisfactory to take a simple sweeping view about your neighbor's life, to give him one broad judgment that has no qualifications, to trample on him in the gutter and never ask how he got there. Then you can freely curse. Then you cannot merely condemn the deed, but utterly denounce the doer.

But men do struggle, even those who fall at last most utterly. It would seem as if anybody needed only to remember his own history and to study his own consciousness to be assured of that. You think of the days when you have sinned most dreadfully. Are you willing to accept any man's judgment of those days who simply sees the sin. You know, though you dare not tell any one besides, of how you fought with your temptation. You know the nights of darkness and the days of hope. You remember the misery of the last yielding, and you say, " He could not curse me if he knew it all."

This is the meaning of the soul's appeal to God. " Let my judgment come forth from Thy presence,"

David cries. Is it that God does not hate sin as man does? Certainly not that. It is that God knows all. The struggle and the fall and the repentance all make one unit of experience to Him. Therefore He may condemn and He may punish but He cannot curse.

And when we thus look at ourselves and into our own consciousness, must we not look abroad on other men and say, " No prejudice shall force or tempt me to a place where I shall see only the blank fact that this man has sinned? No desire of my own soul to simplify and emphasize his life shall shut out of my sight the wrestling before the fall, the good which pleaded against his resistance, and which, though out-raged and insulted, is in him still, and will not leave him at peace in his wickedness?"

There is indeed the other vice. Sometimes a man insists that you shall stand where you can see nothing except the good in him with whom you are to deal. He insists on having you make such allowance for the temptation that you shall disregard the sin, or having you give such value to the struggle that the defeat shall seem a small affair. That is not what we want. The easy apology or even the profuse admiration which may come down from that point of observation is not the true and serious man's greeting and judg-ment of the life of his brother-man. It is as foolish and false as the curse, however more generous and kindly it may be.

Neither of these is just and true, because neither of them is complete. Both of them are partial. It is a " blessing " that man wants to give to man, and the quality of a true blessing is that it is complete. Whenever man blesses his brother-man, if he is doing the act in all its fulness, it is the completeness of one nature taking in all the completeness of the other. Whatever it is, — the mother giving her blessing to her boy as he goes out from the home-gate into the dangerous world, the friend who finds no words of sympathy for his friend in his great sorrow except "God bless you," the priest consecrating the hero as he rushes to his duty in the field, the king who looks across the millions of his people and pours upon them all the blessing of his kingly heart, the people who set their king or president into his place of burdensome honor with shouts of benediction, the neighbor who greets his neighbor with sacred words which have not lost their meaning, or the children who gather round their father's grave and drop their blessings on his dear memory along with their tears, — wherever there is real blessing there is the sight of the whole nature, there is the comprehension of the total life. Weaknesses are not forgotten. It is the remembrance of their presence which makes the voice tremble as it blesses. Struggle is not ignored. It keeps the blessing hopeful when it is trembling on the margin of despair. The whole pathetic mixture of the human life is gathered up together. Its evil and its good are both in sight. The danger and the possibility, the fear and the hope, the darkness and the light, are blended in one great profound conception of what this wonderful human life is; and when, standing where it is all clear before him, one human being says to another, "I bless you," it is the largest act which man can do to man. Rebuke, and pity, and exhortation, and encouragement, and warning, and exaltation, and prayer —all are in it. It is soul meeting soul in the highest region and with the closest grasp.

Jesus "led His disciples out as far as Bethany, and He lifted up His hands and blessed them." There was no curse on His lips as He left the poor, frightened, wilful, ignorant, and stumbling men. "He lifted up His hands and blessed them." So may the total result of the pressure of our lives upon our brethren's lives be blessing! May we see them so largely that a curse shall be impossible!

I must say a few words upon two other applications of our truth that it is the limited and partial sight of the things which makes the curse.

The first of them refers to the way in which men form their judgments about religion. We listen to the platform orator, we read the novel of the day, and what impresses us is this: the way in which a hundred misconceptions have their origin in the perpetual tendency to see a part and not the whole, and utter vehement and sometimes furious judgments on that which finds its reasonableness and meaning only when it is set into the system of which it rightly makes a portion. Religion is the whole larger life of man, seen in the presence and the light of God. The Christian religion is the life of man, seen in the broad illumination of the supreme and wondrous Christ. In Him it finds its wholeness, and its parts grow into reconciliation and significance.

Take for a single instance what is called the fact of miracle ; not this or that miraculous event, but the whole element of miracle as it appears pervading everywhere and coloring the Christian story. I wish that I could tell in simple words how the whole matter seems to me to stand concerning miracles. "The trouble with miracles is that they don't happen," is the cry. And men look up and say, "Yes, that is true. They do not happen. All moves on unmiraculously. We see no wonders." Is that all? Have those eyes, looking up, beheld the whole of Christianity? Have they seen a Being, strange, unique, unprecedented, moving majestically among men with whom He certainly is one, and yet from whom, both by the words He says about Himself and by the self-witness which His figure bears, is greater than the men He walks among, greater than any man who ever walked upon the earth? Have they seen Him, living His most exceptional and lofty life, and then looked, ready for whatever they might witness, to see whether obedient Nature had no response to make to Him greater and richer than she makes to the long, crowded generations of ordinary human life? If not, is it not right to say that they have shut out a part, and then judged of the part which still was left as if it were the whole?

Here is the true philosophy of miracle. All the history of the earth is full of the record of what Nature has to say to man, of what she does and says in answer to his invitations, to his very presence in her courts. That is her natural history as it relates to man. But what man? Who is he that speaks to her and whom she answers? Is it man in his common capacity and character, the ordinary man, man as he has been for ages? For him miracles do not happen. To him Nature replies in the same old sweet and solemn voices in which for ages she has spoken. But when a new man comes, a new manhood, a divine man, his newness and divinity being attested for us not by his miracles, but by his character, then miracles do happen; nay, more than that, it is altogether probable that miracles must happen, being the natural outflow of his life — being, we almost may say, no miracles for him — being as natural in the world of power where he lives as it is in our world that the echo should fly back from the mountain, or the seed we planted should come piercing through the soil.

You must see Christ and the tomb, both of them, before it can seem possible that Lazarus will rise. Let any one take you where you will see the tomb only and not see Christ, and you will of course reject the thought of resurrection and declare it a superstition or a fraud. You have got the task without the power, the load without the lifting-strength. Power and task make one great whole. They greet and answer to each other. Stand where you see Him, and miracle is not merely explained — it is demanded. He is miraculous, and miracle surrounds Him as the sunshine issues from the sun.

The same is true of many of the questions of religion. Stand where you cannot see man's greatness, and the incarnation seems a wild, inexplicable dream. Stand where no music reaches you from the deep harmonies of man's present spiritual life, and it is out of your power to believe in heaven. Lose sight of sin, and the darker possibilities of eternity are hideous impossibilities. The religious truth which you see by itself, out of its position in the great whole which ought to hold it, fails to bear witness of its truth. Strive then for wholes, and let the parts reveal themselves within them. Strive for God, who is the whole. Not immediately for particular religious doctrines, but for that vast religious and divine conception of existence which shall make special religious doctrines credible. By obedience, by communion, climb to the height where you shall be with God, and then the truths about God shall open their reasonableness, their richness, and their harmony. So, I think, Jesus was religious. So may we be.

I must do little more than allude to the one other application of our truth which is in my mind; but I must not let you go without alluding to it. It is the saddest and most terrible of all. I am thinking of the desperation and bitterness which come with the sight of pain without the sight of the higher consequences and results of pain. It is the old tragedy of the Book of Job, and of the books of thousands of tortured lives. "Curse God and die," seems sometimes to be the only outcome of it all. Perhaps, nay almost certainly, there are some to whom it seems so here this morning. It is the only outcome of it all, if the pain you feel or see is all. But if the whole of a man's life from its beginning to its endless end, from its surface in to its inmost heart, is capable of being taken into account, then that desperate outcome is not the only one. There is a blessing and a thankfulness which may overcome and drown the curse. Suppose that, looking at pain, and with the curse just growing into shape upon your lips, a great hand takes you up and lifts you. And as you rise your vision widens. And slowly education grows into your view, surrounding pain, and drawing out its sense of cruelty, and crowding in upon it its own sense of love and purpose. Then, in the larger vision, must not the curse perish? And if the lips are not strong enough to open into thankfulness, at least the eyes, still full of pity, may wait in peace.

This is the fear we have to-day. The sense of human pain grows stronger all the time. And it sometimes seems as if the sense of purpose and education grew weaker in a multitude of souls. It is the heart of man taken, Balaam-like, to a place whence it can see the part and not the whole ; and who that listens does not hear the muttering of the curse? Where is the help, first for your soul, then for the whole great world? Not in saying that pain is not pain, not in shutting the eyes to the part which is so awfully manifest, but in seeing, in insisting upon seeing, the whole.

> " To feel, although no tongue can prove,
> That every cloud that spreads above,
> And veileth love, itself is love."

That is the only help. He who lets his heart bear witness, he who lets the experience of countless sufferers bear witness, he who lets Christ bear witness, that no suffering ever yet came to any human creature by which it was not possible that that human creature should be made better and purer and greater, — he has caught sight of the whole; and though he walks in silence and perplexity and suspense, he does not curse.

And so we come to this, — the sacredness and graciousness of the whole. He who sees the part, grows bitter. He who sees the whole, is full of hope. We curse the part, but not the whole. The reason must be that he who grasps the whole, touches God, and the human soul cannot really curse Him. The whole is sacred. It is more than the sum of its parts. It has its own quality and character. It is great and mysterious. In it is peace. He who sees it all finds rest unto his soul. He who catches glimpses of how he shall see it all some day has something of the power of that rest already.

Remember I have not preached to you blind satisfaction and complacency. I have tried to press on you the old noble and ennobling exhortation, "Lift up your eyes," see all you can. What you cannot see with your eyes, see with your faith. Then go through life not feebly scattering curses by the way, but bravely hopeful, strong in God whose being and love surround it all, blessing and being blessed, at every step and at the end.

XIII.

HIGHER AND LOWER STANDARDS.

"Demas hath forsaken me, having loved this Present World." — II TIMOTHY iv: 10.

OF Demas we know almost nothing except what is suggested in these words. Once in the Epistle to the Colossians, and once in the Epistle to Philemon, St. Paul alludes to him as his own fellow-worker, in tones of sympathy and love. Then in the Epistle to Timothy there comes this statement of his follower's defection.

With so few facts to restrain us, we may give some play to our imagination. We may ask ourselves why and how it was that Demas turned back from the company of Paul, and gave himself to "this present world." It may have been mere lightness of nature, which grew weary of the severe and lofty life which the apostle lived. On the other hand, there may have been something more than that. Demas may certainly have been a man of some degree of seriousness. I can think of him as being first drawn to Paul and Paul's Christ with real enthusiasm. His heart was touched. His mind was fascinated. Lo! here was something greater than the ordinary life. Here was the true life of man. I can imagine him thinking that for a long time, and then I can imagine a misgiving creeping in upon him. "After all," I can picture him saying to himself, " what is this life of Paul, my master? Is there any hope that he can make the world that which he thinks it ought to be? Is he not striving for an impossibility? Is he not before his time? Is he not so far apart from common standards that all his teaching and work must be only a powerless episode, out of which, when it is over, no permanent result can come? Will not the true, the healthy, the practical man rather seek the best standards of his time and live in them?" With thoughts like these, I can conceive this vague and shadowy Demas, by and by, perhaps with deep regret and courteous farewells, forsaking Paul, his master, "having loved this present world."

If any such picture of his history were true, should we not have in Demas a very interesting study of the comparative power of Higher and Lower Standards, and of their relation to one another? We should see a man pressed on by the immediate conditions of his place and time urged to behave and live as his contemporaries and his fellow-citizens were living and behaving; then tempted out beyond these immediate surroundings by the sight of vaster experiences and the more ideal possibilities of man; and then again deliberately leaving and disowning these, and coming back and saying: "No! Beautiful as it is, it is a delusion. Man must live in his own place, and in his own time. The universal and the eternal must not bewilder him. He can identify and integrate his life only in the moulds of his own race, his own family, his own class. Let him find his standards there. Let the bird be the best bird, and the mole the best mole, that it can; but let neither lose its distinctness and special value by aspiring after some vague dream of universal animal life." This is what we should see in Demas if our imagination concerning him were right. And so we should understand the scene when on some dim and hazy morning he turned his back on Paul, and went back to the " present world " which he loved.

Was there ever a restlessness in his soul afterwards? Did the heaven which he once had dared to seek haunt him in his lower life? We are almost sure it must have haunted him, for not by any one resolution does a man shut the windows on the higher standards which once have shone upon him. He cannot so look to earth that he will not be aware of the heaven, any more than he can so fix his eyes on the heaven that he will not know there is an earth. An old mediæval legend says that mankind are the incorporation, the embodiments, of the angels who in the strife between God and Lucifer could not determine on which side they ought to be. They never have finally decided. And so this special fallen angel Demas may, as well as any other man, give us the starting-point from which to think about the true relation of the higher and the lower, the universal and the special, standards to the life of man. That is what I should like to do this morning.

Let us start, then, with the fact that every human being is born into a group of local, ready-made standards, to which, in the absence of any broader and more absolute ideas of life, he naturally and legitimately conforms. The child takes it for granted that what his father and his mother do is right. The ways of the household represent for him the perfect life. As he goes forth from the house door into the school, into the city life, into the Church's teaching, it is all right for him that each of them should welcome him into a set of standards all formed and accepted, which should be presumably the best. He does not know enough to question them. The presumption is enormously upon their side. The very fact of his being born into the midst of them implies a certain kind of evidence that he brings such a nature as will be best suited to them, and such as they will best suit. They represent the same stage in the development of man. And so the child in the household, and the scholar in the school, and the citizen in the State, and the Christian in the Church, starts with a cordial acceptance of the local standard, and desires to live as other men are living in the institution of which he finds himself a part.

In a yet larger way, the same is true about the age in which a man finds himself set. I am here in the nineteenth century, and I am presumably in its spirit, and think it the best century which the world has seen. The same causes have produced it and me and the men who are living in it at my side. I see its light; I feel its nobleness. Other centuries I must go abroad to seek. This century is here. I breathe its breath; its blood is in my veins; its passions are my passions; its ideas are my ideas. And so presumptively, and by the first natural disposition of my life, I am a man of my time and adopt its standards.

This is not something which applies only to weak and waxen characters, such as easily take the impression of their immediate surroundings. Great genius all the more vividly catches the color of its time. Plato is a man of all time, but he is also a man of the fourth century before Christ. Luther is a German of the sixteenth century. Shakespeare is part of the age of Elizabeth. Nay, if we come to that Life of which it might have been expected above all others that it would leave all local and temporary influences and associations on one side, and be simply and universally the life of the Son of Man, Christ Jesus was a Jew; He was a Nazarene; He spoke the language, He thought the thought, of His own people; He reverenced the authority of the Scribes and Pharisees; He justified Himself out of the Jewish law. It was not merely a humanity, but a Hebrew humanity of that especial age, through which He uttered the wisdom and the love of God.

Influences are powerful, not merely in virtue of their intrinsic force, but also in proportion to their nearness or their distance. An idea which ever, in any remotest age, has held the thought of men is powerful forever in the world; but an idea of far less intrinsic force prevailing here and now will conquer it, and sweep the life of the world out of its power. A man in college knows that the standards of the great world of men are wiser, loftier, and freer than those which are the masters in his little world; but the immediate holds him in its power, and he thinks that he is helpless. It is in vain to argue with this first power of the present life. That a man should feel it, is the first condition of successful energy. Now and then a man comes who does not feel it, or who pretends not to feel it. "I will not be an American of the nineteenth century," he says. "I will be a Greek of the time of Pericles. I will be a Jew of the time of Moses. I will be a barbarian of the forest, or an Arab of the desert." And what is the result? How he becomes useless and insignificant and good for nothing! The great age takes no notice of the foreign particle. He adds nothing to its force. He shares nothing of its glory.

Be men of your time. Let no perverseness and no affectation isolate you from it. There is the man behind his time, and the man before his time; and the time gains something from them both, but neither of them makes a true part of its vital strength. There is the other man whom we all know, who stands with the very genius of his time inspiring his life. He will stand always in history, to show what the special humanity of this particular period was. And now the age for which he stands is more real for his characteristic life, and does its real work, in this brief day of his existence, by him and such as he; and he himself is real and strong and solid by this identification with his time.

We say all this with confidence, and then there come misgivings. After all, will not all this make a limited and meagre life? Shall I, because I happen to have been born in this especial century, or because I live in this especial land, or because I am a member of this especial class in college, accept the standards of my time, my place, my class, and ask no larger questions?   I cannot, if I am a man.   It cannot be that it is right that I should do so.   It cannot be that I am doomed to bigotry because I live in one place or time, or to scepticism if I live in another.   " That would make me a puny slave, and make all progress of the world impossible."   So men reason, and they reason well.   Sometimes they act upon their reasoning very badly.   Sometimes the only thing which they can see to do is to throw themselves violently outside their local temporary standards and live in pure defiance of the state of things about them, which is nothing but another kind of slavery.

There is a better way.   There is a calm, deliberate search for other standards, which shall not destroy, but ripen and enlarge, the standards to which we are immediately committed.   There is a way in which, still clinging to our time and place, we may fulfil their influence upon us by more general and more personal influence, so that they shall not hold us in slavery and cramp us, but be the starting-point for larger range and deeper depth.   Let us see what such other standards are.   In general, I think that they are two, which we may call:

First.   The universal human experience ; and

Second.   The personal conscience.

Let us look at both.

First.   What do we mean, then, by the universal

human experience as an enlargement of the standards of our time or place? Why, this! Here you and all the people about you are living in a certain fashion. You were born into its ways of living, and have followed it ever since you were a child. You have never seen any other. The consequence is, you have come to think of it as if it were intrinsically the best way, almost as if it were the only way. You have practically come to feel as if a man could not be clean and upright and intelligent and a gentleman and live in any other way. Now suppose your range of vision widens, suppose you come to see that there are hosts of men who are true, honest, pure, and fine who never heard of your pet ways of living. Suppose the curtain of history is lifted, and you see that whole generations wrought out strong, healthy human lives thinking things wrong which you think right, thinking things right which you think wrong. What is the result? You do not cast your standards instantly away, but you revise them. Their tyranny, their absoluteness, is mitigated. You say, "They may not be right." You have stepped forth into the presence of the great humanity.

Take your religious opinions. They are heterodox or orthodox, but they are absolute to you because they are the opinions of your place and time. You have so thoroughly, so totally, accepted them that you with greatest difficulty are able to believe that any man is a good man and a true man who believes that which you disbelieve, or disbelieves that which you hold true. But lo, across the ocean, if not nearer, there are men who find what you believe all unbelievable, and there are men who hold what is to you incredible, with all their hearts, who yet are altogether brave and spiritual and devout. What shall that mean to you? It must not make you think all truth indifferent. It must not give you into the power of the silly idea that it matters not what a man believes. It must not make me doubt my truth, but it must make me hold my truth more largely, and be sure that there are other aspects of it which may make good and strong men. It must make me know the larger relations of charity and faith.

Thus every conviction and conception, when it is taken out into the broad air of human life, grows clearer and grows truer. "I know this because men know it," I declare. "I am sure of it because men are sure of it." But what men? Why, first of all, these sharp, clear men whom I meet every day, these men who must of necessity immediately represent humanity to me. But what about those other men who lived ten centuries ago? What about these other men who live to-day in China or Paris? Shall they have nothing to say in forming my opinion? If I take any conception of my own and travel far up along the stream of history, and there in the far-away thickets where the stream is very small find men holding the same thing to be true; or if I sail with it across the ocean, and find men of other colors and other tongues believing it and living by it, — is not my faith in it confirmed? Is not the local temporary stand-ard strengthened when the standards of all time and all the world gather around it and agree with it? Must it not also be that the local and temporary standards are regulated and enlarged when the standards of other times and of the whole world show that they are not in accordance with the great and deliberate and long-continued movements of the human mind and soul?

Securus judicat orbis terrarum. The judgments of the world are right. What a great power that principle has always had over the minds of men! It really is at the heart of all appeals to the judgment-seats of the past or the future. It is the principle which, consecrated, builds the Church. Under the power of this principle the standard of the time, the sect, the set, the land, is always being drawn out for refreshment and for enlargement and for rectification into the long and broad standards of humanity. A boy gets to believe, from the society he lives among, that all bright men despise religion. He happens to live in a little narrow, local, temporary set, where clever wits are sneering at the supreme divine relations of the soul. He is all ready to fix it as one of the first conditions of his thought, that one must be either foolish or blind to say that he believes in God. Let that poor boy's horizon be enlarged. Let him see ages filled with the glory of religion. Let him behold multitudes of the world's noblest souls finding their highest nobleness in obedience to an acknowledged God, and is he not set free? Is he not set at liberty to search and find out for himself the larger spiritual life of man? A certain sin is current in a certain land. The exact point of development which that land has reached tends to make that sin seem excusable, perhaps almost to make it seem necessary   A man, full of the sympathy of his time and ready to accept its standards, travels to other lands; and lo, whatever other sins are tolerated there, this sin is counted a disgrace.   Men turn away from him who transgresses in this special fashion with contempt or disgust.   Is not the traveller's spell broken?   Does he not go back to his own land with the standards which it has inspired set right and made large by what the world has shown him?   These are illustrations of what I mean by the power over local and temporary standards of the universal experience of humanity.

Second. I said that also the local and temporary standard was subject to enlargement and correction by the personal conscience.   At first the group of which a human being makes a part — the family, the school, the age — overcomes and conceals his self.   It almost is his self.   But the true self is there all the while.   This is a human being, different from all the other beings that have ever lived or are living on the earth to-day.   What is the result of that?   Some day some decision which the family, the school, the church has made is so important or so strange that it breaks through the outer crust of life, and finds this true self, this personal self, down below and wakens it.   And, once awake, it never goes absolutely to sleep again.   The man's own sense of right and wrong, of wise and foolish, utters its commendations or its condemnations on the standards of the time or of the place; and just in proportion to the true personalness with which he speaks, his utterances are more large and absolute.

For it is true that every real man is more eternal and more universal than his time and place. Every real man is fresh from the creative hand of God. He has not come down simply through the generations. He is the son of Him who was, and is, and is to be. Therefore those standards, which have in them the limitations of the time and place where they were born, come to him for their judgment. They are the utterances of the convictions of all men. And there is a true sense in which every real man is wiser, as there is another sense in which he is more foolish, than his race. At any rate, he is responsible for his own life. His conscience claims this freedom and makes of it a duty. " What is this world that I should take its judgments absolutely? Behold, my time says that this is right, but I, the heart of me, the conscience of me, know that it is wrong. What is the age but multitudes of Me's? Shall not this Me have its own rights which it cannot surrender?" And so the personal conscience revises and enlarges and corrects the standards which the time and place have formed.

The illustrations which I used before might serve us perfectly again. The boy, all ready to be overcome by the flippant and scornful scepticism of his time, hears the remonstrance which comes not merely from the utmost bounds of human life, but also up from the depths of his own soul. The doer of the accepted sin of the day does it in the face not merely of a rebuking humanity, but also of his own nature, which knows and says that it is wrong.   Thus the heart of a man, which is eternal, is always asserting the eternal standards, and so intensively as well as extensively, in the depth of his personal conscience as well as in the breadth of his share in the universal manhood, he is finding the correction and enlargement of the standards of his life.

Let us see, then, what we have reached.   Here is a certain man, — you, we will say, living your daily life.   Where will the standards of that life come from?   First of all out of your surroundings.   You will do what your household, your class, your time, your place think right.   But on these standards will be always pressing the claims of the general human judgments, what men in other times and in other places have thought and are thinking to be right, and the claims of your own conscience, that which God has shown you to be right in your own soul.   The result will be a character of your own time, of your own place, and yet of all times and of all places, or rather of that universal being which underlies all times and all places and manifests itself in each, but loses itself in and becomes the slave of none.

May I just suggest one or two simple illustrations which will make more clear and less abstract what I have been saying.   Suppose a young man born in a certain region of society has adopted a certain scale of personal expense without a question.   He is rich, and all his friends are rich, and luxury is in the very air they breathe.   He really thinks that a man cannot live comfortably on less than he spends every year. Is he to be all his life a slave of those delusions just because he was born in a particular street and of a

special class ?   The things which must save him must
be the widest sight of how the noblest men on earth
are living to-day on not more than a tenth of what he
thinks necessary, and of how luxury has been in ages
the curse of human life, and the protest of his own
conscience that wanton extravagance in a world
where men and women are starving is a sin and
shame.

Here is a community where everybody drinks.
You live in it, and you drink too. Why should you
not? What call or right have you to set yourself up
for an exception? None, if you get your standard
wholly from your time ; but surely reason enough, if
all the world and all the ages speak to you and tell you
how the curse of drink is at the root of a large part of
human misery, and that the earth would almost burst
to blossom if the blight of drunkenness were taken
off. Reason enough, if your own conscience speaks
to you and tells you that you have no right to degrade
your own nature from its best activity, or to put one
grain more of temptation in the way of your hindered
and burdened fellow-men.

There are groups of men, at least, who see no harm
in gambling. Has any man a right to shut his life
into the standards of those groups and give no value
to the fact that the great mass of civilized mankind
has thoroughly believed and proclaimed that for a
man to come into possession of the property of his fellow-man by a process which is neither bargain nor
gift, but the mere working of accident and chance,
is demoralizing and wrong? Has any man a right to
let his soul be deafened to its own instincts, which tell

it that for a man to gain money so is wicked? Here
is where the breaking of the spell must come. Men
in all ages have doubted or denounced the gambler's
life. The gambler's own conscience, if he sets it free,
denounces it. Before the universal human experience and the personal conscience, the standard of
the gaming-house finds'itself corrected and rebuked.

I will not multiply illustrations. Do you not see
how they all point the same way, how they all tend
to urge the same kind of life, — a life profoundly
rooted in the here and now, a life that is in quick and
earnest sympathy with what is close about it, a life
that altogether is disposed to think its own time and
its standards right, and yet a life which is always looking wider and looking deeper, — wider to the universal
experience of man, deeper to the personal conscience
which it carries in itself?

I appeal to you whether what I have described is
not the character, the kind of man, whom the community most trusts and honors, on whom it most
learns to depend. The servant of the hour, but not
its slave; in sympathy with the day, the place, the
business, the party, the circle of society in which it
stands, but not in blind subserviency to it; ready
to protest and having a recognized right to protest
because of an undoubted sympathy and love; always
bringing in new elements and forms of nobleness
out of the fields of history, and up from the depths
of its own nature, — is not this the character of
the man of his own age, the man of his own class,
who makes the whole world and all time more rich?
Is not this the timely and yet universal man whom

it may well stir the ambition of any young man to become.

I know but one step more to make, and that, while it need not take us long to describe it, is a great step, for it brings all our subject out into the rich land of religion. We talk about getting into association with the universal human experience, and about listening to one's own conscience, and then some one starts up and says, " Ah, yes, that is all well, but what am I to do ? I, who am no scholar, who can be no traveller, and who, when I listen for my con- science, hear only a turmoil of doubts and perplex- ities all in confusion down below." When I hear questions such as that my thought goes back to Jesus, and the question which the people asked one another about Him, " How knoweth this man letters, having never learned," seems to throw light upon it all. He was no scholar. They had never seen Him in their schools. But He knew man and knew Himself, and by and by they learned that it was because He knew God.

What does that mean for us ? That if we know God, if we are forever trying to find out what is His will, if we are seeking for it in the Bible, if we are seeking for it in Christ, we find in knowing Him the true enlargement and corrections of the present standards ; we find, in knowing Him, the revelation of the universal experience of man and the awaken- ing of the personal conscience.

How true that is ! In every man of God there is a breadth and depth which makes him free of the world in which he yet most intimately lives. In God there

is the universal man and the true life of every individual child of His. Therefore, whoever loves and
serves Him finds in Him the constant enlargement
and adjustment of his life. Demas need not leave
Paul and Paul's Christ in order that he may love
this present world. He will know how to love and
serve this present world all the more completely if
he knows Christ and the great Revelation of God
which is in him.

Oh if I only could make you young men see how
there is here the true solution of the problem of your
lives ! Shall you be God's or the world's ? Be both !
Not in any low miserable compromise. Not by the
effort to serve God and mammon. But by a brave and
filial questioning of God that He may tell you just
how He wants a child of His to live in this peculiar
time and under these peculiar circumstances of yours.
There is a type of universal human life in harmony
with the best life of all the ages. In tune with the
sublimest and finest spiritual music of the universe,
in harmony also with the profoundest dictates of your
own personal conscience, which you can live in your
parlor and your shop; and that life you can reach if
you are consecrated to God in your own place and
time. If you live that life, the world of the present
owns you and claims you and rejoices in you. The
most distant life of man looks in on you and recognizes you as a part of itself, and says, " Well done ! "
Up from your own conscience speaks your self-
approval. And God your Father bends His love
around you, and out of His blessing feeds you with
His strength.

Compared with such a life, what miserable things are these feverish efforts either to suit the present world or to reject it and rebel against it. Either Demas strolling once more in the streets of Thessalonica with his sight of divine things faded from him like a dream, or some poor starved hermit sitting in his cave and trying to think that he despises that life to which his human heart still tells him that he belongs. How miserable are they both beside the life which goes like Christ's, from duty on to duty, from experience to experience, heartily in them all, and yet above, beyond them all, in hourly communion with God, with the complete humanity, and with Himself.

May we so live! May we be men here, now, and yet men there and then; in the infinite, in the eternal, while yet the duties of the present world are claiming us, and we are doing them with hands made faithful and skilful by the fire of God!

XIV.

THE NATURAL AND THE SPIRITUAL.

Howbeit that was not first which is Spiritual, but that which is
Natural; and afterward that which is Spiritual. — I. Cor. xv. 46.

"The Adam comes before the Christ," St. Paul
declares. And he is simply telling the story of the
Bible. The man of the Garden, untrained, undisci-
plined, self-indulgent, incapable of self-control, comes
before the Man of the Cross, who willingly surrenders
the present for the future, the body for the soul, and
Himself for others. And the earthly life comes before the life of heaven. The life of temptation, and
resistance, and surrender comes before the life of
spontaneity, and freedom, and attainment!

These are St. Paul's two great examples; and then
he seems to gather out of them the wide and general
truth which they contain. He surveys the universe
and finds the same truth everywhere. Everywhere the
higher comes to make the lower perfect. Everywhere
the lower is provided first, to be the basis and opportunity of the higher coming by and by. Everywhere
the lips must be before the speech; the canvas must
be before the picture; the candle must be before the
flame; the brain must be before the thought. It is
the teaching which natural science is giving us pro-
fusely. She traces the long progress in which the

material, at first hard and sterile, has grown fertile with mysterious emanation and clothed itself with higher and higher life. From the coarser to the finer she watches the growth of the ever-ripening world. Her message is the same as Paul's: "That is not first which is Spiritual, but that which is Natural; and afterward that which is Spiritual."

The first suggestion which would come from such a truth is very crude and unsatisfactory. It is that the natural is helpless until the spiritual comes to help it. Let the Adam go on in his mere physical manhood till the Christ appears. Let the mortal live its lower life until death opens to it the doors of immortality. The material must lie in its torpidity until the spiritual form without itself comes and puts into it a life of which it was all destitute before. But our deeper observation teaches us a deeper truth, and the Bible asserts that deeper truth convincingly. The material has within itself the power of spiritual life. Its total story has not been told until a waiting impulse has been felt within it dimly conscious of incompleteness, until it has answered to the spiritual call and roused itself to life. The lips are not complete lips till they have spoken; the brain is not a whole brain till it has thought. So in the Bible the first Adam is full of blind reachings and desires, which the second Adam alone fulfils. The Life of man here upon the earth is capable of a heavenliness which heaven alone can bring to its completeness. The whole secret of the physical has not been read until its power of becoming spiritual by service of the spirit has been discerned. This is what Baptism means.   It is the declaration that this new-born life, which seems only a new-born animal, has in it, bound up with it, a divine nature.   Baptism is the claiming of that nature.   It is the assertion of the regeneration, the deeper and higher birth, the birth from heaven which is coincident with the birth from earth, and which is to use the physical basis for its servant and its power of development.

I hope that I make this plain, for it seems to me to be all-important.   A man sees the great world of spiritual life.   He believes in God and godlikeness. He thinks of genius and of sainthood.   He knows that there are such things as great self-sacrifices and surrenders.   He knows of this spiritual world, but he also thoroughly believes that he does not belong to it.   He is of the earth, earthy.   He is physical, material, limited to the interests and needs and experiences of the lower world.   "Sometime, perhaps at death," he says, "the Power may come which will snatch me up and carry me away and put me in another world, in which now I have no share.   But now that other world is to me as if it did not exist. I have nothing to do with it, or it with me.   I am a creature of the earth, and must live on as such until God perhaps in His own good time carries me to heaven."

Is not that the simple creed about themselves by which multitudes of men are practically living?   It is in protest against that creed that we are bound, with St. Paul for our teacher, to try to understand the true relation between the lower and the higher lives, between the natural and the spiritual as he describes them. That is what I want to do this morning.

The truth from which we start is this, that so far as the life of this world is concerned, every spiritual operation has its physical basis, in close connection with which it lives its life and does its work. The illustrations of that truth are everywhere. The growth of the tree is a mysterious and spiritual power. No man has ever seen it. It cannot be detected at its labor when with a sudden stroke of the axe you tear the tree's trunk open. You are not quick enough to find it. Your sight is not keen enough to catch it. And yet how closely, how inextricably it is bound up with the grosser elements, in connection with which alone it does its work. There must be the black earth and the brown seed, or nothing comes. What growth-power ever made manifestation of itself, creating out of nothing, in the air, a tree that had no history and no progenitor? The material is first, and then the spiritual. Or if we look in quite a different direction — the character of a nation, its advance in cultivation, and in the production of that special type of national being which constitutes its spiritual power, and makes it a real presence, not merely on the map, but among the spiritual forces of the world — this has its physical basis. The soil and situation of the country where that nation lives, the amount and kind of its material prosperity, these are the first elements which tell in the production of the nation's life, and in deciding of what sort its most spiritual productions are to be. The songs of its singers and the raptures of its saints will get their tone from the mountains from which they are echoed, or from the waters across which they float. And need I even suggest to you how every man has in his bodily constitution the physical basis of the most subtle and transcendent parts of his profoundest life? Out from the very marrow of his bones comes something which his finest affections never outgo, and which gives a color to his soul's loftiest visions. His dreams are different from other men's because of the texture of his muscles and the color of his blood. It is on the harp of his nervous system that the Psalm of his life is played. There is a physical correspondent to everything that he thinks or fancies. There is a physical basis to his most spiritual life.

In the story of man's creation in the Book of Genesis, a story which, whatever be its relation to history, contains the Ideas of Human Life most picturesquely and graphically set forth, this truth of the physical basis for the spiritual life appears most vividly. "The Lord God formed man of the dust of the ground and breathed into his nostrils the breath of life, and man became a living soul." The scene is almost visible before us. We can almost see the clay-cold figure laid upon the ground, the corpse which never yet has lived; we can almost feel, that which we cannot see, the awful presence bending above the perfect body and sending through all its limbs and organs the mysterious thrill of life. Each limb and organ is ready for the power which occupies it. Each has within itself the unused fitness for its special work. The Breath of Life finds each responsive to its sum-

mons, " And man becomes a living soul! " How
true it is to all we know! The Perfect Body offering
itself for the medium of the Perfect Soul. I do not
know, I cannot guess, what was the nature of the
historical event to which that verse refers. But I do
know that it is absolutely true to that great order
which pervades the universe. Everywhere the earthly
conditions offer their opportunities to the celestial
miracle. The fuel is cut in the woods of earth; it
is piled, hard and lifeless, on the altar of unheeding
stone, and then from it the flame arises a live aspiring column and lays its fiery tribute at the feet of
God. "That is not first which is spiritual, but that
which is natural; and afterward that which is spiritual."

There are two truths here, then. The first is that
every lower life is made to reach up and fulfil itself
in a higher, and the second is that every higher life
must have its basis and find its conditions in a lower.
Let us look at these truths in turn, and see if they
are not both rich in practical suggestion.

• 1. Every lower life is made to reach up and fulfil
itself in a higher. I do not know anything which
furnishes more food for thought than the perplexity
with which men talk about the care of their human
bodies. Is it a noble or ignoble thing? One generation devotes itself to athletic culture as if there were
no loftier religion; another generation despises exercise, and goes limping and coughing among the
groves of its academy as if to care for health
or sickness were unworthy of a thinking man. A
thousand theories cross and recross one another as

they lie tumbled in upon each other in chaotic confusion. Would it not be good, indeed, if these words should be written in golden letters on the walls of every gymnasium and also on the walls of every school of learning and cell of meditation in the world: "That is not first which is spiritual, but that which is natural." As they stood on the walls of the gymnasium, what they declared would be the need of a strong body for all best spiritual life. As they stood written on the study wall, they would mean the utter failure of the strongest body unless a spiritual life came down from above and occupied it, came out from within and clothed it with a worthy purpose. There are two young men who walk our streets, both of whom have their admirers, each of whom seems in some eyes to be an admirable fulfilment of humanity, both of whom, judged with the fullest judgment, are pitiable failures. One of them is the young student who has burnt out the strength of his body in his midnight oil. The other is the young athlete who has given away to muscle the care and culture which was meant for mind. The staggering scholar and the stupid athlete, what failures they both are! what sad and helpless fragments of humanity! The Body trained as thoroughly, as superbly as may be for the spirit uses. Health gathered like a great reservoir of waters to be set free and turn the wheels of high thoughts, and generous emotions, and benignant charities, — there is the true relationship, there is the perfect man, there is the balance and proportion which is written in the noble maxim of St. Paul.

What is the strongest thing to say to a poor young

fool who is wasting his bodily strength in dissipation ? Tell him about an early grave, and what does he care ? He talks his easy philosophy about "Let us live while we live." Scare him with threats of physical reaction and decay, and he buries his face in the wine-cup and dreams of suicide. But so long as there is any spark of nobleness left in him, it must be that there is a chance that the picture of an intellect weakened, and a moral sense dimmed, and a soul made unfit for any high enterprise by the insufficiency of the physical basis, out of which their efforts must take their start and spring, will waken him and make him think.

Do you know, O young men, that there are old men all through this city whose minds are powerless for any public work or private pleasure because of the wrong they did their bodies when they were of your age ? Do honor to your bodies. Reverence your physical natures, not simply for themselves. Only as ends they are not worthy of it, but because in health and strength lies the true basis of noble thoughts and glorious devotion. A man thinks well and loves well and prays well because of the red running of his blood. A community will have higher tastes and better government and less sordidness and less crime when its alleys and tenement-houses are no longer breeding-places of cholera and fever. We build our schools and our hospitals, and we keep them apart from one another as if they had no true connection. Only when in our thought they make one single system, — and health for the sake of intelligence and character is what we seek, — only then shall we be sure that we are serving and saving the whole man.

There is a health of the Community which corresponds to the health of the physical body and shares in many of its laws. It is what is called in general Material Prosperity. It has its failures and recoveries, its fevers and its paralyses, its full-blooded vitality and its white-faced decline. What shall we say about the Material Prosperity of a Community? Sometimes it is depreciated and defamed. Sometimes we are told that all the building of houses and laying out of roads and increase of the comforts and conveniences of life is base and has no true connection with the higher life of man. All that is foolish. The connection between the lower and the higher is a certain fact, and cannot be ignored. And yet the whole way in which men have asserted and denied that connection is most significant and well deserves our study. Man's treatment of wealth has been one of the strangest indications of his mental and spiritual condition. Think what it has been. He has denounced wealth in all his most exalted moods. He has mused and declaimed upon its worthlessness. And yet it has been the passion of his life to get it, and to get it more and more. Let the moralist stand at the corner of the street and tell men as they pass that money will not bring happiness, and every man who passes will pause just long enough to nod to the sermon a melancholy assent, and then the whole river of human life will pour on to take possession of the last newly opened field of profitable investment and make a little more money. Let the satirist utter his stinging denunciation of the way in which men pursue that which they despise, and despise that which they pursue. Let all men say in certain moods that money-getting is a snare ; nevertheless the pursuit goes on, and in spite of their contempt of wealth-seeking, the mass of men spend their nights in dreaming and their days in working for the universally desired prize of wealth.

Have we ever carefully asked ourselves what all this means, — this practical assertion that wealth is good, running along with the theoretical assertion that the pursuit of wealth is bad? If we do ask ourselves what it all means, are we not led immediately to this, that it is exactly the state of things which would be brought about if some power which ought to develop into high and fine results were constantly pursued, without the demand for such development being forced upon it; a restlessness which yet should never be strong enough to shake the pursuer free from his pursuit; a search and struggle which should never grow complacently sure of itself and its own justification; a spasmodic shame, a constantly recurring misgiving and yet a constant pressing forward in the dubious way? This would be the inevitable consequence of such an unsatisfactory condition.

I take just this to be exactly the state of things concerning the pursuit of money among men. There is a wide and deep conviction that material well-being may be the basis of fine character and noble life. A rich man has opportunities of goodness which a poor man does not have. Self-culture and the care for others lie open to him in his opulent and well-provided home. The getting of wealth and the using of wealth both open the chance for the cultivation of precious qualities. Therefore no baseness of the actual business world has ever led men's soundest thought to condemn money-getting universally and in unsparing terms. On the other hand, the search for wealth has evidently not been always or generally conscious of its possibilities and responsibilities. It has been sordid and selfish. It has not always or generally produced refinement or charity. It has rested contented in its immediate results. It has vulgarly jingled its dollars and not won from them the true gold of character.

Does not all that suggest what the true issue of it all must be? Not by abusing money-getting, but by insisting that money-getting must have ends beyond itself. Not by calling wealth wicked, but by calling wicked the selfish, the licentious, the oppressive use of wealth. Not by trying to make all men poor, but by demanding of rich men that they shall be fine, broad, helpful, in proportion to their riches. So must the problem of wealth be ultimately solved. None but a theorizer or a dreamer pictures to himself the time when either the craving for large personal property will be eradicated from men's souls, or when by artificial legislation it will become impossible for any man in the community to accumulate great riches. But it is not absurd to hope; sometimes we see already glimpses and promises that it may come. It is not absurd to hope for the growth of a private conscience and a public sentiment which shall some day denounce and discredit the rich man who, in his riches keeps a vulgar soul or a stingy hand. The tree must bear its fruit, or else it is a cumberer of the ground. The fountain must not turn into a pool. "That is not first which is spiritual, but that which is natural; and afterward that which is spiritual." The natural is all right and good if it is reaching toward the spiritual; but the natural, the material which desires and promises no spiritual result, is failure and deserves contempt. That is the application of our truth to personal or national well-being and success.

What is true of wealth is true of all the manifold experiences of life. Experiences are the material of Character, the physical basis of feeling and thought. Something happens to you, and you thereby enter into the possibility of a higher and completer nature. The man of many experiences has the opportunity of being a man of manifold life. But yet, as we all know, as we all see, the opening of experiences into character is by no means a necessary or inevitable thing. What shall we say about the man who has gone up and down the world, had part in a vast variety of occupations, crossed many seas, climbed many mountains, walked the streets of many cities, talked with a thousand men, been tossed hither and thither on the distracting billows of all kinds of life, and yet is, after all, the same meagre, narrow, unsympathetic, unrefined mortal which he was at the beginning? His History is nothing but a Diary. He himself is only like a much-travelled log. What can we say except that, in him, experience has failed of its result. It has not opened into Character. The man has gathered nothing but recollections. He is no more a man.   He has gathered no strength.   The Natural has never come into the Spiritual.

You see the difference whenever you talk with two men who have come home from their tour in Europe, or who have passed through great suffering and sorrow, or who are nearing the shore which lies the other side of life.   You know at once which of them has transmuted experiences into intelligence and character, and which of them brings his experiences like so many hard jewels held in his hand, his treasure, but in no sense a part of him.   The first man might forget everything which has happened to him, and all that happened to him would still remain in its essential power in his life.   If the other man forgot the facts of his life, there would be nothing left.   He might as well not have lived.

It is good to multiply experiences.   It is good to do many things and to have manifold relations with the world.   It is good to touch many people and to see many sights ; but it is good, it is necessary, to be content with no experience which remains simply as experience and does not pass on and into character. Events are great if they make dispositions.   The Natural is precious if " afterward," out of it, comes the Spiritual.   The experienced man is happy, if he has really drunk the rain and sunshine of the experiences which have come to him into his heart and is the ripened man, otherwise he is only like the rock on which every passer-by has scrawled his name.

Thus everywhere the lower furnishes opportunities for the higher, and is a failure unless the higher blooms out of the ground which the lower has made ready. It is Paul's groaning and travailing creation. It is the unity of the universe in which, from end to end, there is no hardest, commonest, and cheapest thing which, living in simple healthiness and self-respect, may not become the gathering point and manifestation point of the most infinite celestial light, — no stone that may not make an altar. Reverence the simple, the prosaic, the natural, the real, but demand of every common thing of life, whether it be your body or your money or your daily experience, that it shall bloom to fine results in your own soul and in your influence upon the world. Freely accept the natural as first, but demand that afterward the spiritual shall not fail.

2. There remains but very little time for me to dwell upon our second truth, which was, you remember, the other side of that of which I have been speaking. As the natural must open into the spiritual or it is a failure, so the spiritual must root itself in the natural or it becomes vague and unreal. I see at once how true this is of the two great illustrative instances which I began by pointing out that St. Paul uses. The second Adam follows the first Adam. Christ comes after and completes the humanity which had been in the world before His Incarnation. And as that Humanity would have been sad indeed had He not come to fulfil its glimpses with His light and to realize its broken hopes, so He, when He has come, needs and demands the humanity behind Him, and roots His own life in the great universal soil of human life. Ah, yes, the Saviour's wonderful career was no mere cloud or

sunbeam flung out of the sky and floating vaguely over a world of which it formed no certain part. He felt our human blood through all His veins. His most transcendent miracles were done with human hands. He loved His age, His city, and His race. The least and meanest Jew, the least and meanest man, interpreted to Him his Sonship to the Father. He knew Himself, and we can know Him only as we believe in Him, and try to understand Him as the Son of Man.

Or, if we take Paul's other illustration, the perfect world rests on and finds its interpretation in this world of imperfection in which we are living now. I cannot understand the man I meet upon the street unless I see in him the man who some day is to walk in the new Jerusalem. And also the man walking in the new Jerusalem is unintelligible unless I know he is the same man who once walked here upon the street. The fights and victories, the fights and defeats, which he made here have passed into his nature and are part and parcel of his life forever.

Here is the key to the true realism. Here is the sign how false the shallow realism is of which its artists on canvas or on paper make such base parade. The real life, what is it? Is it the wretched, sordid details of earthly living, uninspired by a single suggestion that in their mud and mire there are the seeds of any spiritual, transcendent fruit or flower? On the other hand, is the real life a vision of some experience beyond the stars which has no connection with the dreariness and degradation of many of the mortal conditions which it has passed through and left behind? Not so. The real life of a man is his highest attainment kept in perpetual association with the meanest and commonest experience out of which it has been fed. When men shall so write and paint the lives of one another, then we shall have the true realism, — a realism in which, to use the Psalmist's words, " Truth shall flourish out of the earth and Righteousness look down from Heaven."

In such a completed realism as this lies the sincerity and healthiness of personal and social life. Get hold thoroughly of this idea that the Spiritual must always feel behind it the Natural from which it proceeds, and from which it is fed, and then how impossible it would be for you to despise any part of your life or to think light of any true work which you are called to do. If your faith in God is stronger for every humble task in which you need and get His aid, then that humble task is necessary to the fulness of your faith in God. You cannot let go of it and fly away. It is redeemed. It will go with you to the world where your Redemption will be perfect. It will make the music of your celestial life more firm and solid. If so, you cannot despise it here or call it slight.

And also there must come a sympathy between the men whose work it is to lay the hard foundations of life and the other men whose hands are bidden to carry up the loftiest pinnacles and spires into the sky. There are those who seem to be doomed to most earthly toil; just to be conscientious, and upright, and thorough, and true. It seems as if that were everything for them. There are other men whose souls leap to triumphant thoughts, and whose eyes are open to ecstatic visions. The great issue of all that I have been saying to you this morning is that these two sorts of men belong together, make one world, are serving the purposes of one God, and making ready one celestial kingdom, and deserve each the other's whole-souled respect. It is not that the lesser man is making his life successful by making possible a higher life which some other man may live, though that is much. It is not possible to look at it in such detail as that. It is that in this universe, where natural and spiritual succeed and minister to one another, he who at any spot is doing good work of any kind is serving the Universal Master and contributing to the Universal Success.

Christ had His word of encouragement and strength to say to every soldier in His army and to every worker at His work. He made both Martha and Mary the servants of His will. It is not only His loftiest disciples at their loftiest tasks. It is all souls, all hands and feet that have duty to perform. They all belong to Him; not merely scholars in their studies, not merely missionaries in their martyrdoms, not merely saints in their closed closets, but every working man and woman everywhere, — they are all His. The spirit which proceeds from Him may pour through the whole mass and find out every particle, and give to each an impetus towards its own next higher stage of life, and so bear the whole along together towards the completion of each man and the completion of the whole business and social life, and politics, and education, and then, as the crown of them all, Religion. "That is not first which is Spiritual, but that which is Natural; and afterward that which is Spiritual!" But they are all God's; and to make each instinct with what measure of His life it is capable of containing, that is to build them all into a flight of shining stairs, sweeping upward into even clearer and intenser light, until he who mounts to the full summit stands by the altar of God's unclouded presence and realizes the blessedness of perfect Communion with Him.

XV.

THE STONE OF SHECHEM.

"And Joshua said unto all the people, Behold, this stone shall be a witness unto us; for it hath heard all the words of the Lord which He spake unto us: it shall be therefore a witness unto you, lest ye deny your God."—JOSHUA xxiv. 27.

JOSHUA had led the people of Israel over the Jordan and into the promised land as far as Shechem. There he halted the host for a most solemn ceremony. It was a poor and insignificant thing; it made their great invasion to be only like any restless movement of one tribe of heathen into the territory of another, unless they entered the promised country and began their new career distinctly as the people of God. Therefore at Shechem Joshua makes them renew their sworn dedication to Jehovah. He gives them once more the old familiar Mosaic message of the Lord: "Now therefore fear the Lord and serve him in sincerity and in truth." And when the people had answered the voice of God with solemn promises of loyalty, then Joshua sealed the whole ceremony with a picturesque and striking figure. He took a great stone and set it up there under an oak which was by the sanctuary of the Lord. He said, "This stone has heard what God has said; here it shall stand as witness to you lest you deny your God." "You may forget," he seemed to say. "Your minds are soft and lose impressions. They are hot and burn with reckless passion." Here is this hard, cold stone. It never will forget, it never will distort the voice that it has listened to. When you need it for encouragement and when you need it for rebuke, this stone which has heard what God has said shall be here to utter forever His unforgotten words.

All readers of the Bible know how common in its pages is this simple, majestic, childlike figure which Joshua employed, — the figure which clothes an inanimate and unintelligent object with perception and memory and the power of utterance. It is the figure which children use in their plays. It is the figure of a primitive and unsophisticated people, and seems to show how near they stand to nature, how close they are in the confidence of the rocks and trees and stars. It is the figure which creates a large part of the mythologies and is at the root of much of the monumental instinct of mankind. And in the Bible it is constantly present in its highest, freshest, and most vivid form. When Cain kills Abel in the book of Genesis it is the actual literal blood of the murdered man that takes a voice and cries out from the ground so that God hears it up in Heaven. When Job tells the story of creation, he makes us hear the very "morning stars sing together in the sky." When the same Job asserts his integrity and justice, he calls upon the very earth that he has tilled to contradict him if he does not speak the truth. "If my land cry against me, or that the furrows thereof complain, let thistles grow instead of wheat, and cockle instead of barley." When David goes out into the morning sunlight he hears the " Heavens declare the glory of God." When Habakkuk is denouncing woes upon the covetous men and the oppressors of the poor, he makes their very houses speak and tell of the iniquity and cruelty which built them. " The stone shall cry out of the wall, and the beam out of the timber shall answer it." When Jesus rides across the rocky ridge of Olivet toward Jerusalem, He declares that the rocks under His feet are all ready to break out in His praises if the voices of the people fail. "I tell you that if these should hold their peace, the stones would immediately cry out." And when St. James upbraids the cruel rich men of his day, even the coins of which they have defrauded their servants take a voice. " Behold the hire of the laborers who have reaped down your fields, which is of you kept back by fraud, crieth." The Bible is preëminently the book of man; but the world in which man lives and the material things he touches are always present in the Bible for his sake.

The splendor of the sunshine, the whisper of the wind, the very smell of the rich ground, are always there, not for their own beauty or sweetness, but for their ministries and messages to man ; and man and nature stand as close to one another as in the child's fairy story or the poet's dream, which keep the Bible tone and coloring for all the ages.

I have referred to all these instances only to remind you how thoroughly Joshua is a man of the Bible when he sets his stone up at Shechem and calls upon the people to endow it in their imaginations with the powers of hearing and of utterance. " This

stone hath heard all the words of the Lord." Crowded
away under its hard substance lay the story and the
Commandments which He had uttered. Nothing until the new wonder of the phonograph, which packs
a human voice into the matter of a bit of lead and
can keep it there for years, and utter it, with all its
first tones and inflections to a generation now unborn,—nothing until this marvel of to-day has so
made an actual material reality of this imagination
of the captain of the Jews. Think what that stone
must have been to all the people! It had heard God
speak. The words of God were in it. No wonder
if they almost made it an idol. How it must have
changed with the changes of their lives! How to
their consciences, acute with certain crime, the word
of God must have spoken out of the stone in stern
and withering rebuke! How when some Jew was
trying to do right, to resist his temptations, he must
have heard God speak to him out of the stone, giving
him approbation and encouragement and strength!
The very rough face of the rock must have seemed
to those simple and susceptible people to smile or
frown on them as they passed before it, carrying
their conscious experiences in them. All the more
because it spoke no audible word, it must have
seemed to have its own voice for every man.

It is no fancy, certainly, to say that there are
always people who are to the world they live in
what that stone in Shechem was to the nation in
the midst of which it stood. Not voluble people,
not people with their glib and ready judgment
upon everything which goes on about them, per-

haps people who seem to the world at large mere stones. But people who "have heard the words of the Lord which He hath spoken," and who henceforth "are witnesses unto us lest we deny our God." Such men or women I am sure that we have known. People who some time in their lives had had the primary truth of God, the Divinity of Righteousness, spoken so into their ears that it has filled their being. Thenceforward they spoke that word in all its simplicity to everybody. All earnest struggle after righteousness feels their approval and sympathy, and counts it really God's. All shuffling, cowardly, and wanton sin hides or hurries away from their rebuking presence. They declare no subtleties and no refinements. They simply, broadly utter right and wrong. Such people have a noble place and function in the world. Men who would not own God's judgments directly, own God's judgments as they come through them. They purify and bless the circle, the community in which they live, as that stone under the oak at Shechem must have seemed to purify and bless the whole land of Israel.

But I do not mean to speak too generally of this piece of picturesque history which seems to me to suggest a very definite and useful subject for our thought. I want to speak to you this afternoon of the real nature and value of association, of that power which gives to the objects which surround mankind a sort of human character and make them vocal with messages of comfort and strength and rebuke. This is the real subject of our verse. Joshua's rock was transformed by the power of association. One hour it was a great dead stone, as silent and uninspiring as any other of the stones among which it lay. The next hour it had been taken up and separated from all its mates forever, a sacred stone, a fountain of inspiration, a fire of poetry and life. It was the association with the solemn self-consecration of the Jews which had transformed it. And our association is always the transforming power. Out of our use of the power of association comes much of our best education and our deepest responsibility.

The work that man does upon the world he lives in, then, is really double. He makes his changes in its outward face. He turns it by his toil of spade or chisel into forms of use or beauty. He sprinkles it with cities and ploughs it up and down with furrows. This is the first work. And then more subtly he fills it with his associations. Without any change in their shape he sends his history in through the mountains and the fields, so that it clings there forever and never can be separated. He twines the things that he has done with the scenery of the earth, so that thereafter they are inseparable. Everybody who has any sensibility sees that this second power of man over nature is the finer and the nobler. It is the greater enrichment of the world by man. Herod builds a temple at Jerusalem. With vast labor he levels the rough places, and hews the great stone blocks into shape. When it is done, his temple shines like a jewel on its hill. Jesus comes right across the little valley to the Mount of Olives. He changes nothing outward. He sticks no spade into its surface. He leaves each bush and olive-tree as He finds it. But there He ofttimes resorts with His disciples. There He lies prostrate in the struggle of Gethsemane. There at last His feet touch the earth as He ascends to Heaven, and ever since those days the mountain burns in the dearest and most sacred memory of man. There are men to whom this seems to be the one value of the external world — to utter the men who have lived and displayed their natures in it. Mere beauty of scenery, mere triumphs of gigantic engineering which have changed the face of the earth, have little charm for them except as they are the background of human history. This is what makes the Old World richer than the New. It is the absence of association in our bays and headlands, in our rivers and our mountains and our prairies, that makes a sort of vast silence in our enormous West, solemn enough and infinitely impressive, but wholly different from the chorus of voiceful memories that thrills one who lands on the shores across the sea and finds

> "Each gray old rock a grand historic thing,
> Each bright wave boasting it has borne a king,
> Undying footprints on each sandy beach,
> Each old wave vocal with heroic speech."

Evidently one great value of this principle of association which clothes the world with the memories of human life, and makes it utter man, is that it keeps in mind and constantly asserts the centralness and rightful superiority of man in the world where he lives. The thinker in whom this principle is strong must always practically hold that man is the centre, that all else on earth exists for him. And without such a faith as that, all human experience seems to testify that man cannot live his best and fullest life. Man is greater than nature,—nature' exists for man. These are truths upon which, thus far at least, in human history has hung man's power of conceiving the sublimest hopes and feeling the most pressing sense of obligation. If ever those truths should be successfully denied and man dislodged from his centralness, I think we cannot know how all the highest life of man would suffer. That self-respect which lies at the root of all moral struggle and all religion, that self-respect which is what makes credible to the Christian the great Christian revelations of the divine fatherhood and the divine redemption, that self-respect which is the real starting-point for true humility, it could not be maintained if man's life should be shown to be coördinate with all the lives around it, no more the purpose and interpreter of the rest than the lives of the lion or the oak. And the actual preservation of this sense of centralness lies very largely in the way in which man covers the earth with his associations and makes the landmarks of nature take their best value from the stories which they have to tell of him.

Nor is this secondary character, this monumental value which the earth acquires, something which comes from a few great exploits which wonderful men have done upon its highest pinnacles of prominence. There is a gradually increasing richness in the earth to which every man who in the humblest station lives a worthy and a faithful life contributes. The outer world gets the voice of God, not only from God directly, but from some Joshua who has spoken it in its presence; and the world in which we live becomes vocal with Him to men in future days whenever any man protests against wickedness, or speaks a word of truth or charity, or utters the God of strength in patience in any corner of the most obscure experience. I know not how real, how practical, this seems to you; but I am sure that the world is a better place for you and me to live in to-day, not merely for the hundred great pattern lives which have passed into the heavens and which we call still by their names, but far more for the countless, nameless multitude of men and women who have wrought into the very substance of the earth, where at last they lay their bodies in unnoticed graves, the great, first, simplest words of God, that man was sacred, that duty was possible, that self-sacrifice was sweet, and that love for one's brother was the crown of life. And you ought not to be satisfied until you find yourself able to feel that the hope of doing something by your living to make the world in a real, although an unappreciable, degree more full of these words for the men who are to follow us, is the noblest and most inspiring promise which can be set before your soul.

The world is too large for some of us to think of. Turn, then, and think about the houses where you live. How large a part of their influence upon you depends upon this principle of association. Of the walls of a house where much life has been lived, where many experiences have been passed through, might not one say exactly what Joshua said about the stone that he set up in Shechem, " They have heard all the words of the Lord which He spake unto you "? And indeed the parallel goes farther. The word which your household walls have heard from God, and which they are still constantly uttering to you if you can only hear it, is the same word which He had spoken in the presence of the old stone at Shechem, and of which that stone was a perpetual witness to the people. What was the witness of that stone ? It was the necessity and the blessing of obedience to God. That was what God had commanded. That was what the people had sworn. That was what the stone had heard and what it bore perpetual witness of afterward to those who passed it and heard with their consciences its silent voice; that not by his own will, but in subjection to a will far greater than his own, the Jew was to occupy this new land and to live the new life which was before him. And not merely this stone, but every monument which had drunk in his nation's history and stood to utter it perpetually, had the same tale to tell. The rock where Abraham had carried up his son and stood with the knife just ready to complete the dreadful sacrifice ; the stone at Bethel where Jacob vowed his vow of consecration ; the twelve stones that the Jews left piled in the bed of Jordan when they crossed dry-shod, — they all told the same story ; they all meant the same thing. It was that Jewish truth of covenant. Since God has done this for us we belong to Him, we hereby acknowledge His ownership and give ourselves to His service. In that truth all the land was steeped. And its utterance came from every rude monument which any Jew or all the Jewish people had set up to commemorate mercy and to proclaim dedication. Now think of any house which by long life of some family in it has become monumental. Its walls have other and far deeper values than these for which you or your fathers paid the architects and carpenters when it was first built. Those walls are steeped in truth, and each room speaks it in its own peculiar voice. What is that truth? Really the same old truth which was spoken from end to end of old Palestine, that house of Israel which had heard and kept so many of the words of God. The necessity and blessing of obedience. The old truth of covenant between man and God. It is not put in the hard old Jewish way as it speaks to you out of the walls of your Christian home. It is richened and deepened. It speaks as something essential and not arbitrary, something which could not be otherwise than as it is; but in its new form it is the same old truth, that man's life belongs to God, and that there is no true life for man except in God, and that man lives in God only by loving obedience. It may be that in the house where you are living is the room where you were born. That chamber must sometimes speak to you of the mere fact of your life; apart from all its circumstances, or rather gathering all its circumstances into the one great fact, the voice of God speaking to you from those walls within which your life began to be must say, "You are," "You live," in such a tone that the wondrousness of life, the blessedness of life, and the tie between all life and Him who is the ever-living and the all-creating one, must come out to you as if a voice that you could hear proclaimed them in your ears. Perhaps there is some room in your house where for the first time you faced the awful mystery of death, where for the first time you watched that slow, sure, gentle, irresistible untwisting of the golden cord and saw mortality fade into immortality before your very eyes. Can that room ever be silent to you again? There is where God gave you at once the keenest pain and the sublimest triumph over pain that the human heart can know. There He taught you at once the necessity and the blessedness of submission. Or perhaps there is some room where you yourself went up once and looked in silence into the very door of death. Some Hezekiah chamber where the message seemed to come to you that you must die, and where you prayed to God that you might live, and told Him how you would give the spared life all to Him. Or perhaps some solemn room where your new birth came to you, where you fought out the struggle of your soul's life, where at last you knew that you, risen as if from very death, had indeed begun to live not for yourself, but unto Him who died for you and rose again. The rooms where your children have been born. The room where you first found yourself rich, the room where you first found yourself poor, the room of your friendships, the room of your daily bread, all of these, and around them the whole house with its associations of quiet, uneventful, but most significant years. They have all "heard the voice of the Lord which He spake unto you;" and if you have ears to hear, they all "bear witness unto you lest you deny your God."

Remember that the more rich and full of experiences your life is, the more the house you live in and all its circumstances and accidents will grow rich. I do not wonder that there are some to whom all that I have been saying will seem unmeaning and absurd. No voices come out of their homes, because no genuine deep life is really lived within them. This surely is part of what is meant by the fickleness and transitoriness of our ordinary life. Men flee from one home to another, from one continent to another, from one occupation to another, not because anything drives them from the old, not because anything really valuable and intelligible draws them in the new, but because they have not lived deeply enough to make themselves associations, because they have felt nothing deeply and thought nothing deeply, enjoyed nothing intensely, suffered nothing very keenly in the old home or the old occupation, and so any morning they can pack up and be off with hardly a suspicion of a pang. Your life cannot be frivolous or vulgar unless you are frivolous or vulgar. He who complains of his circumstances really complains of himself and is his own accuser. He who tires of his house really tires of himself. The restlessness that comes of a divine desire presses deeper down into the rock on which it stands to find the springs of life. It keeps you where you are. The restlessness that comes of human thirst wanders over the surface of the earth, filling its dipper from every little pool caught in the hollows of the rocks. It sends you all abroad. One is sure that all increase of depth in life must bring a greater stability of life, fill our towns with more hereditary and ancestral homes, and give more sacredness to the whole character of a community.

I cannot help saying how the same thing is true of churches, and of the easy wandering from church to church of which we see so much. He who has lived deeply in any church connection, he whose church building and whose pew are bound up with the most profound experiences that man can ever undergo, may change his old church for a new, but if he does, it will be a solemn, thoughtful act done only under the certain stress of duty and true spiritual conviction. The church where he has repented and trusted and grown in grace, the church where he has met Christ, where he has known himself, will be his home, from which only some deepest change can separate him. It may come, for there are demands of duty to one's soul which cut through all associations and compel a man to leave the dearest things behind. But such a change from church to church as that is wholly different from the flippant and unmeaning changes which show, not so much what the new church may hope to do for the wanderer, as what the deserted church has failed to do.

It ought to be harder and harder for men to do wrong the older that they grow. For all around them ought to gather the restraining power of associations. The voice of the Lord ought to speak out

T

of more and more of the things about us, bearing a continual witness to us, lest we " deny our God." Remember that to deny our God is not to be what men call sceptical. It is not to blaspheme. It is simply to live as if there were no God, — no God to help us, no God to be responsible to, no God for us to trust and love. There is no man who does not know that danger, who does not feel it every day. In your schools, in your homes, in your stores, everywhere, the terrible danger of denying God! Against that danger God bears ever fresh and present witness of Himself in your hearts. Every morning His voice is new. Every evening His voice pursues you to your rest. But besides this direct continual presence, there is this other testimony of Himself which I have spoken of to-day. He fills the world of association with utterances of Himself. Oh, as we grow in life, the world ought to be becoming to us more and more full of monumental pictures of human nobleness, patience, self-sacrifice, courage, meekness, so that we shall be more and more sure that goodness and heroism are possible for man. It ought to be always more and more full of the recollection of times when we ourselves mounted to enthusiastic faith and earnest resolution and unselfish action, so that it shall be less and less possible for us to hide behind a low conception, a low expectation of ourselves. It ought to grow bright with more and more luminous points that never cease to burn with the memory of some certain experience of the deep, deep, dear love of God. These are the things which men are tempted to doubt and to deny, — that it is possible for men to be true and good, that each man is himself bound to goodness and truth, and that God loves us. Believe these really, believe these constantly, and it must be very hard to sin. Blessed is he whose life fills itself with monumental memories on which these truths are graven deep. For him the great wide open plain of life, where his wandering sight and steps seemed lost, narrows itself till he finds himself walking between the shining walls of righteousness along the certain road of duty. Less and less does he seek to wander. Duty, dear for itself and dear for the memories that hallow it, satisfies him and inspires him. The past is to him not burden, but wings; and when he comes to God at last, it is a whole lifetime rich with accumulated thankfulness that he lays down at the Saviour's feet.

And think how with the successive generations of mankind, each leaving countless new monuments of divine love and human possibility upon the earth, the earth itself is growing richer every year. Every year some new valley gets its consecration from some new soul's struggle with sin. Every year some new mountain-top burns with another soul's rapture of salvation. We read of the promise of the new heavens and the new earth wherein righteousness shall dwell. Are not the heavens and the earth ever growing new, newer, and more full of righteousness every day? When the time shall come that every star in heaven and every stone on earth shall be vocal with some word of God which it has heard, and in their midst shall live the race of men, no longer deaf and obstinate, but quick-eared to hear and loving-hearted to obey those words as they come crowding in, making the air sacred on every side — when that shall come — which the world's best pictures of Christian life now suggest and prophesy — shall not the promise then have been fulfilled, and the " New Heavens and the New Earth wherein dwelleth righteousness " be a sublime reality?

What is it possible for us to do? These two things, oh, my friends :

First, to hear every voice of God that speaks to us out of any consecrated bit of this old earth where men have lived so long, and to learn from them all these first truths of human life, that man can be very good and brave, that we ourselves are debtors to all our old resolutions and to the loftiest moments of our past, and that God loves us.

Second, to live such lives so true, so deep, so rich, so pure, that the world shall get new monuments by us, that in some little circle where we lived the result of our living, when the certain day comes and we pass on to other unseen fields of service, may be that some stone which our lives touched shall be a witness to the men and women whom we leave behind us, because it has heard the words of the Lord that He spake through our lives, that it may be a witness unto them to help them, to restrain them, to inspire them when they are tempted to deny their God.

Certainly every life to which blessings like these are given is a rich success.

XVI.

THE NEARNESS OF CHRIST.

"Howbeit, we know this man whence He is : but when Christ cometh, no man knoweth whence He is." — JOHN vii. 27.

VERY different and contradictory are the demands which men make of that to which they are moved to give their reverence and service. Most men ask of their religion that it shall be familiar, that it shall have to do with daily life, that it shall seem to issue from the heart of common things and clothe those things with a light which makes them radiant. They dread mystery. They hate to be bidden to lift up their eyes and to look far away. This verse out of the Gospel of St. John has just the other story. In it the men of Galilee are speaking and telling why Christ is not acceptable to them. He is too familiar. They knew him from His childhood. He has come out of a household which they have seen beside them all their lives. "We know this man, whence He is." All this seemed to make it incredible to them that He should be the Christ for whom their people have been waiting all these years. The fulfilment of a hundred prophecies, the answer to a million prayers, it could not be that when at last He came it should be thus. The sun had shone in glory, the mighty clouds had gathered, and the luxuriant rain poured down. They had stood and waited for a worthy issue of it all, and here came quietly, piercing through the sod which the sun had mellowed, a little flower which the rain had fed. Where was the chariot of the skies? Where was the awful mystery? It was all too simple, too familiar. "When Christ cometh no man knoweth whence He is. But we know this man whence He is. This cannot be the Christ!"

There is one distinction in the world's geography which comes immediately to our minds when we thus state the different thoughts and desires of men concerning their religion. We remember how the whole world is in general divided into two hemispheres upon this matter. One half of the world, the great dim East, is mystic. It insists upon not seeing anything too clearly. Make any one of the great ideas of life distinct and clear, and immediately it seems to the Oriental to be untrue. He has an instinct which tells him that the vastest thoughts are too vast for the human mind, and that if they are made to present themselves in forms of statement which the human mind can comprehend, their nature is violated and their strength is lost.

On the other hand, the Occidental, the man of the West, demands clearness and is impatient with mystery. He loves a definite statement as much as his brother of the East dislikes it. He insists on knowing what the eternal and infinite forces mean to his personal life, how they will make him personally happier and better, almost how they will build the house over his head, and cook the dinner on his hearth. This is the difference between the East and the West, between man on the banks of the Ganges and man on the banks of the Mississippi. Plenty of exceptions of course there are. Mystics in Boston and St. Louis. Hard-headed men of facts in Bombay and Calcutta. The two great dispositions cannot be shut off from one another by an ocean or a range of mountains. In some nations and places, as for instance among the Jews and in our own New England, they notably commingle. But in general they thus divide the world between them. The East lives in the moonlight of mystery, the West in the sunlight of scientific fact. The East cries out to the Eternal for vague impulses. The West seizes the present with light hands, and will not let it go till it has furnished it with reasonable, intelligible motives. Each misunderstands, distrusts, and in large degree despises the other. But the two hemispheres together, and not either one by itself, make up the total world.

But of course such geographical suggestions are most immediately interesting as they represent what reappears in every man. There is an east and a west in each of us. In one hemisphere of our being each of us is mystic and transcendental, and in the other hemisphere of our being each of us is limited and practical and concrete, demanding the tangible and clear. No man is destitute of either side. You think you have found the man in whom one side or the other is totally absent; but watch him long enough and some day the missing hemisphere catches a flash of light and shows that it is there, little as you dreamed of it, stoutly as he may have denied that it was there himself. The problem of every man's character and career is what the coming problem of the world's life evidently is, how these two halves, the east and the west, are to be proportioned and related to each other, and into what sort of union they may come to make something greater and more human than either of them is by itself. The foot set on one present spot of present earth, and the eye which ranges the world of stars, to see which way the foot should walk. Imagination which questions the remotest possibilities and prudence, which studies the immediate conditions. Hope which perishes if it defines itself, and Duty which must know the very thing which now needs to be done. It is the proportion and relationship of these in a man's life which mark what sort of a man he is. Every education of a man's life, every consciousness which a man has of himself, every religion which seeks to be a man's illumination, and leaves out either side of a man's nature, is partial and so false. The world's religions have failed, and are failing here to-day. They have been too much either mystic exaltations or hard methods of economy. Surely there is something better which they might be by being both. Such the complete religion must be when it is perfectly revealed.

The perfect religion which will do its work for the whole human nature — the coming of the Son of Man, which, as Jesus said, must be " as the lightning which cometh out of the east and shineth even unto the west " — will comprehend within itself all that the partial religions ever had of good. It will be no mere compromise. The base meetings of ideas or men are in the region of compromise. Their noble meetings are in the region of comprehension. Compromise leaves out the essence and strength of two truths and then makes a barren union of the colorless remainders. Comprehension unites the spiritual substance of both with a larger truth than either, and then lets the new unity create its new form with perfect freedom. One grows to believe in methods of compromise less and less, in methods of comprehension more and more. We talk of reconciling one truth with another. How impertinent it is! Who are we that we should thrust in our petty persons between Kings, and think that we can make them know each other? Who are we that we should dare to undertake to tell majestic truths what each of them must give up in order that the other shall not be offended? Such reconciliations by compromise always fail. No! let us give the great truths souls and lives large enough to meet in, and they will know each other without our help, and mingle as two kingly streams mingle their water in the sunshine to make the yet more royal river.

Here, then, are these two truths, both of them certainly true. One of them is that religion is sublime and far away, and outgoes our life. The other, that religion is familiar and close at hand. One is forever looking for the Son of Man coming in the clouds of Heaven. The other is always craving the presence of Jesus of Nazareth at the fireside of the home. Each truth demands assertion. Each grows restless when the other seems to be taking possession of the field and monopolizing Christianity.

When we ask after the comprehensive conception of religion which shall freely include both these truths, at once we recognize that before we can get hold of it we must first grasp more fully than we do the largeness, the many-sidedness, of the nature of man. Religion is for man. To discuss religion apart from man, as if it were a system of abstract truth, is futile. It is not a religious system, but a religious man, that we are after. Religion is a life, a nature, a being, not a system or a law. Therefore to understand religion you must understand man ; and to see how the great ultimate religion must freely comprehend both of the two truths which have claimed religious thought by turns, we must first take in the largeness of human nature wherein both of these thoughts are embodied, and which the great perfect religion, when it comes, must fully satisfy.

And now, of all the facts concerning man, none is more manifest than this, that in his nature are two elements, to his life there are two sides. One is familiar and domestic, the other is sublime and transcendental. Look at him! See how he deals both with the earth and with the heavens. With the earth which is his daily home. He treads upon its soil ; he delves into its bosom ; he plants his seed in it and eats the fruit that it produces ; he drinks of its streams ; he sails upon its oceans ; he builds his house upon its plains ; he trades in its wealth ; he flourishes or fails according to its changing fortunes ; and then, while he is walking on the earth, all the while his head is among the stars, and his sight goes far beyond them. His deeds are clear, definite, concrete, but his motives go out into regions where he cannot follow them. His principles, which come to the most commonplace applications, are themselves but reënactments of the foundations of the universe. The lightning strikes this special, hard, visible, tangible piece of timber, and sets it into flame. But the lightning was born in the mysterious bosom of a cloud which no eye can penetrate. The sunlight shines upon the tools of man's most ordinary task ; but the sun from which the sunlight comes is a deep world of fire which withers and flings back his gaze. Everywhere man is this double thing. The living which he makes is narrow, practical, prosaic. The life which he lives is a fragment of the life of God. Now he is busy with the multiplication table to count up his income or his rent ; and now he is on the summit of Sinai with Moses, taking the tables of the Eternal Law out of the hands of God.

I do not say that these two elements of his nature, these two sides of his life, stand wholly separate from one another, as they appear when I thus describe them. It is not so. They are in closest connection. The familiar task is always being elevated and enlarged by the greatness of the infinite principle. And the infinite principle is always being concentrated and embodied in the familiar task. The dream and the duty, the prayer and the bargain, are always claiming each other as portions of the one same life. But do you not know how they still are two, and how strangely they divide your human life between them?

It is one of the first results of this fact concerning man, that he is to himself at once intelligible and mysterious, mysterious and intelligible. "As unknown and yet well known," said St. Paul about himself; and he might have said it about any man. Do you not know what I mean? Are there not moments in your life when it seems as if you understood and knew yourself through and through? You have listened to this clank of your machinery so long, that you know every sound it makes. You have handled it and watched it, and are entirely familiar with the way in which every shaft of habit moves, and how each toothed wheel fits into the next toothed wheel, and what you did yesterday gave birth to what you are doing to-day, and will have its grandchild in what you are to do to-morrow. And just then, when everything seemed perfectly transparent, has the distance never opened round you, and deepened and deepened till you felt that if there was anything which you did not know, it was yourself — this self which had to do with the ends of the universe and the eternity behind you and the eternity before? "Know myself!" You say, "Indeed I do," grasping your own warm, hard flesh. " Am I not this, which lives thus? Why should I think myself mysterious?" And then instantly, " Know myself! God forbid! Who am I that I should enter into the bosom of the Eternal purpose, and study there what only there has real and final being? Let me stand in awe before my unknown self and wonder." Poor and mangled is the life which has not thus seemed both to understand and to be ignorant about itself. It must be either useless or visionless.

And now, to come at last to the point for which all this long study has been undertaken. This nature of man decrees the necessary nature of his religion. Here is man, familiar and mysterious, known and unknown to himself and to his brethren. What must the Christ be who shall be that man's Saviour? Must He not come to man in both parts of his double life? Must He not speak to man here, where all is definite and plain, here by his work-bench and his fireside; here where man needs a brother's sympathy; here where duty must be just as clear as daylight; here where man must know whether he is doing right or wrong by unmistakable words of rebuke or praise spoken directly in his listening ear? And then, no less, is it not true that in the farthest depths of his own mystery to which he can go, man still must find Christ waiting and hear Christ speak? Out of the heart of the unknown must come the Christ he knows so well, saying, "I am here too." He who is Son of Man must be also Son of God.

It is not possible to lose either of those hemispheres of His power and not lose Christ. Lose one, and He is a vague wind haunting the universe, disturbing, not directing, us. Lose the other, and He is a prudent counsellor who has nothing to say to our highest aspirations, and no answer to our deepest questions. Keep both, and He is the whole Christ, the Alpha and Omega, so enfolding and outgoing any possible reach of our existence, that we dare go forth to our farthest possibility, sure that we shall find Him there, and dare come in to our most familiar domesticity, sure that there, too, He will be present with His sympathy, His understanding, and His help.

I read the Gospels, and this Christ is there. Who is this that feeds the hungry crowd at the lakeside, and that same night comes walking on the water to His frightened followers? Nay, who in the very feeding of the crowd is close to their human hunger on one side, and close to the heart and power of God upon the other? Did any soul come near Him and not hear at once the voice of the brother Jew and the voice of the celestial wisdom in the tones, so intimate and yet so strange, which fell upon his ear?

I open the story of the Christian Church, and there too is this Christ. He is the rule of life and the infinite satisfaction of the soul through all the Christian ages. When the Church has allowed Him or bidden Him to be only the one or only the other, she has lost His power. Both periods there have been in her history. Sometimes she has made her Christ a beautiful, impracticable vision. Sometimes she has harnessed Him to human machineries, and made Him almost a drudge; but always He has claimed the fulness of his Saviourship, and been, in spite of her, at once the known and unknown, the familiar friend and the transcendent inspiration of the Church's life. May the Christ of the Gospels and the Christ of the Church be our Christ, my friends, our whole Christ, in all the fulness of His Christhood!

I have spoken thus of the double presentation of the Christian faith, and we have seen how the result is that dangers present themselves on either side. It is the danger upon one side only which our text records, and of that I would now speak exclusively in the remainder of my sermon. The Jews complained of Jesus that He was too familiar, that there was too little of distance and mystery about Him. "We know this man whence He is." Is not our first thought about their complaint this: that it shows how little in earnest they were? If they had really been in earnest, the nearer they could have got to Christ, the closer they could have brought Him to themselves, the more familiar He could have seemed, the more they would have rejoiced. While your faith is a subject of speculation, or an object of personal pride, you are ready enough to throne it in some far-off splendor, and drape the curtains of darkness around it where it sits; but when the time comes that you need it, that you must have it or you will die, then you cry out for it to come down from its high seat and be close to your aching want, and open to you the very secrets of its inmost being.

Oh, what a history is here of the experience of many souls! They were jealous for the divinity of Christ. In asserting His divinity they would separate Him from the sordidness and turmoil of our commonplace existence. They would make Him different in sort from us. They would deny that we could know Him by what we found in ourselves. And then some day there came the stress and strain. The commonplace became transfigured and became tragical. The ordinary human incidents — birth, death, success, failure, love, hate, aye food, and drink, and poverty, and wealth — were things of spiritual criticalness. And then their Christ could no longer sit upon a distant throne. The mystery must open; we must have Him here and now. The Son of God must be the Son of Man. We must know by our own hearts what He is. His pity, and patience, and indignation, and delight in faithfulness, whether it succeed or fail, must be revealed to us by these same powers, as they feebly display themselves in us. We will not drag Him down, but our whole life mounts up and claims Him. It is worthy of a God, and so the God enters into it; and lo ! we know Him whence He is. He ceases not to be God, but He is Man, all the more human because of His divinity.

This is the revelation, and the light, and the change which has come to countless souls. When they intensely needed a Christ whom they could know, then the Christ whom they had thought it reverence not to pretend to know, revealed Himself and claimed their knowledge. The great difference in men's theology is this: To one man, theology is totally different from life; to another man, theology is the culmination and fulfilment of life. To one man, Deity hovers over humanity as a foreign heaven, made of other substance, unintelligible by any sympathy of common being; to another man, Deity underlies humanity as the earth underlies the countless trees which grow out of its bosom, bearing witness of what it is, making its silent qualities vocal in the chorus of their shooting branches and whispering leaves. Great, infinitely precious, is the hour when that revelation comes to a young man's soul. Sometimes in sunny stillness, creeping on with the bright growth of gradual life. Sometimes with a sudden tempest, smiting the clouds asunder and letting the broad light pour in. Come how it will, the hour when a young man knows that Christ wants to be known of him, that all his life is full of revelation of Christ if he can hear it, that hour is the hour of his new birth, henceforth there is no common or unclean for him — Christ is glorious in everything, and everything is glorious in Christ.

Such an illumination of a man's Christianity, of his whole thought of Christ, when it has once come, runs everywhere ; it sends its power through all he does and is. The close association of Christ with human life does not degrade Christ, but exalts human life, because Christ is stronger than life and dominates it. See one or two places in which this is true.

Sometimes we shrink from recognizing that Christ is the Saviour of society. It seems to make Christianity a mere police force if we say that men live more peaceably with one another, and are more thrifty, and more independent, and more helpful to each other where the Christian Church is thriving and the Christian Gospel is earnestly preached and thoroughly believed. But surely such a feeling as that must come from too base an estimate of the value of a community and of its best life. If society is sacred, if the living together of a group of God's children on God's earth has infinite meaning and infinite issues, then that Christ, the power and wisdom of God, should be power and wisdom in society is not strange. It would be strange and dreadful if He did not come to it and purify and elevate all its life. When the people of Nazareth said, " He cannot be the Christ, for He is one of us. His brothers and sisters, are they not here with us?" it was not Christ, but Nazareth and brotherhood and sisterhood, that they were dishonoring. If they could have seen how essentially sacred those things were, then Christ would have been all the more Christ because of His sympathy in their sacredness.

And so of your own personal life. You say, in some moods, " What can Christ care for my temptations and my struggles? I should think less of Him if He did care for them. Let the great Master lead the army and lay out the broad campaign, but it is not work of His to be going up and down among the tents seeing how it fares with the sick soldiers, strengthening the cowards, and comforting the lonely hearts." But then, perhaps, the fact becomes indisputably manifest to you that He does do just that. And the fact that He does do it brings you revelation. You see what a soul is. What the peril of a soul is in the light of Christ's strange watchfulness for it. And when you have once seen that, then the watchfulness is strange no longer. The Cross on which Christ dies for man shows man that man is worth dying for. So the Cross makes itself credible, and bows the sceptic, proud and yet humble, at its foot.

And even of things less critical than struggles and

temptations, if, indeed, there be anything in which struggle and temptation are not consciously or unconsciously included. Does it disturb your thought of Christ when you ask yourself to consider whether he cares how your house stands, how your table is spread, how your trade prospers, whether you get or miss the learning which you aim at, whether you gain or lose the game you play? Ah, is not the story of Christ feeding the hungry people at Gennesaret a true part of the Christian Gospel? Could you tear it out of the New Testament, and have the whole Gospel still? Does it disturb and lessen? Does it not confirm and enlarge the truth of Christ to you as you read it between the death of John the Baptist and the sermon to the Pharisees? "He was known to them in the breaking of bread." Remember that. You must know what you, the whole of you, are to Christ, the whole of Him. And then it will be clear how even your comfort and your joy concern Him — how He will care for them, ready still to call for their sacrifice if higher things demand, but showing you His Christhood in one of its most precious sides as He sympathizes with those interests which make so large a portion of His brethren's lives.

Even in the great question of the soul's forgiveness for its sins, does there not sometimes come misgiving? Does it not sometimes seem as if men thought that God would be greater and more awful if He did not stoop to forgive? Who are we that He should care for us? What is it whether we enjoy or suffer, that the Infinite Goodness and Happiness should go out of its way to save us from the consequence of our iniquity? The heathen deity who sits sublime and watches while things take their resistless course, Nature pitiless in all her bounty, these sometimes seem the types of grandeur, and all that is different from them has a touch of weakness in it. Then comes Christ with His revelation to the heart which listens and is convinced. "Lo!" He says, "God does care for man, and is most God when He cares most tenderly. Lo! pity is not weakness: it is strength." IIe lets us see the purpose of forgiveness, which is not release from punishment and pain, but entrance into life, and shows us how well worth forgiving man is, by showing us what man forgiven may become.

Thus everywhere Christ comes to man's commonest and most familiar needs, and there, in them, bears witness of His power. How shall that make us think of Him? Shall it make Him seem less than God's anointed? "As for this man, we know whence He is; but when Christ cometh, no man knoweth." That will depend, as I think that we have seen, on how man seems to us. If he is mysterious in his very nature, then the mystery of the Christ is not lost in the Christ's entrance on man's homeliest estate. Did those Jews know of Jesus, as they said they did, "whence He was"? Ought not His birth and life among them to have so revealed to them the essential wonder of birth and life that they should have willingly accepted His and stood in awe before their own? Is not this the whole lesson of the In-carnation, that when man is himself God can dwell in him?

If you knew the hand which fed the child Shakespeare, would you not honor it? Would you not know that to have been allowed to minister to the humblest wants of that sublime nature was a privilege which king or queen need not refuse? It was to help to make possible Hamlet and Macbeth; and the real wonder of Shakespeare was not that he was Shakespeare, but that he was man. Be sure that you mount up to Christ by gaining His view of yourself, and that you do not drag Him down to yourself by your selfishness, and then you may freely claim Him in your commonest life, and bid Him do, and honor Him for doing, the work which He craves and delights in when He says, "I am among you as He that serveth."

I know full well how all this doctrine may appear, how it has often appeared, to many men; how it has seemed as if we made for ourselves a Christ out of our own necessities, and said, "He must be this, because this is what I need." People have said, "Ah, you believe in Christ because you want to. He comes not out of the certainty of demonstrated truth, but out of your own fancies concerning your own wants. You think you must have Him, and so you bid Him be." I know the delusion which those words expose, and yet I gladly accept the account which those words give of at least one of the ways in which Christ comes to the soul. It is because the soul needs Him that it finds Him. There is no revelation from the sky which could bring Him to our knowledge if the heart with conscious want did not demand the very salvation which He brings. I will be studiously on my guard not to mistake the cravings of my nature for the voice of the coming Christ, but I will not silence those cravings of my nature when they welcome the coming Christ, — I will bid them speak, I will listen for God's answer to them, and when Christ does come it shall make the witness of His coming perfectly conclusive and complete that it is not merely in the clouds of heaven, but through the worn and torn avenues of my conscious human necessities, that He comes.

Has He come so to you, my friend? Do you believe in Jesus Christ to-day, not simply because of the great splendid evidences which all the world can read, not merely because of the trumpet-voice of Christian history and the convincing splendor of the life of miracle, but because of the witness which He has borne to your own soul in His answer to your soul's own needs? Do you believe in Him because when you wanted comfort He comforted you, and when you wanted wisdom He enlightened you, and when you were a coward He made you brave, and when you were weak He made you strong? Do not distrust that evidence. It is good proof. When Christ comes out of Nazareth it is not Christ that is dishonored, but Nazareth that is glorified. Let your whole nature glow and burn with the mysterious capacity which it has shown to need and long for Christ, and then accept Christ because, first having made your nature fit to long for Him, He has then rejoiced to satisfy your nature with Himself.

Other truths about Christ there are which we will preach on other days. I have tried to preach this truth to-day, that no familiarity of religion, no presentation of it as a regulative force, no offer by Christ of Himself as the friend of daily life, must seem to us to depreciate the power of our salvation or make it appear to us other than the touch of God. There will come to you hours of great exaltation; you will go up to mountain-tops of vision. The Divine Voice will speak to you out of the sun and out of the cloud. Those will come in their time as it is best. But let no experience and no expectation of them make you careless or distrustful when out of commonest things, out of daily tasks, and daily difficulties, and daily joys, and the simplest needs of your nature, and the most domestic familiarities of life, God speaks to you and offers you His Son. Know His voice so truly that you cannot mistake it from whatever unexpected quarter it may speak. Watch for the Divine Light so anxiously that you may never say that it is not divine from whatever humblest quarter it may shine.

XVII.

PRAYER.

"If ye abide in Me, and My words abide in you, ye shall ask
what ye will, and it shall be done unto you." — JOHN xv. 7.

In one shape or another the religious question
which gives thoughtful, religious people the most
trouble is probably the question of Prayer. We
cannot doubt that it has always been so. We feel
sure that in every condition of religion, down to the
lowest, in which men are moved to supplicate God
at all, the struggle between the two feelings, between the instinct that God must hear and answer,
and the doubt whether God can hear and answer, has
been always going on. It is not a struggle of our
days alone ; it is not a question which certain peculiar tendencies of our time have brought out. It is
as old as David; nay, as old as Job, as old as all
religion.

Is it possible for the great First Cause to lay Himself open to appeals which originate in human wills,
and so to yield to causes behind Himself in governing
his action? You see our very jealousness for God's
honor comes and lays itself across the path by which
our timid souls are creeping to His mercy-seat. The
very greatness which tempts us to trust Him seems to
forbid us to ask Him. Is prayer, then, all a delusion?
Is it a mere arrangement for a soul's own discipline,

incapable of influence upon the action of God? Is there a possible reality about it? We cannot help feeling that in trying to give answers to these questions, Christians too often bewilder their minds with hopeless speculations, instead of going to Christ and seeing just what He has said about this hard subject of prayer. Let us take up one verse of His this afternoon, and see how clearly He deals with the whole difficulty, how exactly He tells us what we want to know.

Christians, who long to pray, but sometimes almost fear to; who are distressed by doubting just how far prayer may go, just how confidently it is to expect its answer; around whose closets natural law and the majesty of the Almighty seem to gather with an oppressiveness that almost stifles the half-formed petitions, — let us come to Jesus and beg as the Disciples did, "Lord, teach us to pray," and see what He means when He tells us in reply, "If ye abide in me, and my words abide in you, ye shall ask what ye will, and it shall be done."

"If ye abide in me." What is it to abide in Christ? That is the first question in settling the qualities of him who can hope to pray successfully. The phrase becomes familiar to us in the New Testament; and indeed we might find a parallel that would explain it to us in several of the different kinds of relation that exist between human beings. For instance, we should all understand, I think, what was meant if it were said of a young and dutiful child that he abode or lived in his parents. The child's earliest years are so completely hidden behind the parents' life that you do not look upon him altogether as a separate individuality, but rather as almost a part of the same organism, one expression of the parents' nature ; so that, just as the arm, the tongue, the eye, are several media for the expression of the parents' will, in the same way, though in a higher degree, the child is another limb of the parental life and utterance of the parental nature. The law owns this, and reaches the child only through the parent. We all expect children's opinions on matters of religion, of politics, of taste, to be echoes of their parents'. The father acts and thinks for the child. The child acts and thinks in the father. Thus, until the time when the gradual departure takes place, the child's home is not merely in his father's house, but in his father's character, — he abides in him.

Or take another case : the army and the common soldier " abide in " the general. The army does what its general does. As an army, it has no thought or action out of him. It moves when he moves, stops moving when he stops moving. We say the general has gone here and there, and we mean the army has gone. It lays aside all faculty of decision, or rather contributes it all to him, and he with the combined responsibility of the great multitude upon him goes his way, carrying their life in his. There is perhaps the most complete and absolute identification of two lives which it is possible to conceive of.

Now, we can get probably a better idea from these examples than we could from any careful definitions of what it is for a human soul to "abide in Christ." The child abides in the father; the soldier abides in the general. For the soul to abide in Christ, then, is for it to be to Him what the child is to the father, what the soldier is to his captain. It is for it to give up its will to His as completely as the surrenders of will are made in the family and in the army. Nay, the "giving up of will" does not entirely express it, because that implies something like reluctance and resistance. But the child has no will except the father; and the soldier's will is so entirely at one with his captain's upon the great general purpose of the war, which is victory, that he rejoices to accept that captain's will in all details and make it his own. Christ is at once our Father and our Captain. Perfect affection and perfect loyalty combine to shape our attitude towards Him; and the result of the two is that complete identification of our life with His life by which we "abide in Him."

Jesus Himself uses another figure for the same idea: "The Branch cannot bear fruit of itself except it abide in the vine." There is the same identification of life, the same complete dependence, and the same transferrence of responsibility.

In this truth of the Believer's "abiding in Christ" there are two notions involved, — of Permanence and of Repose. It is not a mere temporary harmony of the human nature with the divine. Not a mere glancing of the Christ-life upon the man-life in some of its higher and more spiritual promontories, but it is an assured, final entrance of the human into the divine. It is the entire abandonment and destruction of man's old homes to take up with and settle down in new. The man who abides in Christ stands on the heights of his new life, and strains his sight forward into eternity, and sees but one will, which is both his and Christ's, which is his reconciled to and swallowed up in Christ's, flowing straight on, beyond his sight, towards the Endless End. Its permanence comes from the fact that it is a new life, an entire change; the soul's deliberate removal from the kingdom of earth into the Kingdom of Heaven, before his entrance upon which a man "must be born again."

With this permanence comes Repose, Rest, an internal harmony with a man's self, answering to the external harmony with Christ, that freedom of the spiritual nature for its best activity, which Christ calls " His Peace." There is a new tranquillity which is not stagnation, but assurance, when a life thus enters into Christ. It is like the hushing of a million babbling, chattering mountain streams as they approach the sea and fill themselves with its deep purposes. It is like the steadying of a lost bird's quivering wings when it at last sees the nest and quiets itself with the certainty of reaching it, and settles smoothly down on level pinions to sweep unswervingly towards it. It is like these to see the calm of a restless soul that discovers Christ and rests its tired wings upon the atmosphere of His truth, and so abides in Him as it goes on towards Him.

It is strange how such a truth, deeply realized, purifies religion, how it clears out of the way with quiet, unnoticed evaporation, removing them, not as the wind removes clouds, but as the sun removes them,—all the morbid and perplexing questions that have blinded the spiritual sight. To the soul that does not "abide in Christ" Christianity seems either a very heartless system on the part of God or a very selfish system on the part of man. The Gospel is to be obeyed. Why? Is it that Christ may be glorified? That is very heartless in God, man says, to shape this hard law of life only for His and His Son's glory. Is it that the obeyer's soul may be saved? That is a very low and selfish motive for the Christian, — just to get out of the region of unhappiness, just to get into the realm of joy. But "enter into Christ" and the difficulty is gone. We are no longer servilely and blindly doing His unknown commandments, nor mercenarily seeking our own good. The two natures are harmonized; our wills unite. We want the world converted, and sin cast out, and the Kingdom of Holiness set up. He is glorified when our souls are saved. The salvation of our souls is in glorifying Him. All is changed when we are made the confidants and sharers as well as the mere agents of His purposes. This is the transfer, the advance which He Himself describes a few verses later in the chapter, when He says, " Henceforth I call you not servants ; for the servant knoweth not what his Lord doeth: but I have called you Friends; for all things which I have received of my Father I have made known unto you." This is what is meant by " If ye abide in me."

And "If my words abide in you." This is the second condition of the successful prayer. The keeping for continual and instinctive reference of the definite, explicit teachings and commands of Christ. We can see, I think, why this second condition must necessarily be added to the first. That first relation, — the abiding of the soul in Christ,—if it were perfect, would be enough. An entire sympathy between you and the Lord would make it impossible for you to do anything but just what was the Lord's will. But that first relation, that sympathy is not complete; it is very imperfect and unreliable here. Therefore God cannot trust to man's oneness with Him to ensure man's always unerringly discovering His will. He must make some positive and definite announcement of it. He must give him not merely His own spirit, but His own words. The soul's abiding in Jesus will make him ready to accept Jesus' words, and then the words will come to lead the soul into a deeper and deeper abiding-place in its Saviour. This gives us the true place of the Bible, its true relation to the more immediate communion of the human soul with God's, where no printed book or spoken word intrudes. And this is perfectly carried out into the two illustrations that we used. The father trusts his child and the captain trusts his soldier, in virtue of the identification of their lives, to do his will entirely; but it is by reason of the imperfect sympathy which hinders the inferior from perfectly apprehending the superior's will that the father and the captain must have codes of government and issue orders of the day for their subordinates.

The Bible is a temporary expedient; the oneness of the soul with God is an essential and eternal necessity. The one we may outgrow, the other we can never do without. In Heaven we shall need no Bibles. Who will be patient to look down upon a page and read that God is Love, when the Eternal Love is burning there upon the throne, and our full eyes may look into His depths unhindered? Who will want to read the faithfulness of Jesus when the "Faithful and True," with feet of brass and holding the stars in His unchanging hands, stands there before us in the midst of the candlesticks? We hold our Bible tightly, full of the precious words of God; but who does not hold them, ready to let them go when the great " Word " Himself shall take us perfectly into His sympathy to abide in Him forever?

But now, for the present, we hold them. We must not merely abide in Him, but have His words abide in us. I will tell you how this last clause seems to me. There seems to be a sort of faintly sketched picture of a solemn council-room in the heart of the true Christian, around which sit in beautiful and holy chairs the judges of our lives, — the words of Jesus. Every act that the true Christian does he compels to pass upon its way from conception to execution through that council-room, and every word of Jesus sitting in its place must give its sanction to every act. No deed must go forth that cannot carry the approval of every utterance of Him to whom the Christian has given up his will. We do not trust even our personal feelings for our master as a final test. So long as we have His words, telling us what we must do and what we must not do, we fear the distortions of feeling that we know too well, and rejoice in that judgment-room within us where the words of Christ are throned.

You see, then, what is added when we are told that we must not only abide in Christ, but also have His words abide in us. We are to keep them as test-words to try our lives by, and see how deeply we abide in Him. "If ye love me, keep my commandments." Is not that Christ's own summary of the two conditions? He in whom they are both fulfilled is the full and symmetrical Christian, keeping affection always true by obedience, and obedience always fresh and glowing with sympathetic love. This is to abide in Christ, and to have His words abide in us.

And now what have we reached? It is this full and symmetrical Christian, — the perfect man in Christ, — of whom Christ says that he "shall ask what he will and it shall be done unto him." Does it seem strange, the large, unconditional promise? The simple question is, "What will this regenerated man, this child in perfect sympathy with his father, this Christian abiding in Christ, — what will he ask of God? Evidently he will ask, he can ask, nothing but Christly things in Christly ways. His will has become an echo of the will of Christ. What can he desire that Christ does not desire? Try to put upon his lips a prayer that God would not grant, — a prayer of presumption, or uncharitableness, or self-indulgence, and it drops off. It will not stay upon, it will not go up to heaven from, lips like those. He cannot pray it so long as he abides in Christ. He must go outside of his abiding-place ; he must separate his will from his Lord's, before his mind can

·shape or his mouth utter an unchristian prayer. True, the most earnest Christian may err about the will of God. He may pray for sunshine when it is the will of God that it should rain. He may ask for comfort when it is God's will that he should suffer. But this can only come in superficial things. In the one central thing of all — his own spiritual life — he cannot err. He knows that "this is the will of God, even his sanctification." He may cry out for that with perfect certainty; and for all other things, if he prays as every Christian ought, submitting his prayer to God's revision, "Nevertheless, not my will but Thine be done;" then, whether the special blessing that he asked is sent or not, the larger petition with which he covered in and included his lesser one is surely answered. The thing he really "willed" is "done unto him."

Or take the other condition. Can he in whom the words of Christ abide pray an unanswered prayer? God leaves unanswered among earnest prayers only those which His own character and plans make it impossible for Him to answer. And can the soul that tests every petition by the Bible pray any such prayers as those? Can he in whom this word of Christ abides — "Seek ye first the Kingdom of God and His righteousness" — go on clamoring with miserable mercenary prayers for houses and lands, for food and drink, as if they were the first things to seek? Can he in whom this word of Christ abides — "I say unto you, love your enemies" — torture his lips into uncharitable and malignant petitions, beseeching God for vengeance on his foes? Or he in whom this everlasting word of Christ abides, — " In the world ye shall have tribulations," — can you conceive of him as vexing God with querulous supplications to be released from suffering, and not delighting God with holy petitions that he may be brave and patient under it, that he may be purified and made perfect by it? Oh, my dear friends, how many of our prayers must go unprayed, if we sent them up to the mercy-seat through that judgment-chamber where the words of Jesus sit! How many times we have complained that our prayer brought no answer, when it was a prayer we never could have prayed unless we first drove out every word of Christ from its abiding-place within us! Is there a Christian here who can declare before God that he ever prayed to God in perfect submission to Christ's will, in perfect conformity to Christ's words, and got no answer? Not here; not in all the world; not in all the ages!

This is the meaning of Christ's promise: The true Christian must always have an answer to his prayer, because he can never pray a prayer incapable of answer. Does it sound like a mere truism? Is it an insignificant conclusion that we have reached? Does it amount to nothing to say that Christ will grant all good men's prayers because they cannot ask anything that He is not willing and anxious to grant already? Surely there is no weakening of the thought of prayer in this. How would you strengthen it? Would you say that the good man may ask of God things that He is unwilling to bestow, and gain them? But why is God unwilling to bestow them except for one of two causes: either that the giving of them would injure the soul that asks them, or that it would interfere with some plan that the divine wisdom has shaped for the universe at large? In either case can you conceive of a true and filial prayer demanding the unwilling boon? Grant that the Christian has the power, will he use it? Must he not in using it depart out of that harmony with Christ which is the very condition of his success, cease to abide in Him, and so fail of the dangerous gift that he desires?

You see it all when you look at a child asking a father for some benefit. Prayer is no fiction between those eager lips that beg and those other gracious lips that cordially bestow the boon. There is no sham in that petition. The whole scene is purely, beautifully real. The blessing really comes in answer to the prayer. But it is not necessary that the idea of a conquered reluctance should come in. The father wants to give as much as the child wants to receive. The child, if he be truly dutiful and intelligent, will desire to receive nothing that the father does not want to give. It will be only as he abides in his father, and his father's words abide in him, that he will expect that he can ask what he will, and it shall be given unto him.

This is imperfect. Take the perfect scene of prayer, the Son of God praying to His Father: was there a conflict of wills? Was there a conquering of reluctance? Nay, that is carefully excluded. Although the Son abides perfectly in the Father, so that He and His Father are one, and therefore He

surely may ask what He will, " and it shall be done,"
yet the very chance of His will conflicting with the
Father's will is anticipated, and the superiority of the
Father's will provided for. " Not my will but thine be
done." In the desert, on the mountain, by the table,
wherever He prayed, there was the picture of the perfect prayer. Towards the condition of the praying
Christ all our prayers strive, and are to be measured by
the nearness with which they approach that union of
perfect sympathy with God and perfect submission to
God with which He laid hold of the divine willingness to help.

The result of our whole study of Prayer to-day
seems to be this, that it involves far more than we
ordinarily think, — a certain necessary relation between the soul and God. The condition of prayer is
personal; it looks to character. How this rebukes our
ordinary slipshod notions of what it is to pray ! God's
mercy-seat is no mere stall set by the vulgar roadside,
where every careless passer-by may put an easy hand
out to snatch any glittering blessing that catches
his eye. It stands in the holiest of holies. We can
come to it only through veils and by altars of puri-
fication. To enter into it, we must enter into God.

O my dear friends, there is not one of us that can
live without praying. We all know that. But praying is not " saying our prayers," not shuffling through
a few petitions morning and evening, nor clamoring
with imperious voices before God's presence, setting
up our own will, however earnestly and vehemently,
against His. " Lord teach us to pray," we ask : and
the first answer is, " If ye abide in me and my

words abide in you," then ye shall pray successfully. We must be Christians first. We must enter into the new life, and, once there, Prayer will grow wonderfully easy; as easy to pray on earth, "Lord Jesus, have mercy upon me," as it will be to praise in heaven, "Thou art worthy, O Lord, for thou hast redeemed us."

XVIII.

THE ETERNAL HUMANITY.

"I am Alpha and Omega, the Beginning and the End the First and the Last." — REV. xxii. 13.

WITH all the other deficiencies in our ordinary Christianity, every earnest Christian thinker is continually thrown back to feel that its fundamental defect is an imperfect knowledge of its great head and centre, Christ. Christ is Christianity. He does not merely teach, He is the religion which we hold. To know it, we must know Him. He is not merely the revealer, but the truth. Hence comes the high ambition to know more of the Saviour in order that our share of the salvation may be more complete. Who is He? What is there in Him that fits Him for His work? When did His work begin? By what continual power does it go on? The New Testament comes in answer to these questions to tell us all that we may know of Christ. This verse from the Revelation of St. John may help us to much knowledge of Him, and I invite you as Christians, this afternoon, to a short study of the truths which it contains.

For the verse comprises Christ's declaration of Himself. He asserts His own eternity. He is the beginning of all things and the end of all things, — an eternity of the past, an eternity of the future. His power for man resides in these, His two eternities, each of which, His life as Alpha and His life as Omega, has its peculiar benefits for us.

And remember, at the very outset, what such a declaration must include. Christ says, "I am Eternal." Now, that must mean not merely that He has existed and shall exist forever, but also that in the forevers of the past and the future He is eternally Christ; that the special nature in which He relates Himself to us as Saviour never had a beginning and shall never have an end. Now, what is that special nature?— Christ! The word includes to our thought such a Divinity as involves the human element. Christ is the Divinely human, the humanly Divine. It is the Deity endowed with a peculiar human sympathy, showing by a genuine brotherhood the experience of man. That is to say, there are two words: God and Man. One describes pure deity, the other pure humanity. Christ is a word not identical with either, but including both. It is the Deity in which the Humanity has part; it is the Humanity in which the Deity resides. It is that special mediatorial nature which has its own double wearing of both, the ability to stand between and reconcile the separated manhood and divinity.

Keep this in mind, and then see what it will mean when we are told that this Christ nature, this divine human, has existed forever. Are we not in the habit of talking as if the redemption which called for an anointed Redeemer were a late thought in the universal history. Untold ages after the dateless time when God began to be, His almighty word was spoken, and a new world with a new race to live on it shaped itself out from the void. In that new world a new experiment of moral life brought a catastrophe unknown before, to meet whose terrible demands the great Creator came Himself and took the nature of this last creature living in His last creation. God was made man, and Christ the God-man was made manifest before the worlds. Here we make man, you see, a late thing in the history of the universe; and how is it possible, then, that Christ, who is God with the element of human sympathy, should be eternal? And just here, as it seems to me, there comes in one of the key-passages of the Bible, which we are always far too apt to overlook. It is that verse in Genesis: " In the image of God created He man." God made man like Himself. Ages before the incarnation made God so wonderfully in the image of man, the creation had made man in the image of God.

Now, if we can comprehend that truth at all, it must be evident that before man was made the man-type existed in God. In some part of His perfect nature there was the image of what the new creation was to be. Already, before man trod the garden in the high glory of his new Godlikeness, the pattern of the thing he was to be existed in the nature of Him who was to make him. Before the clay was fashioned and the breath was given, this humanity existed in the Divinity; already there was a union of the Divine and human ; and thus already there was the eternal Christ.

Stop here one minute, and see how this exalts the human nature that we wear. In the midst of the eternity of God, there bursts forth into being the new life of man. What shall we say of it? Is it just a creature of the moment which witnesses its birth? Is it just another of the world's ephemera, with a little longer span of life than some of its tinier brethren? Is it a new type of being made to be born and die? What if this other truth be true? What if the type of this life I live were part and parcel of the everlasting Godhead? What if it be the peculiar glory of one of the persons of that Godhead that He has worn forever, bound with His perfect deity, the perfect archetype and pattern of this humanity of mine? What if there be a Christ who is the Alpha, the beginning of all things; who only brought out into exhibition when He came in human flesh that genuine human brotherhood which had been in him forever? At once is not my insignificance redeemed? Every power in me grows dignified and worthy, catching some of the importance of the eternal type it represents. My love, — poor, feeble, grovelling thing, that licks the dust and twines itself round rubbish, — lo, it is one with, it is capable of being like, the perfect affection with which from all eternity the holy Christ has loved all holy things! My indignation, that blazes its strength away in all sorts of impotent furies, has a sublime identity with the sacred wrath which burns in Christ's bosom when He looks at sin. My hope is the dimmed copy of His power of eternal prophecy. I go through my nature, and I trace out in these blurred and dimmed lines the copies whose originals are all in Him. Here is the tragedy of human life, dear friends. When the

swine wallows in his mire, or the butterfly trifles his
sunny life away, it is a base or little nature given up
to base or little ends.   When you or I live the lives
of brutes or butterflies we are taking that man-
nature which is eternal, whose image and plan was
a part of Godhead through all the infinite forever of
the past; we are taking that man-nature which
copies on earth the uncreated life of Christ in Heaven,
nay, (shall we say it?) we are taking Christ and
making Him contemptible with the drunkenness of
low debauchery, or setting Him in the idle whirl and
meaningless waste of fashionable folly.   Oh, with
what shame and reverence we should carry through
the world this human nature if we really knew that
it did not begin to be with Adam, but existed forever in the eternal Christ!

I hold, then, that the Incarnation was God's commentary on that verse in Genesis, " In the image
of God created He man."   Yes, " from the beginning " there had been a second person in the Trinity,
— a Christ, whose nature included the man-type.   In
due time this man-type was copied and incorporated
in the special exhibition of a race.   There it degen-
erated and went off into sin.   And then the Christ,
who had been what He was forever, came and brought
the pattern and set it down beside the degenerate
copy, and wrought men's hearts to shame and penitence when they saw the everlasting type of what
they had been meant to be, walking among the miserable shows of what they were.

If this truth be so, then we cannot but feel that
there is much in it to enable us to feel rightly with

regard to every one of the new theories which look to a confusion and a loss of the distinctive type of manhood. We have all had our interest excited by the apparent tendencies of modern science towards a depreciation of what has always been considered the unshared honor of humanity. Wise men come forward and tell us of a course of structural development, wherein man becomes not a new creation, for whom a new word was spoken from the creative lips, a new gesture made by the creative hand, but merely the present completion of the natural progress of lower natures working up thus far by some process of selection whose law is resident within itself. The gorilla in his generations is seen climbing through the gradations of a more and more perfect apehood, to attain the summit of his life in man. "Man is in structure one with the brutes." "All are but coördinated terms of nature's great progression from the formless to the formed; from the inorganic to the organic; from blind force to conscious intellect and will." These are the theories that men are talking of. However they differ in details, the one first effect of all of them must be, the depreciation of the individuality of man, the loss of his special type of being, and inevitably the confusion of his human responsibility in the intricate series of the apes. What am I? Anything but one link in an endless chain, that over self-moved wheels runs on forever, working out a progress so mechanical that in it morality is lost? What am I? Only a higher attainment of these poor, dumb brutes, digging the earth a little deeper for the roots I am to eat, piling a little more delicately the den I am to live in, crying a little more articulately the pain or pleasure that I feel? And then suppose I go to Revelation to see what it can say about these things. Suppose I find there this sublime truth, that the man-type for which I am so anxious has had an eternal existence as a part and parcel of the Deity; that, however this manifestation of it has been reached, there is manifest in every man the image of a pattern-life that is in God. Let me carry away from Revelation the supreme truth of the eternal humanity of Christ, and then my moral life, my reverence for the nature which I share, my high ambition after its perfection, all this is unimpaired. Let science show me my affinities with the lower life: a mightier hand points me to my connections with the higher. I go back beyond the first rudiment that curious hands have found buried in the slime of formless worlds; I go back beyond the forming of the world in which man was to live, back to the beginningless Alpha of all being, and lo, in Him I find the eternal pattern after which my nature was to be fashioned, the eternal perfection which my nature was to seek.

But the highest importance of this truth of Christ's past eternity must always be to the great Christian doctrine of the Atonement. You know what that doctrine is. It tells us that when man fell from holiness to sin, there appeared in the whole universe only one nature which had in itself a fitness to undertake the work of reconciliation and restoral. Only one nature stood forth saying, " Lo, I come ! " Christ the incarnate God assumed the work and manifested the one necessary fitness in His union of the divine and human natures. Then comes the question, When did that fitness of the Christ begin? Was it a nature given Him when He was born of Mary? Was it a new assumption of an element of life which had before been wholly unfamiliar? If so, the atonement becomes — what? A late expedient for patching up the breach in God's experiment; a special provision for an unforeseen catastrophe. The precious element of Christ's humanity becomes only the tardy and pitiful consequence of human sin. But take the deeper view. What if this fitness of nature were an everlasting thing in Christ, only coming to special utterance when He was born Jesus the child of the Hebrew Virgin? What if He had borne forever the human element in His Divinity, anointed Christ from all eternity? What if there had been forever a Saviourhood in the Deity, an everlasting readiness which made it always certain that, if such a catastrophe as Eden ever came, such a remedy as Calvary must follow? Does not this deepen all our thoughts of our salvation? Does it not teach us what is meant by " the Lamb slain from the foundation of the world " ?

And see how such a truth tallies with all God's ways. This natural body of ours has in itself the fitness for two sets of processes, — the processes of growth and the processes of repair. You keep your arm unbroken, and nature feeds it with continual health, makes it grow hearty, vigorous, and strong, rounds it out from the baby's feebleness into the full, robust arm of manhood. You break that same arm, and the same nature sets her new efficiencies at work, she gathers up and reshapes the vexed and lacerated flesh, she bridges over the chasm in the broken bone, she restores the lost powers of motion and sensation, and beautifully testifies her completeness, which includes the power of the Healer as well as the Supplier. So it is to me a noble thought, that in an everlasting Christhood in the Deity we have from all eternity a provision for the exigency which came at last, — a provision, not temporary and spasmodic, but existing forever, and only called out into operation by the occurrence of the need.

It seems to me that all this must increase the impressiveness of the thought of the Atonement, both for its rejecters and its accepters, and must increase its deep solemnity for all who preach it. A man puts aside the offer of Salvation by Christ Jesus. What is it he rejects? Is it a sudden thought, a new expedient of God? Is it a hurried plan which God has made ready on the moment to repair this failure in His fallen world? If this were all, it would be bad enough. But when I see a man deliberately raise his hand and ward off from his life the operation of one part of the divine nature which has been aiming at the result of his salvation from eternity, how shall I utter the fearfulness of his sin and of his peril? I look back to the untold times before the world was made. Then, then, before man was, lo, Christ already is, with the provisions of salvation in His nature! Among all other lives His life is unique, for it alone contains the fitness to save — if it should ever need it — the yet unborn world. I see man spring to life. I see him sin. I see, born of his sinning stock and sinning like your fathers, in these late generations, you, man in your capacity, man in your reality of sin. And then comes forward this Eternal Saviour. I see Him lay His long-kept mercy on your soul, born in these latter days to need it. At last the mercy that has waited all through eternity has found its purpose. It comes to save you. And if you will not be saved, if you turn your poor soul away, what can I say but that you are insulting God? What can I do but tremble for you? O my dear brother, how shall you escape if you neglect so great salvation?

And when an earnest soul accepts this everlasting Christ, is there not a new glory in his salvation when he thinks that it has been from everlasting. He looks back, and lo, the Saviour was his Saviour before the worlds were made! The covenant to which he clings had its sublime conditions written in the very constitution of the Godhead. It was not spoken first on Calvary; nay, it did not begin when it was told to David, or to Moses, or to poor Adam crushed into the dust with his new sinfulness outside the garden-gate. Before them all, in the very nature of the Deity, was written the prophecy that if ever in the unfolding of the ages one poor human soul like mine should need salvation, the eternal Christ, bringing His credential of Eternal Human Brotherhood, should come to save it. The ages rolled along; my soul was born, and sinned; it cried out to be saved, and lo, Christ came! What is there left for me to do but cling to Him with a love strong as His precious promises and a faith firm as His Everlasting Saviour-ship?

Let these be the lessons which we gather up as we think upon the Christ of the eternal past. He is the Alpha of our faith. See what it means. It is the Truth of an eternal manhood in the Godhead. It teaches us the glory of this human life we wear as being a thing whose type and pattern was eternal, and it teaches us the magnitude of the grace which saves us as being the necessary effort of one part of the uncreated Deity. He who has learned all the great lesson of this Christ the Alpha must be filled with a sublime reverence for his own humanity, must reverence it and keep it pure and sacred as a holy thing; and he must lay hold with a sublime confidence on that redemption which he sees stretching back and anchoring itself in the uncaused purposes and qualities of God.

And now, if the term "Alpha" asserts a past eternity for Christ, it remains for us to go on and see how the other term " Omega " declares for Him an eternity in the future. He is not merely the beginning, but the end; not only the first, but the last; not merely there has always been, but there shall always be, a Divine Human in the Godhead. This, too, is a truth which we are liable to forget. As we think the marvellous nature of the Saviour began in the manger, so we sometimes feel as if its elements were sundered in the last agony of the cross. Practically a great many of us believe in a Trinity only for thirty-three years of history. Is not this the value of those passages in the New Testament which show us the ascended Saviour speaking or acting still in the same genuine humanity which He had worn on earth? While Stephen stands waiting for the crash of murderous stones, " he looks up steadfastly into heaven and sees Jesus the Son of Man standing on the right hand of God." Saul, prostrate on the Damascus road, cries out to the rebuking voice, " Who art thou, Lord?" and the answer is, "I am Jesus." And as the last Revelation closes and the curtains are gathered together, to be opened again only for the final coming of the Judge, the last voice that comes forth is the voice of Christ, still wearing His human name and lineage, " I Jesus have sent my angel. I am the root and offspring of David." What is all this for, but to assure us of the everlasting manhood in our Lord? The human hand still weighs ; the human voice still speaks; the human heart still loves. He is not only Alpha, but Omega. As all our hope shines from the truth that there ever has been, so it all centres in the truth that there forever shall be, a divine and human Christ.

The highest use of this truth of Christ, the Omega, must be the light which it sheds upon the realities of the judgment day. Christ Himself said, " The Father judgeth no man, but hath committed all judgment unto the Son." Why is this? Is it just because He has worn, is it not rather because He shall forever wear, the human nature which shall make Him fit to judge, with the intelligence and sympathy of brotherhood, the lives of men? I think that none of us have any idea how much we shelter ourselves away from the terrors of the judgment day behind the unfamiliarity of God. He is so far off, so different from us. We cannot really think that He is going to take these acts and motives of ours, so different from His, and test them accurately, judging us all according to the deeds done in the body. How can He, — He is so different from us, so far away? We do not put it to ourselves thus; we do not put it to ourselves at all; but at the bottom this is the way that half of us escape the pressure of responsibility. But take this truth: What if it be a true man that is to judge you, not merely with the far-off memory, but with the present consciousness of manhood? What if the conviction that awaits us there is no other but just that with which brother-man condemns our sin? As a pure human look makes our impurity blush its own sentence to the guilty face; as a true eye loosens the sophistries of falsehood and makes it own its lie; as our humanity quails before a brother-humanity that knows its impulses and temptations through and through, — so shall we quail before the Christ. He is to be our judge, passing by His manhood into a knowledge of the sin which in His Godhood He will punish.

And if human sin needs a humanity to judge it, do not these weak and struggling efforts of our life after goodness crave some sympathy to which they can appeal as they go up to judgment? What! shall I send these poor pretences of holiness up to heaven, this ineffective virtue which is not a being good, but only a trying to try to be so, — shall I send them up to lay themselves against the fiery purity of God and be burnt off like spots of blemish from the white

light of His perfectness? Oh, no, give me a man!
Though He be perfect, He will know what human imperfection is. Though holiness be divine without a
struggle in Him, at least He will comprehend what
my poor struggles mean, and take them as the feeble
efforts of a soul that is trying, not to purchase heaven,
but just to praise Him who has already bought it. If
we look deep enough we ought to feel every time we
see a little child at night trustfully laying his day's
life, made up of faint desires, feeble efforts, and continual failures, into the hands of God, what a blessed
thing it is that there is in that God an everlasting
Christ, an undying humanity, which will take that
day's life into a brother's hands and count it precious
with all the intelligence of sympathy.

And is there not great beauty in this truth of
Christ, the Omega, as we relate it to the dead? We
have all lost dear friends out of this world. We
have all stood upon the margin which was the farthest, which feet untransfigured by death might reach,
and sent some beloved soul into the unknown world.
Where have we sent it? To God, we say, bowing
our heads with resignation. But is there no bleak-
ness, no forlornness in our answer? God is so far off.
However loving, kind, or wise, He is all God; the
child we sent Him was all man in his fresh, genuine
humanity. But what if there be a humanity in God
to which they go? What if, since it went out from us,
that human nature, made first in the image of Christ
the human, has touched again that perfect nature
out of which it sprang and finds itself at home?
Yes, let me set this Christ eternally in the midst of

the other world, and then the human soul that goes there goes to its own. It meets no strangeness on the other shore. The human affections just loosened on the one side fasten into a completer unity and assurance on the other. The child is gathered into the arms of a fatherhood and knows no strangeness or surprise. The brother clasps hands with a newer and more trusty brotherhood. We can commit them to a God who knows them and is waiting for them. They go to Jesus and rest in Him, and wait for us till our humanity, made perfect too by death, shall find its place beside them.

This, then, we mean by Christ the Omega, a Christ of the everlasting future, Alpha and Omega together. His life bridges all eternity, and bearing our hope backward fixes it firmly in a security which has no beginning; bearing it forward crowns it with promises that have no end.

There is another view of this whole subject, which we must not enlarge upon, but which we must not entirely omit. We have spoken of the eternal life of Christ as rounding and embracing the great life of the world. Is it not true likewise of every single Christian experience that Christ is its Alpha and Omega, its beginning and its end? A soul enters on the higher life, passes by the doorway of conversion from disobedience to obedience. When does that soul find Christ? Is it after it has passed, by some power of its own, over the threshold, that there, on the inside, it finds the Lord waiting to be its leader? Oh, no! it looks back and cannot tell the moment when it was not led by Him. It finds no earliest act of its which did not spring out of some yet earlier act of His. It came, but He called. It answered, but first He spoke. It said, "I will;" but before that He said, "Wilt thou?" Yes, we begin, but Christ always began before us. As before all humanity the primal human was in Him forever, so before all Christianity the source and root of all is Christ, out of whom all Christianity must flow. He is the Alpha of our religious life, antedating every act of man's obedience by the eternal promptings of His spirit and the eternal freeness of His grace.

And, then, He is its Omega too. As all Christian influence has its spring in Christ, so no Christian duty has any result except in Him. We look forward, dear friends, into the perfectness that is promised us, and what is it? Simply that we should attain to Him. We may go far in the eternal developments of holiness, but we can never outgo Him. He will be present at the end of every period of everlasting progress, to round and close it for us and to introduce us to a new one as He introduced us to the first, for He is exhaustless.

Oh that we could learn this truth of an exhaustless Christ. We build our Christian lives out from themselves as if Christ were the starting-point from which the first joint grew; but every new joint must hang itself upon its predecessor in the lengthening chain. Oh that we could learn that the life of Christ, the Alpha and Omega, the beginning and the end, stretches from beginning to end under this life of ours, and that each of our weak acts, instead of fastening itself on the consistency of the weak acts that have gone before it, ought to pierce down and root itself directly and freshly in Him. May I plead with you for this! Strive for continual freshness in the higher life. Let it not build itself upon itself as mere habit. Let it grow ever out of Him as a true life. Let each act distinctly find its motive, find its strength in Him. Keep striking roots into His personal helpfulness all the way along. Make Him your Alpha and Omega; from Alpha to Omega make Him the source of every strength and truth your nature seeks.

"Of Him, and through Him, and to Him are all things, to whom be glory forever." That is Paul's summary of our truth. "Of Him," the Alpha — "To Him," the Omega—"Through Him," from Alpha to Omega, the Everlasting Christ. The fault of our religion is that we do not know enough of Christ. May God grant that if we have at all learned how He begins the Christian life in man we may go on learning new lessons of His wondrous power every day, till some day, in the perfect world, we learn the perfect lesson of how He can glorify a poor, weak, human creature with Himself, and, gathering all its culture into Him, take our souls for His and be our Omega, our End as He has been our Beginning, the last complete fulfilment of the last prayer that we shall ever pray, when prayer ceases because need has ceased forever!

XIX.

THE CHRISTIAN MINISTRY.

" And the Evening and the Morning were the First Day."

GENESIS i. 5.

THERE are many mysteries about the days of
Genesis concerning which we need not trouble ourselves to-night.   But this one verse may guide our
thoughts in the direction in which we have come expecting that they should be led.   It is a noble beginning of the world's history.   It declares of the
first day that it was made up of an evening and a
morning.   It is not so that we ordinarily reckon the
world's days.   We think of them as moving on from
morning to evening, opening in freshness, and exu-
berance, and hope, ripening through hours of activity
and strength, and at last closing in peaceful exhaus-
tion, like a fire that has burned itself out to ashes.
Not such is the first day of all the days.   It begins
with evening, with the fulfilment and completeness
of the dayless period which had gone before, and
moves forward into the morning, into the exuber-
ance, and hope, and freshness of untried ambitions
and attempts.   " Evening and Morning were the first
day."   As time went on, within each of those unities
which we call days was summed up and pictured this
truth, that every fulfilment has at its heart the power
of a new beginning, that nothing is ever finally done,

that all is ever doing, that all the gathering of the results of one period's experience has for its purpose and natural issue the opening of a new period in which that experience shall become effective with new form and face.

It is a depressing doctrine in some moods, that nothing is ever done, that all is ever doing, that nothing finishes except that it may instantly begin again. It is a noble and inspiring doctrine when we are at our best, for the absolutely done would be the absolutely dead, only the thing to be, stirring at its heart, proves that the thing which has been is still alive. The evening gathers with its dusky peace; work ceases; men sit by quiet firesides; they count the gains and losses of the completed hours under the quiet stars; the glare and rush grow dim and still. It would be dreadful if it only meant a finished day. It is glorious and beautiful because it means a day all ready to open; nay, already opening in this calm completion. It is St. Paul's great teaching that " Experience worketh Hope."

Is not this first day, then, the type of what all days of human life should be? Does it not, set there in the forefront of history, bear perpetual testimony to the truth that no completion is complete or can be truly understood, unless it stands in close connection with a new commencement. Does it not give us the suggestion which we want when we are gathered here to-night to commemorate the honored completion of a long period of faithful work? You close your youth and pass on into middle life. You close by and by your middle active life and pass on into old age.

You leave one place where you have lived and move into another. You are no longer able to hold one form of faith but a more generous faith opens to welcome you. One sort of company in which you have been much at home dismisses you, and your life henceforth is to be lived among new faces. You finish a piece of work which has long occupied you and take up new tools to work on new materials. At last you go from life to life, and with one " longing, lingering look behind " resign this " pleasing anxious being." In every case it means a vast difference whether you join together in your thought only the old beginning and this fulfilment, or this fulfilment and the new beginning which it makes possible, upon whether the morning and the evening or the evening and the morning are your day, upon whether the forty years of journey as they close are filled more with recollection of the Egyptout of which he came or the Canaan into which they have brought the traveller.

If we get at the real heart of the difference it lies in this, that he who has lived in the form of an experience looks back, while he who has entered into the substance and soul of an experience looks forward. " The outward man perishes," as Paul says, " but the inward man is renewed day by day." The perishing of a form and method in which we have lived may naturally bring a pensive sadness like that which always comes to us as we watch a setting of the sun, but he who is in the true spirit of the sunset turns instantly from the westward to the eastern look. The things the day has given him, — its knowledge, and its inspirations, and its friendship, and its faith,—

these the departing sun is powerless to carry with it. They claim the new day in which to show their power and to do their work. Live deeply and you must live hopefully. That is the law of life. I should like to try to make this clear and real to you by a few illustrations.

1.   Here is a man who has believed a truth, and it has been clear to him as daylight; its lines have been invariably distinct; its colors have been always bright and vivid. But by and by there comes a change, — the lines grow dim and wavering; the colors become faint and blurred; it is not all as definite and certain as it used to be; the twilight, the evening of his faith, has come. Many of you know that of which I speak, and you know how to two men who stand side by side, this evening of their faith, which comes to both alike, means totally different things. To one it means blank unbelief, the melancholy death of faith. To the other out of the dimmed obscured doctrine came a light even richer than it had ever shed in its clearest days. The character which he had gathered in believing it grew stronger and claimed richer truth to satisfy it. His faithfulness grew greater while his formal faith grew less. And visions came to him with wonderful assurance of a new dawn of faith in which he should believe again as he had never believed before. So it has been with many of us about the Bible, and about the nature and the work of Christ. The evening of some half faith which we used to hold has bound itself close to the morning of a new and precious and completer faith which we know that we shall hold forever.

2. Or let it be not your faith, but your fortune. The evening of your abundant prosperity arrived. The darkness gathered in about the radiant luxurious life which you had lived. No longer did it seem as if the sun shone and the flowers bloomed and the seasons came and went for you. You said, " It is all over. I have had my day." I cannot help hoping, I cannot help believing, that to some of you, since you said that, there has come a great surprise. What seemed all over has proved to be but just begun. The day which you thought you had had, you can see now that you had hardly touched. Prosperity has come to mean to you another thing. The hours in which it meant plenty of money, plenty of friends, seem now so thin and superficial. To work, to help and to be helped, to learn sympathy by suffering, to learn faith by perplexity, to reach truth through wonder, behold! this is what it is to prosper, this is what it is to live. You did not really begin to live till the darkening of your happiness brought you into the knowledge of a happiness which can never darken. The evening and the morning have been your first day.

3. I need do no more than just allude to the way in which all this is illustrated in the best friendships, which make so large a part of our lives. The evening gathers round a friendship. Some circumstance suspends the daily intercourse which has been our daily satisfaction and delight. Perhaps the great circumstance of death comes in; and then it is proved whether our intercourse with that friend of ours has been only a thing of outward contacts, or

a thing of spiritual sympathy. If it has been a thing of spiritual sympathy, no circumstance, not even death, can break it. It has been gathered, with all its past history, into that great, cold hand, only that thence it may be given out into a larger and more abundant life. Who of us has not known the dead in closer knowledge than he ever knew them when they were living? To which of us has there not come the certainty, as he stood by some friend's dying bed, that his intercourse with that friend and his understanding of him was but just beginning; that all they had been to each other was really precious as the foundation and the promise of what they were to be to each other in the unseen life forever? The eye through its tears looked backward for an instant, and then strained its gaze forward with eager curiosity and hope.

When Jesus was parting from His disciples all this was very real to Him. " These are in the world and I come to Thee," He said to His Father; and then to His disciples, "Lo, I am with you always." The evening gathered round His active, patient life, but the Christian world has always thought of those last chapters of His incarnate story, not with reference to the past which went before them, but with reference to the future for which they prepared; not as an end, but as a beginning. The evening of the Passion and the morning of the Resurrection are the first day of the Lord's power. It was "expedient that He should go away," not because His work was done, but in order that He might begin it.

This is the value of experiences. They are enfolded into the transitional moments of life, and thence their essential power goes forth to make itself felt in new achievement. Such moments are like locks upon the stream of time. They lift the boat to a new level, and then send it forth, the same boat, on the same stream, still to swim on up towards the springs among the hills.

If experiences were not capable of being thus enfolded and transmuted, how insignificant they would be. Mere facts without fertility, mere stones, not seeds, encumbering the soil. Whether there were few or many of them would make but little matter; whether the man died at twenty years old or at eighty would be hardly worth the asking. But if every experience makes a new element in the great complex future, never lost, contributing something which it alone can give, then this instinctive desire for a full life, for many experiences, which is in us all is natural and right. Then to lose any of the legitimate experiences of a full human career is a loss for which one will be poorer forever. This is the reason of the sadness which no faith in immortality can dissipate, belonging to the death of those who die in youth, — the sense of untimeliness which we cannot reason down. You, a man of sixty, recall to-day some friend of your boyhood with whom you started life forty years ago. He died at twenty-one. The two brave ships had scarcely started side by side upon their voyage before one was drawn off by an irresistible current out of the broad sunlit stream into the mysterious ocean which lies always dark beside our human life. What do you think of as you remember him, and remember what a rich thing life has been for you since he departed? Do you not pity him for what he has missed? Whatever eternity may bring him he will never know what it is to be a human being here upon the earth, first twenty-five years old, then thirty, then forty, then fifty. Each of these ages is a separate experience. It means something special. It contributes something distinct. That contribution his career and character will never get. We do not doubt the compensations. Something has come to him in the unseen, celestial life which has made up for the loss; but still the loss is there. That special thing he can never be. That particular knowledge he can never have. But you who have passed through each of these regions with sensitive, receptive nature have the power of them in you forever. No dream of celestial life will ever drown them. No fire of the unveiled sight of God will ever burn them out of you. Their form is gone past all recovery; but their substance is more than your possession; it is part of you. The experiences, in all the real vitality they had, have been enfolded into you, and shall be unfolded into the work which you shall do, the life which you shall live forever.

When one thinks of this, he feels like turning aside and exhorting the young people to live as fully and vividly as possible at every period of life, that there may be as much of power as possible to be enfolded into the evening of life and opened into the eternal morning. It is good to multiply experiences, if only they are things of the substance and not merely of the form. Do not let the certainty that you will outgrow any period of life keep you from making the most of it and getting the most out of it while it lasts. The bee takes the honey and is content to leave the flower. Live as abundantly as you can. The kind of life is most essential, but the amount of life, that, too, is vastly important. The direction of the stream is the first thing to care for; but when it is pointed the right way, then do all you can to increase its volume. The stronger it runs, the more it will keep the right direction.

But now I want to turn a little more closely to what is in our minds to-night by asking you to see how all that I have said of long-continued life in general is especially true of a life long-lived in the Christian ministry. There, most of all, experiences gather themselves into character, and so make the material of future living. I should expect this to be so, because in its idea the ministry is not merely a noble form of human life, — it is identical with noble life. All noble life is ministry. All ministry is noble life. Every true man is a minister. In proportion as a minister is a true minister, he is a true man. Therefore I should expect that in the Christian ministry more than anywhere else experiences would richen the life they come to and make great futures possible.

I want to claim that no other occupation of mankind can compare in the richness of its experiences with the Ministry of the Christian Gospel. Let me sing for a few moments, in the presence of this beloved and venerated pastorship, the excellence and abundance of the life which the Christian pastor and priest is given the privilege of living. It ripens to its full maturity like a growing tree. It has its seed-time and its leaf-time and its bud-time and its blossom-time and its fruit-time, and each of them sends forward its contribution and makes its preparation for that which is to follow. And in each of them the minister who lives in it has at least the opportunity of the richest relations with the two great sources of human strength, — the divine life on one side of it, and the human life upon the other.

Think of the minister's possible relation, nay, if he is trying to be a true minister, his necessary relation, to God. God is the granary from which he must be immediately fed, the armory from which his weapons must be immediately drawn. Study and thought and contemplation of divine things are not merely his occasional luxury, they are his perpetual necessity. He must sanctify himself that the people may be sanctified through him. He is forever being driven into the deep waters of humiliation for his weakness and of penitence for his sins. He is always trying to understand God's will. " What is the divine intention in this man's joy, in that man's tribulation?" He is kept constantly aware of the infinite and perfect purposes by conscious sympathy with them. " What God wants he wants." He is forever being rebuked and encouraged and enlightened and disturbed and settled, and then redisturbed by influences which come directly out of the heart of God into his heart which is laid upon it. Can you conceive of a life richer in the profoundest experiences than that. Beneath the calm surface what tempest and what sunshine, what tumult and what peace!

And then turn the other way and think of the Christian minister's relation to mankind. Everything which touches man touches him. The dramas of his people's lives are all replayed on the stage of his sympathies. He triumphs with the conqueror, and is beaten with the vanquished soul. He goes into business with the venturesome boy, and seeks truth with the enthusiastic student, and goes to Congress with the politician, and grows rich with the prosperous merchant, and fails with the bankrupt, and enters into peace with the old man who has weathered the storms and anchored in the harbor of his fireside. Whatever tells upon his people's characters he shares with them. Their temptations and their victories are his. He goes with them up into the heavens and down into the depths. His personal life is multiplied by theirs. And then what sight and study of the effects of circumstances on character! What admiration of silent, secret heroism which no other eyes see but his and God's! What knowledge of human strength and human weakness, — strength often where the world thinks that all is pitiably weak, weakness often where the world thinks that everything is absolutely strong! What anxious feeling here and there all over a nature with eager hands to find the spring which shall set free its better life! What glimpses of unexpected educations of God! What fears and hopes, what visions of the mystery of man!

I am not talking of this or that actual minister.

Certainly I am not daring to intrude into the sacred secrecy of that long and rich ministry which we have gathered to congratulate to-night. I am not even limiting my picture to what any actual minister has ever actually attained. I am talking of the idea of our profession. I am talking of that which glows before the eyes when the young men see their visions and the old men dream their dreams. There are base hours in the ministry in which the minister's relation to the world is mean and meagre, perhaps there are whole base ministries to which any of this richness of experience never comes; but I am talking of the ministry as it is in its idea and as it is in large degree realized by every earnest laborer for the souls of men. There is no stupider mistake than that which pretends to think that the minister is an innocent, ignorant, amiable soul, shut out from life, living in cushioned security, where no tumult of the wicked world and no breath from the breezy hilltops of speculative doubt ever can intrude. It is not true. He is no silly optimist in spite of all his hope. He is no dead log of belief in spite of all his faith. Oh, my friends, do not think that because a minister sees the capacity of human nature in the light of the Gospel, he does not therefore see its danger. I hope the tragical peril of existence does not seem to other men more terrible than it always seems to him. I hope the faces which they meet upon the street are not more pitiable or pathetic to other eyes than they are to his. I hope the house-fronts do not grow transparent and reveal the mean and miserable life within, the corpses and the skeletons, to other men as the minister sees them after his long service in the crowded town.

And will you talk of him as if his ordination had been a spell which had placed him forever beyond the reach of doubt? Will you think that he has had somewhere in a Book or in a Bishop the ready answers to all the fierce questions which tear the souls of other men? It is not so. Just in proportion to his love for the truth must be the intensity of his wrestling for it, his sense of the strength of all its enemies. He sits upon no mountain of assurance looking down upon the world of struggling men. He is in the thick and centre of the struggle. He has no scorn of doubt. He knows its strength too well.

And yet while he is in the midst of sin and doubt —here is the privilege of his position — he cannot cease also to see goodness and faith. The wonders of patience that he meets! The splendid victories of spiritual assurance which he sees! Ah, my friends, it is not possible to talk of such a life as that man lives in the way in which foolish people sometimes talk of it. It is no dead break on the wheels of time. It is no burnt-out cinder among the glowing coals of life. It is a very wheel itself. It is the livest coal in all the furnace, making the other coals seem cold beside it. As Christ in Jerusalem made the hot Hebrew life look tame and worthless; as Paul in Athens "frustrated the tokens of liars and made diviners mad, and turned the wise men backward and made their knowledge foolish."

The time must come again, as it has come in other days, when our young men shall feel the vitality of the Christian ministry, and seek it with the heroic consecration of their lives. If they could only know that it is of all lives richest in experience, that in it the passion to live finds fullest satisfaction ! What is it to live? To crawl on in the dust, leaving a trail which the next shower hastens to wash away? Is it to breathe the breath of heaven as the tortoise does, and to bask in the sunshine like the lizard? Or is it to leap and run and quiver with vitality to do things, to learn things, to become things every day? Is it to touch the eternal forces which are behind everything with one hand, and to lay the other on the quivering needles and the beating hammers of this common life ? Is it to deal with God and to deal with man? Is it to use powers to their utmost and to find ever new power coming out in them constantly with their use? If this is life, then there is no man who lives more than the minister; and the generous youth whose cry is, " Let me live while I live," must some day feel the vitality of great service of God and man, and press in through the sacred doors saying, " Let me, too, be a Minister."

I must come back out of my eulogy, my Psalm of the Ministry, which I hope has not carried me too far. We must return to the truth on which we were dwelling, and see how in this life of the ministry, the richest in experiences, the law of the evening and the morning, the law of the enfolding and unfolding of experience, especially applies. No life, I think, more than the ministry has a true continuousness, and yet none more distinctly divides itself into periods, each of which unfolds into new activity the experience which has been enfolded by the period which went before. It goes back almost to the beginning of the life. First came the personal religious history, before the boy had begun to think of ministries or rectorships. The early touching of the nature by the grace of God, the first mysterious knowledge of the greatness of the world and of the Sonship to the Father that gathered itself into a focus and revealed a " call to the ministry," the only call which has any true significance or value, the earnest desire to bring Christ to men and men to Christ, the " Woe is me, if I preach not the Gospel." The call to the ministry completely recognized opened the long and happy time of education, the search for truth and the discovery from year to year of the subtile and rich correspondences of truth with the soul of man. Education in this special phrase of it being completed, then came ordination, the ever-remembered day, separate always among all the days of life, in which the young man brought all that he had and was, and gave it to the service of his Lord. It is not a day merely, — it is a stage in the career. It is not a point only, but a period, so clear a series of spiritual activities does it include, — recognition, gratitude, humility, submission, privilege. It is like the sunrise as it stands between the dawning and the day. Then comes the earliest ministry, — that which our church means to express by the Diaconate, — that first delighted awestruck touch upon the souls of fellow-men. What minister ever forgets it? To what minister does it not stand forever separate and distinct? All that first ministry expands then into the richness of a full Priesthood, — those broad glorious days of the noontime of life, when, rector, pastor, servant, friend, the minister goes in and out among the people with a recognized right which yet never loses his sense of his own privilege nor his reverence for their sacredness, and sees them in their joys and sorrows, by their joys and sorrow, ripen and deepen through the grace of God. There is nothing to compare in richness with those years in any life of any man, and yet the end has not been reached. Another unfolding comes as the minister's life attains its full maturity, and at last he stands a veteran, perhaps in the same parish where once he stood a boy, and a new influence goes forth from him, which is the power of all the enfolded experience of all the finished years. "At evening time it shall be light." That promise, which has been again and again fulfilled for him, finds its completest fulfilment at the end.

Is there not here a most remarkable power of renewal? Does not each evening open into its morning with ever fresh vitality? It never ends, — the minister never retires from the ministry, and is a minister no longer. His ministry changes and enlarges, but never dies. Our Bishop Williams in Japan gives up the cares of his Episcopate, but it is only that he may go on with all his rich experience into some native village and begin again, burying himself like a seed that has in it all the packed richness of the sunshine in which it has ripened. "The man was above forty years old, upon whom this miracle was showed." So cries the author of the Book of Acts in wonder as he sees Peter and John heal the lame man at the Gate of the Temple. Upon the ministry of forty years still comes new influence. It never loses the capacity of newness. It is ever receptive. It is never dead. " Thy raiment waxed not old upon thee, neither did thy foot swell those forty years." That is not merely a record of the past demanding gratitude. It is a prophecy of the future bestowing hope. At the very end comes Pisgah, the mountain of the evening and the morning. The Desert lies behind, — the Promised land before. The servant of the Lord sees for the people of the Lord here on the earth great regions of faith and life into which he cannot lead them, into which they will not enter till he has passed away. He is thankful for them. And for himself the old servant of the Lord catches dim inspiring glimpses of an uninterrupted and ever-deepening service which he shall render to his God in the unseen world, of a ministry which shall be his privilege forever, —and so he is content, thankful, and hopeful.

Thus I have asked you to think to-night upon the ever-renewing power of all good life, and especially of the life of the Christian Minister. I will not close till in a few last words I beg you to remember what is the secret of that power of renewal. It is the persistency, the eternity of God. Not the minister's life nor any other life renews itself. The life which has nothing but itself to drink of dries up. It is only as it draws forever of the timeless and eternal life that any life gets freshness and perpetual renewal. If I am right in what I have been saying to you, and the life of the ministry has this special power of renewal, it is solely because it dares to stand, because in some sense it is compelled to stand, in peculiarly intimate and conscious relationship with the eternal God. The ministry which is not near to God, and tries to subsist upon itself, lives feebler and dies quicker than any other work of man. But it is not only on the ministry that there rests this necessity. All life which would not grow stale and monotonous must feed itself from God. All life which would make to-day the transmutation place where yesterday shall give its power to Forever must be full of the felt presence, of the love and fear of Him in whom yesterday, to-day, and forever all are one.

I beg you, oh, my friends, if sometimes you are trembling at the possible degeneracy and drying up of your life as you grow old, to see that here is your salvation. Fasten your life to God, and it must be young with his perpetual youth; it must be forever renewed in Him. Remember how He promised by His prophet that "They who wait on the Lord shall renew their strength." Only the soul which waits on Him knows such renewal. It cannot conceive of, certainly it cannot dread, senility. It sees in its vision perpetual renewal securing perpetual youth to all eternity. It lays down each task to take up a greater. It goes out of each room to enter into a larger. It sees each evening set, only to turn instantly and look for a new sunrise. To us, whatever be our life, may life be that! Then thankfulness and expectation shall meet in every crystal moment. At every moment we shall say as Christ said, both "I have glorified thee. I have finished the work that thou gavest me," and also, " Now, oh Father, glorify thou me with thine own self." To be able to say the two together is to hold Evening and Morning blended together in one great Day of the Lord. Such lives which cannot die, may it be given to us all to live!

XX.

FOREIGN MISSIONS.

"And He said unto them : ' Go ye into all the world and preach the Gospel to every creature.' " — MARK xvi. 15.

ONCE more, this morning, these old familiar words press forward and demand our hearing. Once more the Master stands with His disciples on the Mount of Olives, and, looking abroad over the wide earth, claims it all for Himself. As we look upon the picture, two other mountain scenes rise up before us, and we recognize that they belong to the same spiritual world with this. First we see Moses on Mount Pisgah looking into the promised land which he might not enter with his people, but into which they should carry the spirit and the strength and the laws and the hopes which he had given them. So Jesus could not go in bodily presence into Christian history. He could not visibly lead down the centuries the ever-increasing army of His disciples. Sometimes we wonder how it would have been had that been possible. What would the Christian ages have been if, somewhere on the earth, there had lived on the bodily presence of the Incarnate Christ. So the Jews, conquering Canaan, must sometimes have stopped in weary march or furious battle and said to one another, "O for a sight of Moses!" but it was better for them, and it is better for us, as God ordained it.

The other picture is the mountain of the Lord's temptation. There, at the beginning of His ministry, Satan had said to Jesus, "All these kingdoms of the earth will I give Thee if Thou wilt fall down and worship me!" Now, standing upon the Mount of Olives, Jesus saw how good it was that He refused the tempter. Behold, they were His without Satan, His by the gift of His father and the redemption of His cross. It was as if He took formal possession of them when He spoke these words, "Go ye into all the world and preach the Gospel to every creature."

We must give these words their full and picturesque importance before we can rightly treat them as declaring Christ's idea and purpose for His Gospel. When we do thus conceive them, they make us see Him standing and surrounding the whole vast circle with one sweep of prophecy. He asserts, not incidentally and casually, but most deliberately and solemnly, that His Gospel is to be preached to all the world. These disciples and their successors are to do it.

When we hear of a determination or a purpose of the divine Christ, we must remind ourselves how much it means. It is not merely a resolution of His will, — it is also a declaration of the necessity of things. God resolves that which must be. His decrees of what shall be, are really announcements of what is. His knowledge and His will are not, as they are with us, two things, — they are but one. When, then, Christ says to His disciples, "This Gospel of mine is to cover all the world," He is really declaring that the nature of His Gospel is universal.

It is such that only in covering the world does it fulfil its being. We are forever trying to make the universal partial, and to make the partial universal. We tug and stretch and pull to make that which has in it only the capacity for some service broad enough and long enough to overspread that for which it is all incompetent, and so it cracks and breaks. On the other hand, we try to narrow and fold some great principle or power and set it to little uses which are not worthy of it, and so " to partly give up what is meant for mankind." There is no such folly in the adaptations which God makes when He says, " O wind, go blow; O sun, go shine unto the uttermost parts of heaven or earth," — it is because there is in wind or sun an energy which only the uttermost parts can satisfy. When He builds around some life a narrow wall, and bids it work its seventy years in that small circuit, if the wall which surrounds it is really of His building, it is because there its concentrated strength can work its best result. And so when Christ said, "This my Gospel is for all mankind," it was an utterance which told of what the Gospel was as well as of what it was to do. Not merely its destiny, but its nature, was universal.

When, then, the Christian faith having begun its life almost immediately began to spread itself abroad, it was doing two things. It was justifying its Lord's prophecy, and it was realizing its own nature. There came at first a moment's pause and hesitation. We can see in those chapters of the Book of Acts how for a few years the faith could not quite believe the story of itself which was speaking at its heart. It heard the ends of the earth calling it, but it could not see beyond the narrow coasts of Judea. But the beauty of those early days is the way in which it could not be content with that. It is not the ends of the earth calling in desperation for something which was not made to help them, which had no vast vocation, which at last started out desperately to do a work which must be done, but for which it felt no fitness in itself. The heart of the church feels the need of going as much as the ends of the world desire that it should come. It is "deep answering to deep!" He who studies the early expansion of the Christian truth feels himself standing between a world which must be saved and a Power of Salvation which must give itself away. The world is only half conscious of its need. The Power of Salvation does not understand the tumult at its heart; but both are real, and they are reaching out for one another. And the student of those days feels the inspiration as he stands between them. It is like standing between the sun and the earth in the morning.

This is the fundamental meaning, the fundamental truth of foreign missions. It goes as deep as the nature of the Gospel. It is written in the necessities of the human soul. And now comes in another principle, which is, that when a force meant for a large expansion is denied the large expansion which its nature craves, it does not merely fail of the larger work which it is not allowed to do, but it loses its best capacity and power in the narrow field to which it is confined. It is unfortunate that we can never speak of foreign missions without remembering and taking into account the objections to them, the disbelief in them, which are in many Christian people's minds. All such objections and disbelief must, as it seems to me, be met by the broad principle which I have just now stated. Any arrested development, any denial to a power, of its true range and scope, not merely limits it, but poisons it; not merely shuts it out of regions where it wants to go, but makes it work feebly or falsely in the region to which it is confined.

You forbid a limit its right to grow to its true size, and your stunted limit is apt to be not merely small, but sickly. You fence a city round with narrow walls, and, shut in on itself, it festers and corrupts and fills its crowded streets with misery. You shut an idea out from all opportunity of application, and it becomes fantastic and insincere. This is where cranks and fanatics are made. It is not in ideas going too far, it is in their being denied some true and legitimate activity that they become unhealthy. Whatever goes in the direction of its nature, and is not pressed beyond the power which it naturally possesses, and is not hindered or obstructed till its work is done, works healthily, and neither grows peevish nor grows dead. It is the fire which you shut in tight that either goes out or explodes.

The glory of liberty is this, that it gives everything its chance, it lets each thing do that which it was made to do. To force anything to do that which it was not made to do is not liberty, though sometimes it usurps the name. It is only another slavery. But the curse of ordinary slavery is the curse which belongs to all arrested development. Not merely it shuts power out of fields which belong to it: it makes it work feebly or falsely in the fields where it is unnaturally confined.

This has always been true in the history of the Christian Church, wherever its outward tendency, its missionary activity, has been hampered, its inward life has suffered. Perhaps there has been no illustration of this more striking than right here in our own New England. The Puritans who came first to our shores were deeply, overwhelmingly religious men. They came here for religious purposes. Their minds were always busy with religious problems. Their souls were eager with the passion for spiritual growth. They tried to live, they did live, very near to God; but they had little immediate missionary spirit. They expected the ultimate submission of the world to Christ, but they felt themselves summoned to very little instant action toward the great result. Their thought was more intensive than extensive in its character. Except where the irrepressible pity of Eliot and his companions touched the Indian life they may be said to have had no missionary work. There is much to account for the fact in their history and their circumstances, but the fact is clear.

And what was the result? The arrested development of that intense religious life wrought its inevitable consequence. You all know something of what a confusion of intricate, complicated, and practically incomprehensible dogma the New England theology became. The endless discussion of fantastic questions occupied a large part of the people's thought. The minute and morbid study of their spiritual conditions distorted and tormented anxious souls. Strange theories of the atonement grew like weeds. A willingness to be lost was made the dreadful condition of salvation. Heresies sprang out of the soil where orthodoxy lay corrupt and almost dead. It was the sad fate of a religious life denied its due development and shut in on itself.

It was not till this century began, not till at Williamstown, behind the summer haystack, the little group of students consecrated themselves to the extension of the Gospel, not till the missionary spirit took possession of the New England churches, that the mists began to scatter and a healthier condition began to prevail in religious thought and life. The old intensity we fain would see again, but not exactly as it was. If the extensive impulse shall go forth unhindered, there must be a new intensity in time which shall be better than the old. Already we think we begin to see some of its signs. They make us dream of what it may be in the fulness of its power. And every sign it shows, every dream which we dream concerning it, connects it closely with the missionary spirit, with the sending of the Christian Gospel abroad throughout the world.

I must not linger long upon my way to bid you think how true all this is with respect to the personal and individual religious life. A man is made a Christian by the grace of God, and for what? Not, as we have said a thousand times, to get him into heaven, but in order that through him the grace of God may go abroad and some piece of the world be saved. Let the new Christian give himself to that idea, and how the religious life thrives in him! How healthily, how vigorously it grows! How it bears witness of itself at every moment that it is the soul's true life! Let it lose that idea and think of itself alone, and two results must follow: first, regions of life which ought to have been blessed by it go without their blessing; and, second, the spirit of selfishness takes possession of the faith itself. Hardness, uncharitableness, bigotry, fantasticalness, that which I think one comes to dread more and more in religion, the loss of simplicity, the loss of humanness, which means the loss of divineness: these invade the precious substance of the man's religion. It is possible to state what occurs in various ways. It is possible to say that the Christian neglects his duty and God punishes him. It is also possible to say that the outgoing flood of life is stopped and hindered and thrown back upon the soul, which, overwhelmed by it, is like the dreary marsh over which the stagnant water spreads itself, which ought to be energetically pressing out to sea.

I like to state the case under this latter form, because it seems to assert the truth, that missions are not an occasional duty, but the essential necessity of Christian life. It is not an exceptional enterprise to which man is occasionally summoned, it is the fundamental condition without which man cannot live. It is not like an army summoned once or twice a century to repulse a special foe, feeling itself unnatural, expecting from the moment of its enlistment, the time when it shall lay down its arms and go back to the works of peace. It is like the daily activity of the city, taken up naturally every morning, constituting the normal expression of the city's life, never to cease while the city lives, the pulse which shows at any moment what degree of vitality the city has, — such is the missionary spirit to the Christian Church.

Of all I have been saying there has been one great, ever-instructive illustration in history which is the experience of the Hebrew race. Have you ever thought how exactly the modern Christian who "does not believe in foreign missions" corresponds to the Jew of the Old Testament? He has not indeed the excuse and self-explanation which the best Jews had. He does not say to himself as they said, that it is for a purpose and a deliberate design of God that his religion is shut up in himself and forbidden to go abroad. But, without the excuse or explanation, his condition is exactly the same as that of the old Jew. His is a perfect modern Judaism. Look at him. Conscious of privilege, perfectly aware that God has given to him truth and light which are inestimably precious, holding the tables of a divine law in his sanctuary, feeling the illumination of a divine wisdom burn in the jewels of his breastplate, he is perpetually aware of how his life belongs to God, and, looking forth from the observatory of his privilege, he sees the whole dark world. Sometimes he pities it, sometimes he despises it, sometimes he almost hates it We can see each of those three emotions, now one and now another, in the wonderfully distinct, expressive face of the Hebrew which looks out from the wondrous Book.

This modern Hebrew sometimes recognizes how the same spirit which is clear and strong in him shows signs of faint and feeble working in the great mass of uncalled, unprivileged humanity, just as the old Jew could not always shut his eyes and ears to the working of the Spirit of God among the Gentiles. Sometimes he hears the beating of the waves on their restriction, and catches glimpses of some possible day when they will break through and claim the world; but, for the present, now, he is here and the world is there, — the river on this side and the sea on that side shut him in. He will not cross either of them to find those who lie beyond. He prays his prayers, and they are real prayers; he believes his truths, and they are real truths; he does his tasks, and they are real tasks, — but what is the spiritual life of the Esquimaux among his snows, or the Asiatic in his jungle, is nothing in the world to him. The very question smites his ear with no reality.

This is our Judaism! Do you remember Peter on the housetop at Joppa? Can you not see that stanch, sturdy Hebrew figure stepping eagerly along the road to Cesarea after he had seen the vision? Can you not hear the words which come pouring out of his lips as he stands at last in the presence of the listening heathen, "God hath shown me that I should not call any man common or unclean"? There is a delight full of surprise, "A wonderful truth," he seems to say, "and yet how strange that I did not see it all the while. How strange that I ever should have imagined that God could think any of his children unclean or common!" So we all feel when our Judaisms at last break open. So we look out on a new life and are amazed that the old life ever satisfied us. So the Christian, made the missionary, seems for the first time to have known what his faith really is.

I have said that when, with the arrest of its development released, the Christian faith goes forth in missionary effort, part of the blessing which results is the increase of health and life in the home Christianity out of which the missionary impulse starts. No part of that return of power is more valuable than the way in which the personalness of the religious life is kept alive. Do you see what I mean? The ordinary long-established Christianity tends to organization. It loses the person in the institution. It seems to trust to forces which have little of individual freedom. It runs to machinery. But the great truth which missionary history bears witness to is that all missionary effort must be supremely personal. It is not an institution, but a man, that hears the appeal of Macedonia and sails across the sea. From Paul all the way down through all the ages it is a line of shining persons, each kindled with his own faith, each working in his own way, that makes the continuity of missions. They own the church; they are the church. But they are the church in that personal expression of its strength which always has been and always will be the most real and powerful. The shutting up, then, of missionary activity is the deadening of the per-

sonal life of the church. The non-missionary church
is the most hide-bound in creed and organization.

As we bear this in mind, our eyes and hearts
become impatient for a sight they long to see. It
is not simply a waking up of the church in a
missionary direction that we covet; it is not
simply the opening of stingy pockets and the pouring
out of vast wealth, — it is the want of men; it is the
standing forth of brave young Christian souls saying,
"I want to go. My message burns upon my lips
until I tell it. Send me!" Are there none here?
The choicest and the best are none too good. Are
there none here? I tell you, friends, the foreign missionary work waits for nothing but that strong, first-
rate, leading men, full of the simple faith that God
is the world's Father, and Christ is the world's King,
— the missionary work only needs them to show its
strength, to claim the souls of waiting multitudes to
the world's end, and the abundant confidence and
support of Christians here at home. Whenever such
a man has appeared, his power has been wonderful.
Men, far inferior, have done enough to show through
all their failures what a great missionary might ac-
complish. That he will come, the Christian heart
believes and waits.

Until he comes the church goes on obedient to
her idea, keeping the field open for his coming.
Here is the real uncertainty of foreign missions.
No man can say when the true missionary will appear. It is not by boards and committees and estab-
lishments that the Gospel of Christ is ultimately to
be spread throughout the world. Only by fiery-

hearted preachers of the truth and workers in the cause of Christ can that be done. Just as it is not by schools and academies, but by great minds, great thinkers, great discoverers, great scholars, that knowledge makes vast advances and ignorance is dispelled. But schools and academies hold fast the ground which has been gained, keep the ideas of learning vivid, and furnish the cradles out of which the great creative geniuses proceed. So all our ordinary missionary operations furnish the basis for great personal work, tempt and make possible the strong efficiency of ardent souls, and occupy that which the pioneer has won with the strong grasp of permanent possession.

But never can we forget that it is not by machineries or institutions, but only by human natures, only by men, that any great victory of light over darkness, of truth over error, is achieved. Therefore we pray and look and long for men. Let them appear, and all the apparatus of work may be most primitive and incomplete, still the work will be done. Let them be wanting, and with the most perfect apparatus there is no result. Institutions embody ideas and offer opportunities and hold results, but only men do the world's work. Very interesting, very precious is the church as an organization, with its history, its order, its symbols, and its forms ; but " how beautiful upon the mountains are the feet of him that bringeth good tidings, that publisheth peace ! "

As a religion becomes more deep and spiritual, the preservation of its essential spirit will of course become at once more difficult and more important; and

if, as I have all along been saying, the effectiveness
of a faith depends upon the absoluteness with which
its spirit is preserved, there will possibly enough
come times when an inferior faith may seem at least
to do a work in which the supreme faith of Christianity appears to fail. This, as I take it, is the real
fact regarding that of which much has been said in
certain quarters very lately. It has been declared
that Islam, the religion of Mohammed, is making
great progress both in India and in Africa, where
Christianity moves very slowly. It is ever pleaded
that perhaps only by a previous conversion to
Mohammedanism can the lowest forms of heathenism mount gradually to the spiritual heights of
Christian faith. It is not easy to learn what the
exact facts are; but if, as it is probable, the lower
faith makes converts where the higher fails, it is
not because the higher is too high, certainly not
because it is less true, but because it needs stronger
men with purer inspirations, and those it has not
found. Let the divine flame of the love of Christ
the Crucified and of all His Father's children for
His sake burn as intensely in a thousand bosoms as
the fanatical enthusiasm of the prophet blazes in a
thousand swords of his disciples, and the victory
cannot be doubtful. That is the temporary weakness of Christianity which must be its final strength,
that it can fight with no false weapons, and is strong
only in proportion as it is pure. Not by an Islam
Christianity of terror, but by a true Christianity of
love the struggle must be carried forward and the
victory finally obtained.

The close association of the quality of Christianity with its quantity, if I may so call it, of the sort in which it exists at the centre with the power which it exerts at the ends, gives great importance, from the missionary point of view, to every change of thought and feeling which Christian faith undergoes where it has longest been established.

In general, it may be said that there are two great conceptions of that faith, within one of which or the other all lesser differences may be included. One of them makes Christ and His religion to be unnatural to man; the other counts them most supremely natural. I do not now argue which is true. I doubt not there is truth in both; I doubt not there are points of view from which the whole idea of incarnation and redemption may have its value in its strangeness, may seem to bring as its appeal, in virtue of its being a terrible necessity, an awful and almost violent remedial interference with the headlong ruin of a rebellious world; I doubt not that there is another point of view from which the coming and the work of Christ must seem to be the flower of all hopes and struggles which humanity has had from the beginning, " the Desire of all Nations," the most natural, perhaps the inevitable utterance of that Divinity, which has always been in and under human life, made violent and tragical in its manifestation only by the false crust of inhuman sin and selfishness through which the divine fire was compelled to break.

I do not now argue which of these conceptions of Christianity is true. I only ask myself, with the second of them so largely, so more and more largely, occupying men's devout and thoughtful minds, what will be the effect on Christian missions? I ask myself, and I cannot doubt the answer. That missions will fail because one aspect of Christian truth, deep, tender, strong, has claimed the Christian heart out of which missionary impulse must proceed, I cannot for a moment think. That truth which, just so far as it is true, enlarges the sympathy of man, breaks down the walls of self-conceited privilege, and makes the lowest true shareholders in the highest, — that truth cannot by any possibility paralyze, it must by every certainty invigorate, the outgoing energy of missionary zeal. It may, it must, change and modify and color, but it cannot destroy, the missionary spirit.

If we believe that, then we may well put to ourselves the questions, — and with the putting of these questions we shall be ready to close our missionary thoughts and pass to our missionary offering, — we may well put to ourselves, I say, the questions, What has the simpler, broader, and more natural Christianity to say to the missionary? what to the heathen? what to the false and imperfect faiths? And what will it expect as the result of missionary work?

What will it say to the missionary? It will say, " Go, like your Master, not to judge, but to redeem and save. Go, not with threats of what will come without your Gospel, but with glowing promise of what may come with it. Go, and make men be, by teaching that they are, the sons of God. Go simply, naturally, not 'carrying Christ' across the sea, but knowing well that you cannot find any darkest spot on earth where He is not already."

What shall it say to the heathen? "Whom ye ignorantly worship, Him declare I unto you. The life you are living is not your true life. You are made for the light. Behold the Light of Life! Let Him redeem you. Lo! through the awful cross He saved you, if you will be saved from death."

What will it say to the false and imperfect faiths? "I cannot hate you. I cannot denounce you, save as the evil of man has mixed itself with your truth. I reverence you; I pity you; I would interpret you to yourself. It is my Christ that you are feeling for. Come, let us seek for Him together."

What will it look for as the result? A great free service of Christ throughout the world. Each continent, each nation, each soul, serving the same Lord in its own way, with its own worship, its own work. One chorus of obedience and growing goodness in a thousand tones, swelling up forever from the redeemed Earth to the King and to the Lamb.

The truth which carries such messages and has such hopes as those must be dear to God's heart, and is a noble truth for men to believe in and live by.

But, after all our thoughts and speculations, may God give us pity for the heathen, and help us to send to them that Gospel which is our Glory and Joy!

A Catalogue

of

Theological Works

published by

Macmillan & Co.

Bedford Street, Strand, London

CONTENTS

MACMILLAN AND CO.'S THEOLOGICAL CATALOGUE

The Bible

HISTORY OF THE BIBLE

THE ENGLISH BIBLE: An External and Critical History of the various English Translations of Scripture. By Prof. JOHN EADIE. 2 vols. 8vo. 28s.

THE BIBLE IN THE CHURCH. By Right Rev. Bishop WESTCOTT. 10th Edition. 18mo. 4s. 6d.

BIBLICAL HISTORY

BIBLE LESSONS. By Rev. E. A. ABBOTT. Crown 8vo. 4s. 6d.

SIDE-LIGHTS UPON BIBLE HISTORY. By Mrs. SYDNEY BUXTON. Illustrated. Crown 8vo. 5s.

STORIES FROM THE BIBLE. By Rev. A. J. CHURCH. Illustrated. Two Series. Crown 8vo. 3s. 6d. each.

BIBLE READINGS SELECTED FROM THE PENTATEUCH AND THE BOOK OF JOSHUA. By Rev. J. A. CROSS. 2nd Edition. Globe 8vo. 2s. 6d.

CHILDREN'S TREASURY OF BIBLE STORIES. By Mrs. H. GASKOIN. 18mo. 1s. each. Part I. Old Testament; II. New Testament; III. Three Apostles.

A CLASS-BOOK OF OLD TESTAMENT HISTORY. By Rev. Canon MACLEAR. With Four Maps. 18mo. 4s. 6d.

A CLASS-BOOK OF NEW TESTAMENT HISTORY. Including the connection of the Old and New Testament. By the same. 18mo. 5s. 6d.

A SHILLING BOOK OF OLD TESTAMENT HISTORY. By the same. 18mo. 1s.

A SHILLING BOOK OF NEW TESTAMENT HISTORY. By the same. 18mo. 1s.

THE OLD TESTAMENT

SCRIPTURE READINGS FOR SCHOOLS AND FAMILIES. By C. M. YONGE. Globe 8vo. 1s. 6d. each; also with comments, 3s. 6d. each.—First Series: GENESIS TO DEUTERONOMY.—Second Series: JOSHUA TO SOLOMON.—Third Series: KINGS AND THE PROPHETS.—Fourth Series: THE GOSPEL TIMES.—Fifth Series: APOSTOLIC TIMES.

The Old Testament—*continued.*

WARBURTONIAN LECTURES ON THE MINOR PROPHETS.
By Rev. A. F. KIRKPATRICK, B.D. Crown 8vo. [*In the Press.*

THE PATRIARCHS AND LAWGIVERS OF THE OLD
TESTAMENT. By FREDERICK DENISON MAURICE. New
Edition. Crown 8vo. 3s. 6d.

THE PROPHETS AND KINGS OF THE OLD TESTAMENT.
By the same. New Edition. Crown 8vo. 3s. 6d.

THE CANON OF THE OLD TESTAMENT. An Essay on the
Growth and Formation of the Hebrew Canon of Scripture. By
Rev. Prof. H. E. RYLE. Crown 8vo. 6s.

THE EARLY NARRATIVES OF GENESIS. By Rev. Prof. H. E.
RYLE. Cr. 8vo. 3s. net.

The Pentateuch—

AN HISTORICO-CRITICAL INQUIRY INTO THE ORIGIN
AND COMPOSITION OF THE HEXATEUCH (PENTA-
TEUCH AND BOOK OF JOSHUA). By Prof. A. KUENEN.
Translated by PHILIP H. WICKSTEED, M.A. 8vo. 14s.

The Psalms—

THE PSALMS CHRONOLOGICALLY ARRANGED. An
Amended Version, with Historical Introductions and Explanatory
Notes. By Four Friends. New Edition. Crown 8vo. 5s. net.

GOLDEN TREASURY PSALTER. The Student's Edition.
Being an Edition with briefer Notes of "The Psalms Chronologically Arranged by Four Friends." 18mo. 3s. 6d.

THE PSALMS. With Introductions and Critical Notes. By A. C.
JENNINGS, M.A., and W. H. LOWE, M.A. In 2 vols. 2nd
Edition. Crown 8vo. 10s. 6d. each.

INTRODUCTION TO THE STUDY AND USE OF THE
PSALMS. By Rev. J. F. THRUPP. 2nd Edition. 2 vols. 8vo. 21s.

Isaiah—

ISAIAH XL.—LXVI. With the Shorter Prophecies allied to it.
By MATTHEW ARNOLD. With Notes. Crown 8vo. 5s.

ISAIAH OF JERUSALEM. In the Authorised English Version, with
Introduction, Corrections, and Notes. By the same. Cr. 8vo. 4s. 6d.

A BIBLE-READING FOR SCHOOLS. The Great Prophecy of
Israel's Restoration (Isaiah xl.-lxvi.) Arranged and Edited for
Young Learners. By the same. 4th Edition. 18mo. 1s.

COMMENTARY ON THE BOOK OF ISAIAH, Critical, Historical,
and Prophetical; including a Revised English Translation. By
T. R. BIRKS. 2nd Edition. 8vo. 12s. 6d.

THE BOOK OF ISAIAH CHRONOLOGICALLY ARRANGED.
By T. K. CHEYNE. Crown 8vo. 7s. 6d.

Zechariah—

THE HEBREW STUDENT'S COMMENTARY ON ZECH-
ARIAH, Hebrew and LXX. By W. H. LOWE, M.A. 8vo. 10s. 6d.

THE NEW TESTAMENT

APOCRYPHAL GOSPEL OF PETER. The Greek Text of the Newly-Discovered Fragment. 8vo. Sewed. 1s.

THE NEW TESTAMENT. Essay on the Right Estimation of MS. Evidence in the Text of the New Testament. By T. R. BIRKS. Crown 8vo. 3s. 6d.

THE SOTERIOLOGY OF THE NEW TESTAMENT. By W. P. DU BOSE, M.A. Crown 8vo. 7s. 6d.

THE MESSAGES OF THE BOOKS. Being Discourses and Notes on the Books of the New Testament. By Ven. Archdeacon FARRAR. 8vo. 14s.

THE CLASSICAL ELEMENT IN THE NEW TESTAMENT. Considered as a Proof of its Genuineness, with an Appendix on the Oldest Authorities used in the Formation of the Canon. By C. H. HOOLE. 8vo. 10s. 6d.

ON A FRESH REVISION OF THE ENGLISH NEW TESTA-MENT. With an Appendix on the last Petition of the Lord's Prayer. By Bishop LIGHTFOOT. Crown 8vo. 7s. 6d.

DISSERTATIONS ON THE APOSTOLIC AGE. By Bishop LIGHTFOOT. 8vo. 14s.

THE UNITY OF THE NEW TESTAMENT. By F. D. MAURICE. 2nd Edition. 2 vols. Crown 8vo. 12s.

A COMPANION TO THE GREEK TESTAMENT AND THE ENGLISH VERSION. By PHILIP SCHAFF, D.D. Cr. 8vo. 12s.

A GENERAL SURVEY OF THE HISTORY OF THE CANON OF THE NEW TESTAMENT DURING THE FIRST FOUR CENTURIES. By Right Rev. Bishop WESTCOTT. 6th Edition. Crown 8vo. 10s. 6d.

THE NEW TESTAMENT IN THE ORIGINAL GREEK. The Text revised by Bishop WESTCOTT, D.D., and Prof. F. J. A. HORT, D.D. 2 vols. Crown 8vo. 10s. 6d. each.—Vol. I. Text; II. Introduction and Appendix.

THE NEW TESTAMENT IN THE ORIGINAL GREEK, for Schools. The Text revised by Bishop WESTCOTT, D.D., and F. J. A. HORT, D.D. 12mo, cloth, 4s. 6d. ; 18mo, roan, red edges, 5s. 6d. ; morocco, gilt edges, 6s. 6d.

THE GOSPELS—

THE COMMON TRADITION OF THE SYNOPTIC GOSPELS, in the Text of the Revised Version. By Rev. E. A. ABBOTT and W. G. RUSHBROOKE. Crown 8vo. 3s. 6d.

SYNOPTICON : An Exposition of the Common Matter of the Synoptic Gospels. By W. G. RUSHBROOKE. Printed in Colours. In Six Parts, and Appendix. 4to.—Part I. 3s. 6d. Parts II. and III. 7s. Parts IV. V. and VI. with Indices, 10s. 6d. Appendices, 10s. 6d. Complete in 1 vol., 35s. Indispensable to a Theological Student.

INTRODUCTION TO THE STUDY OF THE FOUR GOSPELS. By Right Rev. Bishop WESTCOTT. 7th Ed. Cr. 8vo. 10s. 6d.

THE COMPOSITION OF THE FOUR GOSPELS. By Rev. ARTHUR WRIGHT. Crown 8vo. 5s.

Gospel of St. Matthew—
THE GOSPEL ACCORDING TO ST. MATTHEW. Greek Text as Revised by Bishop WESTCOTT and Dr. HORT. With Introduction and Notes by Rev. A. SLOMAN, M.A. Fcap. 8vo. 2s. 6d.
CHOICE NOTES ON ST. MATTHEW, drawn from Old and New Sources. Crown 8vo. 4s. 6d. (St. Matthew and St. Mark in 1 vol. 9s.)

Gospel of St. Mark—
SCHOOL READINGS IN THE GREEK TESTAMENT. Being the Outlines of the Life of our Lord as given by St. Mark, with additions from the Text of the other Evangelists. Edited, with Notes and Vocabulary, by Rev. A. CALVERT, M.A. Fcap. 8vo. 2s. 6d.
CHOICE NOTES ON ST. MARK, drawn from Old and New Sources. Cr. 8vo. 4s. 6d. (St. Matthew and St. Mark in 1 vol. 9s.)

Gospel of St. Luke—
THE GOSPEL ACCORDING TO ST. LUKE. The Greek Text as Revised by Bishop WESTCOTT and Dr. HORT. With Introduction and Notes by Rev. J. BOND, M.A. Fcap. 8vo. 2s. 6d.
CHOICE NOTES ON ST. LUKE, drawn from Old and New Sources. Crown 8vo. 4s. 6d.
THE GOSPEL OF THE KINGDOM OF HEAVEN. A Course of Lectures on the Gospel of St. Luke. By F. D. MAURICE. 3rd Edition. Crown 8vo. 6s.

Gospel of St. John—
THE CENTRAL TEACHING OF CHRIST. Being a Study and Exposition of St. John, Chapters XIII. to XVII. By Rev. CANON BERNARD, M.A. Crown 8vo. 7s. 6d.
THE GOSPEL OF ST. JOHN. By F. D. MAURICE. 8th Ed. Cr. 8vo. 6s.
CHOICE NOTES ON ST. JOHN, drawn from Old and New Sources. Crown 8vo. 4s. 6d.

THE ACTS OF THE APOSTLES—
THE ACTS OF THE APOSTLES. Being the Greek Text as Revised by Bishop WESTCOTT and Dr. HORT. With Explanatory Notes by T. E. PAGE, M.A. Fcap. 8vo. 3s. 6d.
THE CHURCH OF THE FIRST DAYS. THE CHURCH OF JERUSALEM. THE CHURCH OF THE GENTILES. THE CHURCH OF THE WORLD. Lectures on the Acts of the Apostles. By Very Rev. C. J. VAUGHAN. Crown 8vo. 10s. 6d.

THE EPISTLES of St. Paul—
ST. PAUL'S EPISTLE TO THE ROMANS. The Greek Text, with English Notes. By Very Rev. C. J. VAUGHAN. 7th Edition. Crown 8vo. 7s. 6d.
A COMMENTARY ON ST. PAUL'S TWO EPISTLES TO THE CORINTHIANS. Greek Text, with Commentary. By Rev. W. KAY. 8vo. 9s.

Of St. Paul—*continued.*

ST. PAUL'S EPISTLE TO THE GALATIANS. A Revised Text, with Introduction, Notes, and Dissertations. By Bishop LIGHTFOOT. 10th Edition. 8vo. 12s.

ST. PAUL'S EPISTLE TO THE PHILIPPIANS. A Revised Text, with Introduction, Notes, and Dissertations. By the same. 9th Edition. 8vo. 12s.

ST. PAUL'S EPISTLE TO THE PHILIPPIANS. With translation, Paraphrase, and Notes for English Readers. By Very Rev. C. J. VAUGHAN. Crown 8vo. 5s.

ST. PAUL'S EPISTLES TO THE COLOSSIANS AND TO PHILEMON. A Revised Text, with Introductions, etc. By Bishop LIGHTFOOT. 9th Edition. 8vo. 12s.

THE EPISTLES OF ST. PAUL TO THE EPHESIANS, THE COLOSSIANS, AND PHILEMON. With Introductions and Notes. By Rev. J. LL. DAVIES. 2nd Edition. 8vo. 7s. 6d.

THE EPISTLES OF ST. PAUL. For English Readers. Part I. containing the First Epistle to the Thessalonians. By Very Rev. C. J. VAUGHAN. 2nd Edition. 8vo. Sewed. 1s. 6d.

ST. PAUL'S EPISTLES TO THE THESSALONIANS, COMMENTARY ON THE GREEK TEXT. By Prof. JOHN EADIE. 8vo. 12s.

The Epistle of St. James—

THE EPISTLE OF ST. JAMES. The Greek Text, with Introduction and Notes. By Rev. JOSEPH MAYOR, M.A. 8vo. 14s.

The Epistles of St. John—

THE EPISTLES OF ST. JOHN. By F. D. MAURICE. 4th Edition. Crown 8vo. 6s.

THE EPISTLES OF ST. JOHN. The Greek Text, with Notes. By Right Rev. Bishop WESTCOTT. 3rd Edition. 8vo. 12s. 6d.

The Epistle to the Hebrews—

THE EPISTLE TO THE HEBREWS IN GREEK AND ENGLISH. With Notes. By Rev. FREDERIC RENDALL. Crown 8vo. 6s.

THE EPISTLE TO THE HEBREWS. English Text, with Commentary. By the same. Crown 8vo. 7s. 6d.

THE EPISTLE TO THE HEBREWS. With Notes. By Very Rev. C. J. VAUGHAN. Crown 8vo. 7s. 6d.

THE EPISTLE TO THE HEBREWS. The Greek Text, with Notes and Essays. By Right Rev. Bishop WESTCOTT. 8vo. 14s.

REVELATION—

LECTURES ON THE APOCALYPSE. By F. D. MAURICE. 2nd Edition. Crown 8vo. 6s.

LECTURES ON THE APOCALYPSE. By Rev. Prof. W. MILLIGAN. Crown 8vo. 5s.

THE REVELATION OF ST. JOHN. By Rev. Prof. W. MILLIGAN. 2nd Edition. Crown 8vo. 7s. 6d.

REVELATION—*continued.*

LECTURES ON THE REVELATION OF ST. JOHN. By Very Rev. C. J. VAUGHAN. 5th Edition. Crown 8vo. 10s. 6d.

THE BIBLE WORD-BOOK. By W. ALDIS WRIGHT. 2nd Edition. Crown 8vo. 7s. 6d.

Christian Church, History of the

Church (Dean).—THE OXFORD MOVEMENT. Twelve Years, 1833-45. Globe 8vo. 5s.

Cunningham (Rev. John).—THE GROWTH OF THE CHURCH IN ITS ORGANISATION AND INSTITUTIONS. 8vo. 9s.

Dale (A. W. W.)—THE SYNOD OF ELVIRA, AND CHRISTIAN LIFE IN THE FOURTH CENTURY. Cr. 8vo. 10s. 6d.

Hardwick (Archdeacon).—A HISTORY OF THE CHRISTIAN CHURCH. Middle Age. Ed. by Bishop STUBBS. Cr. 8vo. 10s. 6d. A HISTORY OF THE CHRISTIAN CHURCH DURING THE REFORMATION. Revised by Bishop STUBBS. Cr. 8vo. 10s. 6d.

Hort (Dr. F. J. A.)—TWO DISSERTATIONS. I. On ΜΟΝΟΓΕΝΗΣ ΘΕΟΣ in Scripture and Tradition. II. On the "Constantinopolitan" Creed and other Eastern Creeds of the Fourth Century. 8vo. 7s. 6d.

Killen (W. D.)—ECCLESIASTICAL HISTORY OF IRELAND, FROM THE EARLIEST DATE TO THE PRESENT TIME. 2 vols. 8vo. 25s.

Simpson (W.)—AN EPITOME OF THE HISTORY OF THE CHRISTIAN CHURCH. Fcap. 8vo. 3s. 6d.

Vaughan (Very Rev. C. J., Dean of Llandaff).—THE CHURCH OF THE FIRST DAYS. THE CHURCH OF JERUSALEM. THE CHURCH OF THE GENTILES. THE CHURCH OF THE WORLD. Crown 8vo. 10s. 6d.

Ward (W.) — WILLIAM GEORGE WARD AND THE OXFORD MOVEMENT. Portrait. 8vo. 14s.

The Church of England

Catechism of—

A CLASS-BOOK OF THE CATECHISM OF THE CHURCH OF ENGLAND. By Rev. Canon MACLEAR. 18mo. 1s. 6d.

A FIRST CLASS-BOOK OF THE CATECHISM OF THE CHURCH OF ENGLAND, with Scripture Proofs for Junior Classes and Schools. By the same. 18mo. 6d.

THE ORDER OF CONFIRMATION, with Prayers and Devotions. By the Rev. Canon MACLEAR. 32mo. 6d.

Collects—

COLLECTS OF THE CHURCH OF ENGLAND. With a Coloured Floral Design to each Collect. Crown 8vo. 12s.

Disestablishment—

DISESTABLISHMENT AND DISENDOWMENT. What are they? By Prof. E. A. FREEMAN. 4th Edition. Crown 8vo. 1s.

DISESTABLISHMENT : or, A Defence of the Principle of a National Church. By GEORGE HARWOOD. 8vo. 12s.

A DEFENCE OF THE CHURCH OF ENGLAND AGAINST DISESTABLISHMENT. By ROUNDELL, EARL OF SELBORNE. Crown 8vo. 2s. 6d.

ANCIENT FACTS & FICTIONS CONCERNING CHURCHES AND TITHES. By the same. 2nd Edition. Crown 8vo. 7s. 6d.

Dissent in its Relation to—

DISSENT IN ITS RELATION TO THE CHURCH OF ENG-LAND. By Rev. G. H. CURTEIS. Bampton Lectures for 1871. Crown 8vo. 7s. 6d.

Holy Communion—

THE COMMUNION SERVICE FROM THE BOOK OF COMMON PRAYER, with Select Readings from the Writings of the Rev. F. D. MAURICE. Edited by Bishop COLENSO. 6th Edition. 16mo. 2s. 6d.

BEFORE THE TABLE : An Inquiry, Historical and Theological, into the Meaning of the Consecration Rubric in the Communion Service of the Church of England. By Very Rev. J. S. HOWSON. 8vo. 7s. 6d.

FIRST COMMUNION, with Prayers and Devotions for the newly Confirmed. By Rev. Canon MACLEAR. 32mo. 6d.

A MANUAL OF INSTRUCTION FOR CONFIRMATION AND FIRST COMMUNION, with Prayers and Devotions. By the same. 32mo. 2s.

Liturgy—

A COMPANION TO THE LECTIONARY. By Rev. W. BENHAM, B.D. Crown 8vo. 4s. 6d.

AN INTRODUCTION TO THE CREEDS. By Rev. Canon MACLEAR. 18mo. 3s. 6d.

AN INTRODUCTION TO THE THIRTY-NINE ARTICLES. By the same. 18mo. *[In the Press.*

A HISTORY OF THE BOOK OF COMMON PRAYER. By Rev. F. PROCTER. 18th Edition. Crown 8vo. 10s. 6d.

AN ELEMENTARY INTRODUCTION TO THE BOOK OF COMMON PRAYER. By Rev. F. PROCTER and Rev. Canon MACLEAR. 18mo. 2s. 6d.

TWELVE DISCOURSES ON SUBJECTS CONNECTED WITH THE LITURGY AND WORSHIP OF THE CHURCH OF ENGLAND. By Very Rev. C. J. VAUGHAN. 4th Edition. Fcap. 8vo. 6s.

Devotional Books

Brooke (S. A.)—FORM OF MORNING AND EVENING PRAYER, and for the Administration of the Lord's Supper, together with the Baptismal and Marriage Services, Bedford Chapel, Bloomsbury. Fcap. 8vo. 1s. net.

Eastlake (Lady).—FELLOWSHIP: LETTERS ADDRESSED TO MY SISTER-MOURNERS. Crown 8vo. 2s. 6d.

IMITATIO CHRISTI, LIBRI IV. Printed in Borders after Holbein, Dürer, and other old Masters, containing Dances of Death, Acts of Mercy, Emblems, etc. Crown 8vo. 7s. 6d.

Kingsley (Charles).—OUT OF THE DEEP: WORDS FOR THE SORROWFUL. From the writings of CHARLES KINGSLEY. Extra fcap. 8vo. 3s. 6d.

DAILY THOUGHTS. Selected from the Writings of CHARLES KINGSLEY. By his Wife. Crown 8vo. 6s.

FROM DEATH TO LIFE. Fragments of Teaching to a Village Congregation. With Letters on the "Life after Death." Edited by his Wife. Fcap. 8vo. 2s. 6d.

Maclear (Rev. Canon).—A MANUAL OF INSTRUCTION FOR CONFIRMATION AND FIRST COMMUNION, WITH PRAYERS AND DEVOTIONS. 32mo. 2s.

THE HOUR OF SORROW; OR, THE OFFICE FOR THE BURIAL OF THE DEAD. 32mo. 2s.

Maurice (Frederick Denison).—LESSONS OF HOPE. Readings from the Works of F. D. MAURICE. Selected by Rev. J. LL. DAVIES, M.A. Crown 8vo. 5s.

RAYS OF SUNLIGHT FOR DARK DAYS. With a Preface by Very Rev. C. J. VAUGHAN, D.D. New Edition. 18mo. 3s. 6d.

Service (Rev. John).—PRAYERS FOR PUBLIC WORSHIP. Crown 8vo. 4s. 6d.

THE WORSHIP OF GOD, AND FELLOWSHIP AMONG MEN. By FREDERICK DENISON MAURICE and others. Fcap. 8vo. 3s. 6d.

Welby-Gregory (The Hon. Lady).—LINKS AND CLUES. 2nd Edition. Crown 8vo. 6s.

Westcott (Rt. Rev. B. F., Bishop of Durham).—THOUGHTS ON REVELATION AND LIFE. Selections from the Writings of Bishop WESTCOTT. Edited by Rev. S. PHILLIPS. Crown 8vo. 6s.

Wilbraham (Frances M.)—IN THE SERE AND YELLOW LEAF: THOUGHTS AND RECOLLECTIONS FOR OLD AND YOUNG. Globe 8vo. 3s. 6d.

The Fathers

Cunningham (Rev. W.)—THE EPISTLE OF ST. BARNABAS. A Dissertation, including a Discussion of its Date and Authorship. Together with the Greek Text, the Latin Version, and a New English Translation and Commentary. Crown 8vo. 7s. 6d.

Donaldson (Prof. James).—THE APOSTOLICAL FATHERS. A Critical Account of their Genuine Writings, and of their Doctrines. 2nd Edition. Crown 8vo. 7s. 6d.

Lightfoot (Bishop).—THE APOSTOLIC FATHERS. Part I. ST. CLEMENT OF ROME. Revised Texts, with Introductions, Notes, Dissertations, and Translations. 2 vols. 8vo. 32s.

THE APOSTOLIC FATHERS. Part II. ST. IGNATIUS to ST. POLY-CARP. Revised Texts, with Introductions, Notes, Dissertations, and Translations. 3 vols. 2nd Edition. Demy 8vo. 48s.

THE APOSTOLIC FATHERS. Abridged Edition. With Short Introductions, Greek Text, and English Translation. 8vo. 16s.

Hymnology

Brooke (S. A.)—CHRISTIAN HYMNS. Edited and arranged. Fcap. 8vo. 2s. net.
This may also be had bound up with the Form of Service at Bedford Chapel, Blooms-bury. Price complete, 3s. net.

Palgrave (Prof. F. T.)—ORIGINAL HYMNS. 18mo. 1s. 6d.

Selborne (Roundell, Earl of)—
THE BOOK OF PRAISE. From the best English Hymn Writers. 18mo. 2s. 6d. net.

A HYMNAL. Chiefly from *The Book of Praise.* In various sizes. —A. Royal 32mo. 6d.—B. Small 18mo, larger type. 1s.—C. Same Edition, fine paper. 1s. 6d.—An Edition with Music, Selected, Harmonised, and Composed by JOHN HULLAH. Square 18mo. 3s. 6d.

Woods (M. A.) — HYMNS FOR SCHOOL WORSHIP. Compiled by M. A. WOODS. 18mo. 1s. 6d.

Sermons, Lectures, Addresses, and Theological Essays

(See also 'Bible,' 'Church of England,' 'Fathers.')

Abbot (Francis)—
SCIENTIFIC THEISM. Crown 8vo. 7s. 6d.
THE WAY OUT OF AGNOSTICISM : or, The Philosophy of Free Religion. Crown 8vo. 4s. 6d.

Abbott (Rev. E. A.)—
CAMBRIDGE SERMONS. 8vo. 6s.
OXFORD SERMONS. 8vo. 7s. 6d.
PHILOMYTHUS. An Antidote against Credulity. A discussion of Cardinal Newman's Essay on Ecclesiastical Miracles. 2nd Edition. Crown 8vo. 3s. 6d.
NEWMANIANISM. A Reply. Crown 8vo. Sewed, 1s. net.

Ainger (Rev. Alfred, Canon of Bristol).—SERMONS PREACHED IN THE TEMPLE CHURCH. Extra fcap. 8vo. 6s.

Alexander (W., Bishop of Derry and Raphoe).—THE LEAD-
ING IDEAS OF THE GOSPELS. New Edition, Revised
and Enlarged. Crown 8vo. 6s.

Baines (Rev. Edward).—SERMONS. With a Preface and
Memoir, by A. BARRY, D.D., late Bishop of Sydney. Crown 8vo. 6s.

Bather (Archdeacon).—ON SOME MINISTERIAL DUTIES,
CATECHISING, PREACHING, ETC. Edited, with a Preface,
by Very Rev. C. J. VAUGHAN, D.D. Fcap. 8vo. 4s. 6d.

Binnie (Rev. William).—SERMONS. Crown 8vo. 6s.

Birks (Thomas Rawson)—
THE DIFFICULTIES OF BELIEF IN CONNECTION WITH
THE CREATION AND THE FALL, REDEMPTION, AND
JUDGMENT. 2nd Edition. Crown 8vo. 5s.
JUSTIFICATION AND IMPUTED RIGHTEOUSNESS. Being
a Review of Ten Sermons on the Nature and Effects of Faith, by
JAMES THOMAS O'BRIEN, D.D., late Bishop of Ossory, Ferns, and
Leighlin. Crown 8vo. 6s.
SUPERNATURAL REVELATION : or, First Principles of Moral
Theology. 8vo. 8s.

Brooke (Rev. Stopford A.)—SHORT SERMONS. Cr. 8vo. 6s.

Brooks (Phillips, Bishop of Massachusetts)—
THE CANDLE OF THE LORD, and other Sermons. Crown 8vo.
6s.
SERMONS PREACHED IN ENGLISH CHURCHES. Crown
8vo. 6s.
TWENTY SERMONS. Crown 8vo. 6s.
TOLERANCE. Crown 8vo. 2s. 6d.
THE LIGHT OF THE WORLD. Crown 8vo. 3s. 6d.

Brunton (T. Lauder). — THE BIBLE AND SCIENCE.
With Illustrations. Crown 8vo. 10s. 6d.

Butler (Rev. George).—SERMONS PREACHED IN CHEL-
TENHAM COLLEGE CHAPEL. 8vo. 7s. 6d.

Butler (W. Archer)—
SERMONS, DOCTRINAL AND PRACTICAL. 11th Edition.
8vo. 8s.
SECOND SERIES OF SERMONS. 8vo. 7s.

Campbell (Dr. John M'Leod)—
THE NATURE OF THE ATONEMENT. 6th Ed. Cr. 8vo. 6s.
REMINISCENCES AND REFLECTIONS. Edited with an
Introductory Narrative, by his Son, DONALD CAMPBELL, M.A.
Crown 8vo. 7s. 6d.
THOUGHTS ON REVELATION. 2nd Edition. Crown 8vo. 5s.
RESPONSIBILITY FOR THE GIFT OF ETERNAL LIFE.
Compiled from Sermons preached at Row, in the years 1829-31.
Crown 8vo. 5s.

Canterbury (Edward White, Archbishop of)—
BOY-LIFE: its Trial, its Strength, its Fulness. Sundays in Wellington College, 1859-73. 4th Edition. Crown 8vo. 6s.
THE SEVEN GIFTS. Addressed to the Diocese of Canterbury in his Primary Visitation. 2nd Edition. Crown 8vo. 6s.
CHRIST AND HIS TIMES. Addressed to the Diocese of Canterbury in his Second Visitation. Crown 8vo. 6s.

Carpenter (W. Boyd, Bishop of Ripon)—
TRUTH IN TALE. Addresses, chiefly to Children. Crown 8vo. 4s. 6d.
THE PERMANENT ELEMENTS OF RELIGION: Bampton Lectures, 1887. 2nd Edition. Crown 8vo. 6s.

Cazenove (J. Gibson).—CONCERNING THE BEING AND ATTRIBUTES OF GOD. 8vo. 5s.

Church (Dean)—
HUMAN LIFE AND ITS CONDITIONS. Crown 8vo. 6s.
THE GIFTS OF CIVILISATION, and other Sermons and Lectures. 2nd Edition. Crown 8vo. 7s. 6d.
DISCIPLINE OF THE CHRISTIAN CHARACTER, and other Sermons. Crown 8vo. 4s. 6d.
ADVENT SERMONS. 1885. Crown 8vo. 4s. 6d.
VILLAGE SERMONS. Crown 8vo. 6s.
CATHEDRAL AND UNIVERSITY SERMONS. Crown 8vo. 6s.
CLERGYMAN'S SELF-EXAMINATION CONCERNING THE APOSTLES' CREED. Extra fcap. 8vo. 1s. 6d.

Congreve (Rev. John).—HIGH HOPES AND PLEADINGS FOR A REASONABLE FAITH, NOBLER THOUGHTS, LARGER CHARITY. Crown 8vo. 5s.

Cooke (Josiah P., Jun.)—RELIGION AND CHEMISTRY. Crown 8vo. 7s. 6d.

Cotton (Bishop).—SERMONS PREACHED TO ENGLISH CONGREGATIONS IN INDIA. Crown 8vo. 7s. 6d.

Cunningham (Rev. W.)—CHRISTIAN CIVILISATION, WITH SPECIAL REFERENCE TO INDIA. Cr. 8vo. 5s.

Curteis (Rev. G. H.)—THE SCIENTIFIC OBSTACLES TO CHRISTIAN BELIEF. The Boyle Lectures, 1884. Cr. 8vo. 6s.

Davies (Rev. J. Llewelyn)—
THE GOSPEL AND MODERN LIFE. 2nd Edition, to which is added Morality according to the Sacrament of the Lord's Supper. Extra fcap. 8vo. 6s.
SOCIAL QUESTIONS FROM THE POINT OF VIEW OF CHRISTIAN THEOLOGY. 2nd Edition. Crown 8vo. 6s.
WARNINGS AGAINST SUPERSTITION. Extra fcap. 8vo. 2s. 6d.
THE CHRISTIAN CALLING. Extra fcap. 8vo. 6s.
ORDER AND GROWTH AS INVOLVED IN THE SPIRITUAL CONSTITUTION OF HUMAN SOCIETY. Crown 8vo. 3s. 6d.

Davies (Rev. J. Llewelyn)—*continued.*
  BAPTISM, CONFIRMATION, AND THE LORD'S SUPPER,
    as interpreted by their Outward Signs. Three Addresses. New
    Edition. 18mo. 1s.
Diggle (Rev. J. W.) — GODLINESS AND MANLINESS.
    A Miscellany of Brief Papers touching the Relation of Religion to
    Life. Crown 8vo. 6s.
Drummond (Prof. James).—INTRODUCTION TO THE
    STUDY OF THEOLOGY. Crown 8vo. 5s.
ECCE HOMO. A Survey of the Life and Work of Jesus Christ.
    20th Edition. Globe 8vo. 6s.
Ellerton (Rev. John). — THE HOLIEST MANHOOD, AND
    ITS LESSONS FOR BUSY LIVES. Crown 8vo. 6s.
FAITH AND CONDUCT : An Essay on Verifiable Religion. Crown
    8vo. 7s. 6d.
Farrar (Ven. F. W., Archdeacon of Westminster)—
  THE HISTORY OF INTERPRETATION. Being the Bampton
    Lectures, 1885. 8vo. 16s.
  Collected Edition of the Sermons, etc. Crown 8vo. 3s. 6d.
    each.
  SEEKERS AFTER GOD.
  ETERNAL HOPE. Sermons Preached in Westminster Abbey.
  THE FALL OF MAN, and other Sermons.
  THE WITNESS OF HISTORY TO CHRIST. Hulsean Lectures.
  THE SILENCE AND VOICES OF GOD.
  IN THE DAYS OF THY YOUTH. Sermons on Practical Subjects.
  SAINTLY WORKERS. Five Lenten Lectures.
  EPHPHATHA : or, The Amelioration of the World.
  MERCY AND JUDGMENT. A few last words on Christian Eschat-
    ology.
  SERMONS AND ADDRESSES delivered in America.
Fiske (John).—MAN'S DESTINY VIEWED IN THE LIGHT
    OF HIS ORIGIN. Crown 8vo. 3s. 6d.
Forbes (Rev. Granville).—THE VOICE OF GOD IN THE
    PSALMS. Crown 8vo. 6s. 6d.
Fowle (Rev. T. W.)—A NEW ANALOGY BETWEEN
    REVEALED RELIGION AND THE COURSE AND CON-
    STITUTION OF NATURE. Crown 8vo. 6s.
Fraser (Bishop). — SERMONS. Edited by Rev. JOHN W.
    DIGGLE. 2 vols. Crown 8vo. 6s. each.
Hamilton (John)—
  ON TRUTH AND ERROR. Crown 8vo. 5s.
  ARTHUR'S SEAT : or, The Church of the Banned. Crown
    8vo. 6s.
  ABOVE AND AROUND : Thoughts on God and Man. 12mo. 2s. 6d.
Hardwick (Archdeacon). — CHRIST AND OTHER MAS-
    TERS. 6th Edition. Crown 8vo. 10s. 6d.

Hare (Julius Charles)—
THE MISSION OF THE COMFORTER. New Edition. Edited by Dean PLUMPTRE. Crown 8vo. 7s. 6d.
THE VICTORY OF FAITH. Edited by Dean PLUMPTRE, with Introductory Notices by Prof. MAURICE and Dean STANLEY. Crown 8vo. 6s. 6d.

Harper (Father Thomas, S.J.)—THE METAPHYSICS OF THE SCHOOL. In 5 vols. Vols. I. and II. 8vo. 18s. each. Vol. III. Part I. 12s.

Harris (Rev. G. C.)—SERMONS. With a Memoir by CHARLOTTE M. YONGE, and Portrait. Extra fcap. 8vo. 6s.

Hutton (R. H.)—
ESSAYS ON SOME OF THE MODERN GUIDES OF ENGLISH THOUGHT IN MATTERS OF FAITH. Globe 8vo. 6s.
THEOLOGICAL ESSAYS. Globe 8vo. 6s.

Illingworth (Rev. J. R.)—SERMONS PREACHED IN A COLLEGE CHAPEL. Crown 8vo. 5s.
UNIVERSITY AND CATHEDRAL SERMONS. Crown 8vo.
[In the Press.

Jacob (Rev. J. A.)—BUILDING IN SILENCE, and other Sermons. Extra fcap. 8vo. 6s.

James (Rev. Herbert).—THE COUNTRY CLERGYMAN AND HIS WORK. Crown 8vo. 6s.

Jeans (Rev. G. E.)—HAILEYBURY CHAPEL, and other Sermons. Fcap. 8vo. 3s. 6d.

Jellett (Rev. Dr.)—
THE ELDER SON, and other Sermons. Crown 8vo. 6s.
THE EFFICACY OF PRAYER. 3rd Edition. Crown 8vo. 5s.

Kellogg (Rev. S. H.)—THE LIGHT OF ASIA AND THE LIGHT OF THE WORLD. Crown 8vo. 7s. 6d.
THE GENESIS AND GROWTH OF RELIGION. Cr. 8vo. 6s.

Kingsley (Charles)—
VILLAGE AND TOWN AND COUNTRY SERMONS. Crown 8vo. 3s. 6d.
THE WATER OF LIFE, and other Sermons. Crown 8vo. 3s. 6d.
SERMONS ON NATIONAL SUBJECTS, AND THE KING OF THE EARTH. Crown 8vo. 3s. 6d.
SERMONS FOR THE TIMES. Crown 8vo. 3s. 6d.
GOOD NEWS OF GOD. Crown 8vo. 3s. 6d.
THE GOSPEL OF THE PENTATEUCH, AND DAVID. Crown 8vo. 3s. 6d.
DISCIPLINE, and other Sermons. Crown 8vo. 3s. 6d.
WESTMINSTER SERMONS. Crown 8vo. 3s. 6d.
ALL SAINTS' DAY, and other Sermons. Crown 8vo. 3s. 6d.

Kirkpatrick (Prof. A. F.)—THE DIVINE LIBRARY OF THE OLD TESTAMENT. Its Origin, Preservation, Inspiration, and Permanent Value. Crown 8vo. 3s. net.

Kirkpatrick (Prof. A. F.)—*continued.*
THE DOCTRINE OF THE PROPHETS. Warburtonian Lectures 1886-1890. Crown 8vo. 6s.

Kynaston (Rev. Herbert, D.D.)—SERMONS PREACHED IN THE COLLEGE CHAPEL, CHELTENHAM. Crown 8vo. 6s.

Lightfoot (Bishop)—
LEADERS IN THE NORTHERN CHURCH : Sermons Preached in the Diocese of Durham. 2nd Edition. Crown 8vo. 6s.
ORDINATION ADDRESSES AND COUNSELS TO CLERGY. Crown 8vo. 6s.
CAMBRIDGE SERMONS. Crown 8vo. 6s.
SERMONS PREACHED IN ST. PAUL'S CATHEDRAL. Crown 8vo. 6s.
SERMONS PREACHED ON SPECIAL OCCASIONS. Crown 8vo. 6s.
A CHARGE DELIVERED TO THE CLERGY OF THE DIOCESE OF DURHAM, 25th Nov. 1886. Demy 8vo. 2s.
ESSAYS ON THE WORK ENTITLED "Supernatural Religion." 8vo. 10s. 6d.
DISSERTATIONS ON THE APOSTOLIC AGE. 8vo. 14s.
BIBLICAL MISCELLANIES. 8vo. [*In the Press.*

Maclaren (Rev. Alexander)—
SERMONS PREACHED AT MANCHESTER. 11th Edition. Fcap. 8vo. 4s. 6d.
A SECOND SERIES OF SERMONS. 7th Ed. Fcap. 8vo. 4s. 6d.
A THIRD SERIES. 6th Edition. Fcap. 8vo. 4s. 6d.
WEEK-DAY EVENING ADDRESSES. 4th Ed. Fcap. 8vo. 2s. 6d.
THE SECRET OF POWER, AND OTHER SERMONS. Fcap. 8vo. 4s. 6d.

Macmillan (Rev. Hugh)—
BIBLE TEACHINGS IN NATURE. 15th Ed. Globe 8vo. 6s.
THE TRUE VINE ; OR, THE ANALOGIES OF OUR LORD'S ALLEGORY. 5th Edition. Globe 8vo. 6s.
THE MINISTRY OF NATURE. 8th Edition. Globe 8vo. 6s.
THE SABBATH OF THE FIELDS. 6th Edition. Globe 8vo. 6s.
THE MARRIAGE IN CANA. Globe 8vo. 6s.
TWO WORLDS ARE OURS. 3rd Edition. Globe 8vo. 6s.
THE OLIVE LEAF. Globe 8vo. 6s.
THE GATE BEAUTIFUL AND OTHER BIBLE TEACHINGS FOR THE YOUNG. Crown 8vo. 3s. 6d.

Mahaffy (Rev. Prof.)—THE DECAY OF MODERN PREACHING : AN ESSAY. Crown 8vo. 3s. 6d.

Maturin (Rev. W.)—THE BLESSEDNESS OF THE DEAD IN CHRIST. Crown 8vo. 7s. 6d.

Maurice (Frederick Denison)—
THE KINGDOM OF CHRIST. 3rd Ed. 2 Vols. Cr. 8vo. 12s.
EXPOSITORY SERMONS ON THE PRAYER-BOOK ; AND ON THE LORD'S PRAYER. New Edition. Crown 8vo. 6s.

Maurice (Frederick Denison)—*continued.*

SERMONS PREACHED IN COUNTRY CHURCHES. 2nd Edition. Crown 8vo. 6s.

THE CONSCIENCE. Lectures on Casuistry. 3rd Ed. Cr. 8vo. 4s. 6d.

DIALOGUES ON FAMILY WORSHIP. Crown 8vo. 4s. 6d.

THE DOCTRINE OF SACRIFICE DEDUCED FROM THE SCRIPTURES. 2nd Edition. Crown 8vo. 6s.

THE RELIGIONS OF THE WORLD. 6th Edition. Cr. 8vo. 4s. 6d.

ON THE SABBATH DAY; THE CHARACTER OF THE WARRIOR; AND ON THE INTERPRETATION OF HISTORY. Fcap. 8vo. 2s. 6d.

LEARNING AND WORKING. Crown 8vo. 4s. 6d.

THE LORD'S PRAYER, THE CREED, AND THE COMMANDMENTS. 18mo. 1s.

SERMONS PREACHED IN LINCOLN'S INN CHAPEL. In Six Volumes. Crown 8vo. 3s. 6d. each.

Collected Works. Monthly Volumes from October 1892. Crown 8vo. 3s. 6d. each.

CHRISTMAS DAY AND OTHER SERMONS.

THEOLOGICAL ESSAYS.

PROPHETS AND KINGS.

PATRIARCHS AND LAWGIVERS.

THE GOSPEL OF THE KINGDOM OF HEAVEN.

GOSPEL OF ST. JOHN.

EPISTLE OF ST. JOHN.

LECTURES ON THE APOCALYPSE.

FRIENDSHIP OF BOOKS.

SOCIAL MORALITY.

PRAYER BOOK AND LORD'S PRAYER.

THE DOCTRINE OF SACRIFICE.

Milligan (Rev. Prof. W.)—THE RESURRECTION OF OUR LORD. Fourth Thousand. Crown 8vo. 5s.

THE ASCENSION AND HEAVENLY PRIESTHOOD OF OUR LORD. *Baird Lectures,* 1891. Crown 8vo. 7s. 6d.

Moorhouse (J., Bishop of Manchester)—

JACOB : Three Sermons. Extra fcap. 8vo. 3s. 6d.

THE TEACHING OF CHRIST. Its Conditions, Secret, and Results. Crown 8vo. 3s. net.

Mylne (L. G., Bishop of Bombay).—SERMONS PREACHED IN ST. THOMAS'S CATHEDRAL, BOMBAY. Crown 8vo. 6s.

NATURAL RELIGION. By the author of "Ecce Homo." 3rd Edition. Globe 8vo. 6s.

Pattison (Mark).—SERMONS. Crown 8vo. 6s.

PAUL OF TARSUS. 8vo. 10s. 6d.

PHILOCHRISTUS. Memoirs of a Disciple of the Lord. 3rd Ed. 8vo. 12s.

Plumptre (Dean). — MOVEMENTS IN RELIGIOUS THOUGHT. Fcap. 8vo. 3s. 6d.

Potter (R.)—THE RELATION OF ETHICS TO RELIGION. Crown 8vo. 2s. 6d.

REASONABLE FAITH : A Short Religious Essay for the Times. By "Three Friends." Crown 8vo. 1s.

Reichel (C. P., Bishop of Meath)—

THE LORD'S PRAYER, and other Sermons. Crown 8vo. 7s. 6d.

CATHEDRAL AND UNIVERSITY SERMONS. Crown 8vo. 6s.

Rendall (Rev. F.)—THE THEOLOGY OF THE HEBREW CHRISTIANS. Crown 8vo. 5s.

Reynolds (H. R.)—NOTES OF THE CHRISTIAN LIFE. Crown 8vo. 7s. 6d.

Robinson (Prebendary H. G.)—MAN IN THE IMAGE OF GOD, and other Sermons. Crown 8vo. 7s. 6d.

Russell (Dean).—THE LIGHT THAT LIGHTETH EVERY MAN : Sermons. With an introduction by Dean PLUMPTRE, D.D. Crown 8vo. 6s.

Salmon (Rev. Prof. George)—

NON-MIRACULOUS CHRISTIANITY, and other Sermons. 2nd Edition. Crown 8vo. 6s.

GNOSTICISM AND AGNOSTICISM, and other Sermons. Crown 8vo. 7s. 6d.

Sandford (C. W., Bishop of Gibraltar). — COUNSEL TO ENGLISH CHURCHMEN ABROAD. Crown 8vo. 6s.

SCOTCH SERMONS, 1880. By Principal CAIRD and others. 3rd Edition. 8vo. 10s. 6d.

Service (Rev. John).—SERMONS. With Portrait. Crown 8vo. 6s.

Shirley (W. N.)—ELIJAH : Four University Sermons. Fcap. 8vo. 2s. 6d.

Smith (Rev. Travers).—MAN'S KNOWLEDGE OF MAN AND OF GOD. Crown 8vo. 6s.

Smith (W. Saumarez).—THE BLOOD OF THE NEW COVENANT : A Theological Essay. Crown 8vo. 2s. 6d.

Stanley (Dean)—

THE NATIONAL THANKSGIVING. Sermons preached in Westminster Abbey. 2nd Edition. Crown 8vo. 2s. 6d.

ADDRESSES AND SERMONS delivered during a visit to the United States and Canada in 1878. Crown 8vo. 6s.

Stewart (Prof. Balfour) and **Tait** (Prof. P. G.)—THE UNSEEN UNIVERSE ; OR, PHYSICAL SPECULATIONS ON A FUTURE STATE. 15th Edition. Crown 8vo. 6s.

PARADOXICAL PHILOSOPHY : A Sequel to "The Unseen Universe." Crown 8vo. 7s. 6d.

Stubbs (Rev. C. W.)—FOR CHRIST AND CITY. Sermons and Addresses. Crown 8vo. 6s.

Tait (Archbishop)—

THE PRESENT POSITION OF THE CHURCH OF ENGLAND. Being the Charge delivered at his Primary Visitation. 8vo. 3s. 6d.

DUTIES OF THE CHURCH OF ENGLAND. Being seven Addresses delivered at his Second Visitation. 8vo. 4s. 6d.

THE CHURCH OF THE FUTURE. Charges delivered at his Third Quadrennial Visitation. 2nd Edition. Crown 8vo. 3s. 6d.

Taylor (Isaac).—THE RESTORATION OF BELIEF. Crown 8vo. 8s. 6d.

Temple (Frederick, Bishop of London)—

SERMONS PREACHED IN THE CHAPEL OF RUGBY SCHOOL. SECOND SERIES. 3rd Edition. Extra fcap. 8vo. 6s.

THIRD SERIES. 4th Edition. Extra fcap. 8vo. 6s.

THE RELATIONS BETWEEN RELIGION AND SCIENCE. Bampton Lectures, 1884. 7th and Cheaper Ed. Cr. 8vo. 6s.

Trench (Archbishop).—HULSEAN LECTURES. 8vo. 7s. 6d.

Tulloch (Principal).—THE CHRIST OF THE GOSPELS AND THE CHRIST OF MODERN CRITICISM. Extra fcap. 8vo. 4s. 6d.

Vaughan (C. J., Dean of Llandaff)—

MEMORIALS OF HARROW SUNDAYS. 5th Edition. Crown 8vo. 10s. 6d.

EPIPHANY, LENT, AND EASTER. 3rd Ed. Cr. 8vo. 10s. 6d.

HEROES OF FAITH. 2nd Edition. Crown 8vo. 6s.

LIFE'S WORK AND GOD'S DISCIPLINE. 3rd Edition. Extra fcap. 8vo. 2s. 6d.

THE WHOLESOME WORDS OF JESUS CHRIST. 2nd Edition. Fcap. 8vo. 3s. 6d.

FOES OF FAITH. 2nd Edition. Fcap. 8vo. 3s. 6d.

CHRIST SATISFYING THE INSTINCTS OF HUMANITY. 2nd Edition. Extra fcap. 8vo. 3s. 6d.

COUNSELS FOR YOUNG STUDENTS. Fcap. 8vo. 2s. 6d.

THE TWO GREAT TEMPTATIONS. 2nd Ed. Fcap. 8vo. 3s. 6d.

ADDRESSES FOR YOUNG CLERGYMEN. Extra fcap. 8vo. 4s. 6d.

"MY SON, GIVE ME THINE HEART." Extra fcap. 8vo. 5s.

REST AWHILE. Addresses to Toilers in the Ministry. Extra fcap. 8vo. 5s.

TEMPLE SERMONS. Crown 8vo. 10s. 6d.

AUTHORISED OR REVISED? Sermons on some of the Texts in which the Revised Version differs from the Authorised. Crown 8vo. 7s. 6d.

LESSONS OF THE CROSS AND PASSION. WORDS FROM THE CROSS. THE REIGN OF SIN. THE LORD'S PRAYER. Four Courses of Lent Lectures. Crown 8vo. 10s. 6d.

UNIVERSITY SERMONS. NEW AND OLD. Cr. 8vo. 10s. 6d.

Vaughan (C. J., Dean of Llandaff)—*continued.*
NOTES FOR LECTURES ON CONFIRMATION. Fcap. 8vo.
   1s. 6d.
   THE PRAYERS OF JESUS CHRIST : a closing volume of Lent
      Lectures delivered in the Temple Church.   Globe 8vo.   3s. 6d.
   DONCASTER SERMONS.   Lessons of Life and Godliness, and
      Words from the Gospels.   Cr. 8vo.   10s. 6d.
   RESTFUL THOUGHTS IN RESTLESS TIMES.   Crown 8vo.
                                                      [*In the Press.*

Vaughan (Rev. D. J.)—THE PRESENT TRIAL OF FAITH.
   Crown 8vo.   9s.
Vaughan (Rev. E. T.)—SOME REASONS OF OUR CHRIS-
   TIAN HOPE.   Hulsean Lectures for 1875.   Crown 8vo.   6s. 6d.
Vaughan (Rev. Robert).—STONES FROM THE QUARRY.
   Sermons.   Crown 8vo.   5s.
Venn (Rev. John).—ON SOME CHARACTERISTICS OF
   BELIEF, SCIENTIFIC AND RELIGIOUS.   8vo.   6s. 6d.
Warington (G.)—THE WEEK OF CREATION. Cr. 8vo. 4s. 6d.
Welldon (Rev.   J.   E.   C.)—THE   SPIRITUAL   LIFE, and
   other Sermons.   Crown 8vo.   6s.
Westcott (B. F., Bishop of Durham)—
   ON THE RELIGIOUS OFFICE OF THE UNIVERSITIES.
      Sermons.   Crown 8vo.   4s. 6d.
   GIFTS FOR MINISTRY.   Addresses to Candidates for Ordination.
      Crown 8vo.   1s. 6d.
   THE VICTORY OF THE CROSS.   Sermons preached during Holy
      Week, 1888, in Hereford Cathedral.   Crown 8vo.   3s. 6d.
   FROM STRENGTH TO STRENGTH.   Three Sermons (In
      Memoriam J. B. D.)   Crown 8vo.   2s.
   THE REVELATION OF THE RISEN LORD.   Cr. 8vo.   6s.
   THE HISTORIC FAITH.   3rd Edition.   Crown 8vo.   6s.
   THE GOSPEL OF THE RESURRECTION. 6th Ed. Cr. 8vo. 6s.
   THE REVELATION OF THE FATHER.   Crown 8vo.   6s.
   CHRISTUS CONSUMMATOR.   2nd Edition.   Crown 8vo.   6s.
   SOME THOUGHTS FROM THE ORDINAL.   Cr. 8vo.   1s. 6d.
   SOCIAL ASPECTS OF CHRISTIANITY.   Crown 8vo.   6s.
   ESSAYS IN THE HISTORY OF RELIGIOUS THOUGHT IN
      THE WEST.   Globe 8vo.   6s.
   THE GOSPEL OF LIFE.   Cr. 8vo.   6s.
Wickham   (Rev.   E.   C.)—WELLINGTON   COLLEGE
   SERMONS.   Crown 8vo.   6s.
Wilkins (Prof. A. S.)—THE LIGHT OF THE WORLD :   an
   Essay.   2nd Edition.   Crown 8vo.   3s. 6d.
Wilson (J. M., Archdeacon of Manchester)—
   SERMONS PREACHED IN CLIFTON COLLEGE CHAPEL.
      Second Series.   1888-90.   Crown 8vo.   6s.
   ESSAYS AND ADDRESSES.   Crown 8vo.   4s. 6d.
   SOME CONTRIBUTIONS TO THE RELIGIOUS THOUGHT
      OF OUR TIME.   Crown 8vo.   6s.

Printed by R. & R. Clark, *Edinburgh*

VI.30.1.93

9 783744 742252